Lecture on the Book of Job - I

MAN OF
FLESH,
MAN OF
SPIRIT

Lecture on the Book of Job - I

MAN OF
FLESH,
MAN OF
SPIRIT

Rev. Dr. Jaerock Lee

URIM
BOOKS

Lecture on the Book of Job – I
Man of Flesh, Man of Spirit
by Dr. Jaerock Lee
Published by Urim Books (Representative: Kyungtae Noh)
73, Yeouidaebang-ro 22-gil, Dongjak-Gu, Seoul, Korea
www.urimbooks.com

Unless otherwise noted, all Scripture quotations are taken from the Holy Bible, NEW AMERICAN STANDARD BIBLE, ®, Copyright © 1960, 1962, 1963, 1968, 1971, 1972, 1973, 1975, 1977, 1995 by The Lockman Foundation. Used by permission.

Copyright © 2007 by Dr. Jaerock Lee ISBN: 978-89-7557-146-6(04230)
Translated by Dr. Esther Kooyoung Chung. Used by permission.
Previously published in Korean by Urim Books, Seoul, Korea.
Copyright © 2006, ISBN: 89-7557-044-4, ISBN: 89-7557-060-6

First Published April 2008
Second Edition August 2009
Edited by Eunmi Lee
Designed by Editorial Bureau of Urim Books
For more information contact at urimbook@hotmail.com

The Old Testament is mainly divided into the Torah, Neviim, and Ketuvim. The Torah is the Five Books of Moses which writes about the law and other teachings. The Neviim is the prophets, and the Ketuvim is the wisdom of the ancient Israel.

The Book of Job belongs to Ketuvim. It talks about the sufferings of man, the providence of God, and the faith of Job. The name, "Job" means 'A man who turns back,' or 'A man who cries,' but the exact meaning is not certain.

Job lived in the area called Uz, and it is somewhere near the border between Iraq and Saudi Arabia. Some scholars think Job is a fictional character appearing in a literary work. But, Job actually did exist. The Bible tells us about his birthplace, the number of his children, and the array of his possessions in detail.

Ezekiel, Noah, and Daniel were all men in history, and the Bible tells us that Job is also an actual man in history (Ezekiel 14:14; 20). James in the New Testament also tells us about the endurance of Job (James 5:11).

The Book of Job contains many Hebrew vocabularies that cannot be found in other Books of the Old Testament. Also, it covers many subjects in depth and with vast knowledge including astrology, geography, zoology, oceanography, mining, travel, and law. It is truly a masterpiece in world literature.

A Book of Wisdom Giving You
Clear Answers to Common Questions of Life
and Leading You to Successful Life

The Book of Job is one of the most difficult books in the Bible. Usually, people think of Job in the context of a man who was upright and blameless; who was tested by God for no reason; he didn't complain; and he passed all the tests very well and received double the amount of blessings that he had formerly possessed. But, with this kind of shallow understanding, we cannot really have the answers to many questions that arise in the book.

I only longed to understand the word of God properly and live according to it. From the time I accepted Jesus, I began to pray to God to explain the Bible to me in detail. Through much fasting and prayers for 7 years, God finally answered my prayer. By the inspiration of the Holy Spirit He let me first understand about the difficult passages of the Bible, and I understood each verse contained such deep spiritual meaning.

The Book of Job scrutinizes the heart of men very deeply and tells us about the evil and our true nature in the depths of our heart, thereby letting us realize ourselves. Ultimately, through this book, we can find out whether we are men of flesh or men of spirit, and it also gives us the methodology on how to change into men of spirit. 'Flesh' means something that changes, untruths, and darkness, and 'spirit' means the truth, unchanging and eternal things, and world of light.

In December 1986, I began to preach what the Lord has

taught me about the Book of Job, in the Friday all night services. It went on for 6 full years until December 11, 1992. While I was preaching about the Book of Job, many church members realized themselves through the word and tried to break their ego and self, and to change themselves with the truth.

The Book of Job deals with the importance of positive words and the politics of proper and successful social interaction. But, the book has such deep spiritual meaning that we can understand the full meaning only when it's interpreted by the inspiration of the Holy Spirit. It covers an extensive range of subjects that are concerned with the various problems of life and extensively details the three way flow of spiritual rules that are applicable between God, men, and Satan. The Book of Job describes the way to receive blessings and how and why Satan is able to bring accusations against men.

God let everything be recorded through Job about how He works in our lives so that we can find our problems and solve them. God let the conversations between Job and his friends be recorded in this book, so there is truth and untruth together in the book. We can discern it and determine whether it is really correct or not when we reflect upon it with the word of God.

If we understand the Book of Job, we can gain wisdom and strength to overcome any kind of hardship or problem in life.

I give thanks to the poetess Eunmi Lee who edited the scripts to publish this work *The Lecture on the Book of Job – I: Man of Flesh, Man of Spirit.* I also give thanks to Christian Press for publishing it. I give all thanks and glory to Father God who blessed us to publish this book.

May all the readers of this book gain greater hope for heavenly kingdom from it, everything go well with them, their souls prosper and they enjoy good health, in the name of the Lord Jesus Christ I pray!

Jaerock Lee

Book
Review

My spiritual sight was opened
through the spiritual interpretation
and I was captured by the literature
and artistry of the book

Job is a symbol of those who suffer. Of course, his suffering cannot match that of Jesus. But having to scratch his boils with potsherd can be the representative example of 'human suffering.'

The Lecture on the Book of Job written by Rev. Dr. Jaerock Lee gave me a completely new theological interpretation that overturned my previous understanding about Job.
Before then, I just knew that Job was a righteous man who rebuked his wife when she said to him, "Curse God and die" (Job 2:9-10). He didn't curse God but overcame the pain of death, and received blessings twice as much as he had possessed before. His friends were the ones who just gave him hard times for no reason.
When I was young, I once wrote a Biblical play about Job in my church. I just wrote simply about Job and the three friends. But Dr. Jaerock Lee's *Lecture on the Book of Job* gave me an awakening. It opened my spiritual sight by quoting from various books in both Old and New Testaments, making easy comparisons of real life situations.

I felt sorry that Job could have just kept quiet when his friends were trying to teach him a lesson, and just accepted his iniquity and shortcomings. Who could have thought Job would reach the level of giving exceedingly unreasonable excuses and complaining against God?

But because the Book of Job and the Book of Revelation are the most difficult Books in the Bible, each one may have different kinds of interpretation. And when Rev. Dr. Jaerock Lee said, "The Book of Job is written in the viewpoint of Job's faith, so not everything written in this Book is truth. Job's wrong ideas are also expressed as he spoke," this is very true.

Then, I had one question. Does suffering come when men sin? Or is it a lash of God?
Considering the advice of Eliphaz, we may think that diseases and sufferings are caused by men's sin. And, Rev. Jaerock Lee gives a very clear answer to this question as well. It's the arrogance of Eliphaz that is condemning Job.
Even when we say something right, we have to say it in an appropriate way according to the word of God that is the truth. I thoroughly realized that we should not speak the right words merely with our knowledge.
Also, I once again realized from this Book that there is nobody who can judge us believers in this world, but only Jesus Christ, who can give us the life and also the judgment.
I tried to understand the subjects that the lecture on Job really means, comparing it with the Bible. Thanks to the detailed and appropriate explanations on each verse, I could understand even the difficult verses, directly applying them to my real life through this book. I was once again captured by its literature and artistry of the Book of Job. I came to realize why the Bible has become a worldwide bestseller.
I would like to recommend this book to all Christians who are living today, to everyone who believes that sufferings are blessings and who never complains against God when he is in trouble.

March 2007
Yoorim Han (A Korean TV Broadcasting writer)

One of the final masterpieces
on the Lectures on the Book of Job

Dr. Jaerock Lee, Senior Pastor of Manmin Central Church seems to be one of the happiest of the world. It is because he has not only raised his church as one of the biggest churches in the world but also gained absolute recognition and favor from his church members.

In addition, he has healed countless sick people at home and outdoors by the power of God he received from God and led them to God. Countless others who are suffering from pains of diseases are still longing to receive his prayer.

But here is one thing that we are not to overlook. The healing through prayer is not the ultimate goal of his ministry. The ultimate purpose he seeks in his ministry is to let those who have been healed through his prayers gain salvation of their souls and possess the hope for heaven. The healing ministry is one of the intermediates en route for the final goal.

Our Lord Jesus spent much of His public ministry, which was counted as valuable as to Him as gold, on the healing ministry for the sick. Then, was it the ultimate purpose of the ministry of the Lord to recover good health of the people? Not at all! The reason that He performed works of God's power was for them to know God, praise His almightiness and reach salvation. In the same way, Dr. Jaerock Lee's healing ministry is for many people to reach the precious kingdom of heaven.

The Lecture on the Book of Job surveys the whole life of Job including his physical diseases, sufferings, and recovery and presents to us a new and spiritual sight for Job who rediscovered God and opened his sight for the hope for heaven.

The understanding that many people usually have of Job is as the following. Job was a man of righteousness in the East and faithfully served God. One day he came to suffer severe trials and diseases because of unreasonable accusation of Satan, but because he was patient until the end without complaining against God, God let him restore everything and receive double blessings. In conclusion, Job was still righteous in the midst of such sufferings but his friends were found unrighteous with their continual judging and condemning him.

Now through this book *"Man of Flesh, Man of Spirit,"* Dr. Jaerock Lee has turned over the superficial understanding of the Book of Job from the beginning. Job was declared to be blameless and upright, but in reality he did not possess the right understanding of heaven nor was he sure of the justice of God because he possessed just fleshly faith. It is true that he did his best to fulfill the perfect deeds, but is found in detail that he failed to have his heart circumcised. Also, the verses saying that he was afraid to lose his possessions and riches and wealth of the earth prove that he lacked the faith and trust in God.

When his faith collapsed down through excessive trials and hardships, he finally burst into his anger and complaints and his evils hidden deep within his heart were revealed. Through the period of the process of trials and sufferings, he became a person with spiritual faith.

Through this magnificent drama about the Book of Job, I have come to understand that the ultimate goal of Rev. Dr. Jaerock Lee's ministry of healing of body and spirit he dreams is to lead as many people to the kingdom of heaven.

This work *"The Lecture on the Book of Job – I: Man of Flesh, Man of Spirit"* is not separated from his other works *"The Measure of Faith,"* *"The Message of the Cross,"* *"Heaven,"* and *"Hell."* It is because the great history of God's redemption of mankind rises like rainbow behind the diseases, trials, healing and recovery of Job. Here is embedded the core point of Dr. Jaerock Lee, Senior Pastor of Manmin Central Church. He has incessantly revealed the secrets of the kingdom of heaven and urged as many people to take the kingdom of heaven by force. He does not aim at making the lame throwing away crutches but is forcefully urging them to march forward towards heaven with their strong legs.

I heard that the author Dr. Jaerock Lee had suffered various kinds of diseases and nicknamed "Department Store of Diseases" in his young days. In time he met the living God and was completely healed of his diseases, and since then he has dedicated himself to the kingdom of the Lord with a burning heart. Because he has suffered severe pains of body and seriously groaned due to physical diseases, he introduces the sufferings of Job more vividly through this work "The Lecture on the Book of Job." The glory of heaven that Job saw after his healing of diseases looks more magnificent in this book.

The message that runs through Dr. Jaerock Lee's books is as simple but strong as his preaching. And because his book is based on his experimental testimonies, the emotions and impressions last long. His preaching sounds charismatic but he appears really gentle and meek at the personal meeting. His life shows enough humbleness and love not to treat even little children recklessly.

I believe that here is the reason that members of Manmin

Central Church love him so much.

Now I am so glad to see this powerful work that can awaken many people from their spiritual slumber, and wish to share this great joy with as many Christians at home and outdoors.

Byung Jong Kim
(Ph.D. & Prof. Seoul National University)

Table of Contents

Chapter 1

Job Was Blameless and Upright

1. Job Was Blameless in Deeds
2. The Origin of Satan
3. Satan Accuses according
   to the law of the Spiritual Realm
4. Job Passed the First Test of Satan

"There was a man in the land of Uz whose name was Job; and that man was blameless, upright, fearing God and turning away from evil." (Job 1:1)

1. Job Was Blameless in Deeds

"There was a man in the land of Uz whose name was Job; and that man was blameless, upright, fearing God and turning away from evil" (1:1).

Men judge by appearances, but God looks at the inner heart, and so, He knows exactly who is honest. When God looked at the heart of Job, he was blameless and upright.

The Webster's Revised Unabridged Dictionary defines the word 'Blameless' as 'Free from blame; without fault; innocent; guiltless.' The word 'to be blameless' spiritually means 'to show gentleness with deeds.' A gentle person has a meek, soft, mild, and warm character along with virtue and the capacity to embrace others. No matter how gentle a person seems to be on the outside, if he gets angry in an extreme situation, such as being slapped by somebody for no reason, we cannot say that he is gentle.

Next, the same dictionary refers to the word 'to be upright' as 'Morally erect; having rectitude; honest; just; as, a man upright in all his ways.' But the spiritual meaning is not just being honest with others, but to be honest and upright with oneself as well. God can recognize anyone as an upright person when he keeps his promises made to others and those made to himself as well. Those who do not cheat their own minds will never harm or do bad things to others.

In the reading passage, Job was blameless and upright, and he feared God. 'To fear' is to respect and revere. Those who fear God believe in God, so they revere Him. They cast off all forms of evil (1 Thessalonians 5:22) and keep all the words of God, leaving behind sins.

Jesus is the Word that became flesh and came to this world. He feared God. He was faithful in all things and responded to God with only 'Yes' and 'Amen' (Revelation 3:14). The patriarchs of faith in the Bible also feared God, and they were able to humble themselves and devote their lives completely. If you live by God's word without going against the truth, we can say you truly fear God.

When you first begin a life in Christ and your faith isn't very strong yet, you may say you fear God, but actually you do not really fear Him yet. But as your faith grows, you learn to fear God. As your faith grows, you come to know more clearly about Him, and you do not sin. Then, you will not be afraid of Him but love Him from the heart.

Job feared God, so he kept the word of God and he turned away from evil. Job did not sin out of the fear of God since he knew that the living God hated sins. We can now understand that Job did not serve God out of his true love and the fear that was awe and reverence, but rather with the fear of apprehension.

"Seven sons and three daughters were born to him. His possessions also were 7, 000 sheep, 3,000 camels, 500 yoke of oxen, 500 female donkeys, and very many servants; and that man was the greatest of all the men of the east. His sons used to go and hold a feast in the house of each one on his day, and they would send and

invite their three sisters to eat and drink with them.
When the days of feasting had completed their cycle, Job
would send and consecrate them, rising up early in the
morning and offering burnt offerings according to the
number of them all; for Job said, 'Perhaps my sons have
sinned and cursed God in their hearts.' Thus Job did
continually" (1:2-5).

This passage tells us about the blessings given to those who fear God and turn away from evil. Job was called the greatest of all the men of the east because he was deemed to fear God and turn away from evil. It's the same today. Those who are recognized by God will be able to enjoy blessings of wealth, children, and health among many other blessings.

In this passage, the numbers 3,000 or 7,000 do not have special meanings. In the Bible, number 3 is the number of being right and 7 is the number of perfection. The reason why number 3 and 7 often appears is to show that God Himself is working for Job because he was a man who feared God and turned away from sins. Namely, it tells us Job was such a blessed man.

Because Job was blameless and upright, his children also loved one another and the relationships among them were very good. If the head of the family sets a good example, the children will grow well at peace with one another. Job's children had feasts and parties in each other's homes and when they had birthdays the brothers even invited their sisters to enjoy the festivities with them.

But the peace they had was not true and spiritual peace but only peace in flesh. Of course, in today's world, where love has cooled down, many families do not even have fleshly joy and peace. Job was rich, but because of his children, he was always worried.

It was because his children did not have fear of God. Job was worried that his children might do something against God, so he always offered God sin offerings for his children. His deeds of this kind never changed, so we can understand that he truly feared God and shunned evil.

During the Old Testament times, they had to be forgiven of their sins by giving sin offerings whenever they sinned. Sin in Old Testament times was only the deeds that were not in accordance with the law. So, Job could be holy in deeds by giving sacrifices. But God looks at the inner hearts, and what He really wants is not just circumcision on the outside, but the circumcision of heart.

In the New Testament times, the Holy Spirit has come to us, and every one of us who believe in the blood of Jesus can circumcise our hearts by the power of the Holy Spirit. Through the power of the Holy Spirit, we can cast off sinful natures and filthy things of heart, and change even unfavorable personalities into truth. The fundamental reason why God allowed Job those trials was that He wanted Job to have a holy and sanctified heart by the circumcising of the heart, rather than just superficial circumcision on the outside by deeds.

2. The Origin of Satan

"Now there was a day when the sons of God came to present themselves before the LORD, and Satan also came among them. The LORD said to Satan, 'From where do you come?' Then Satan answered the LORD and said, 'From roaming about on the earth and walking

around on it.' The LORD said to Satan, 'Have you considered My servant Job? For there is no one like him on the earth, a blameless and upright man, fearing God and turning away from evil'" (1:6-8).

About the 'sons of God' in this passage, some Bible scholars say that they were angels. But Hebrews 1:5 says, "For to which of the angels did He ever say, 'You are My Son, Today I have begotten You'? And again, 'I will be a Father to Him And He shall be a Son to Me'?"

God never calls angels or other spiritual beings His sons. In Genesis chapter 1 is recorded the Creation of God. Genesis 1:26 says, "Let Us make man in Our image, according to Our likeness," and we can understand that God the Father, the Son, and the Holy Spirit also took part in the Creation.

Also, Job 38:6-7 says, "On what were its bases sunk? Or who laid its cornerstone, when the morning stars sang together and all the sons of God shouted for joy?" It also mentions the 'sons of God.' When God laid the foundations to make earth and during the process of the Creation, the sons of God were rejoicing.

Namely, here, the 'sons of God' refers to Jesus Christ, the one and only Son of God, and the Holy Spirit who would work as our Helper. Therefore, the 'sons of God' in Job chapter 1 refers to 'God the Son Jesus Christ,' and 'God the Holy Spirit,' the two entities.

Some may wonder, "God is perfectly holy Being, and how can He have conversations with evil Satan?" It's because they think Satan can also go to the place where God is and talk to Him. But Satan cannot enter into even the Garden of Eden, not to mention the heavenly kingdom or before the throne of God. God searches everything in the universe. His throne is located in the heavenly kingdom, but He can move around anywhere He wants. In the spiritual realm, if God wants, He can talk to Satan wherever it may be.

Now, what kind of being is Satan? The Bible writes about the origin of Satan.

"How you have fallen from heaven, O star of the morning, son of the dawn! You have been cut down to the earth, you who have weakened the nations! But you said in your heart, 'I will ascend to heaven; I will raise my throne above the stars of God, and I will sit on the mount of assembly In the recesses of the north. I will ascend above the heights of the clouds; I will make myself like the Most High'" (Isaiah 14:12-14).

King James Version uses the word 'Lucifer' for the morning star. Lucifer was an archangel who had the duty of praising God, before God created men. Lucifer had been loved by God for a long time, but Lucifer developed pride inside thinking that it could also be like God.

In time, Lucifer tempted the angels under its control, the dragons, which were in leadership positions among the cherubim, and also other beasts that were under the control of the dragons and along with them it plotted scheme of rebelling against God. Revelation 12:9 says, "And the great dragon was thrown down, the serpent of old who is called the devil and Satan, who deceives the whole world; he was thrown down to the earth, and his angels were thrown down with him."

The reason why the Bible mentions detestable animals is because they were the kinds of beasts that participated in the rebellion against God along with Lucifer (Leviticus chapter

11). But Lucifer lost the battle against the army of God and was driven out from the position of escorting the throne of God to the air. After Lucifer was driven out, it formed the organization of the world of evil spirits. It began to control the evil spirits such as the dragons and its angels, Satan, and the devil to stand against God.

Satan Accuses Day and Night

When men sin or do something that is not right in God's sight, Satan accuses them before God day and night (Revelation 12:10). The God of justice rules everything according to the law of the spiritual realm, so if we do untruths in God's sight, God has to allow the trials to be inflicted upon us through the enemy devil and Satan.

But God does not allow Satan to accuse us and to bring on us tests and trials without proper reason. Adam violated the law of the spiritual realm by eating the forbidden fruit. God prohibited him from eating from the tree of the knowledge of good and evil, but he violated the word of God, so he had to hand over his authority as the lord of all creation to Satan.

God gave the curse to serpent that it would eat dust all the days of its life (Genesis 3:14), and dust here means men who are made from the dust of the ground, and the serpent is the enemy devil and Satan. Namely, it means that those who live in darkness and untruth committing sins will be prey of the enemy devil and Satan.

Satan accuses men before God as long as they commit sins and brings on them trials and tests, and controls them as it wants. But it cannot touch those who have cast off all forms of evil, walk in the light and live by the word of God.

3. Satan Accuses according to the Law of the Spiritual Realm

The Book of Job tells us about the law of the spiritual realm through the triangular relationships that exist between God, men, and Satan. In chapter 1 verse 7, God asks Satan where he came from. It's not that the almighty God did not know where Satan had been, but the Bible just writes these conversations in detail to let us know how Satan's accusations against man takes place.

As God commanded Satan to eat dust, Satan consumes those people who depart from God's word and commit sins. But even when they are sinners, Satan can devour men only after getting the permission from God, the God of justice and love.

That is why Satan prowled around everywhere to find someone to devour and came before God to make accusations (1 Peter 5:8). God of justice has to allow Satan's accusations if it is just according to the law of the spiritual realm. Satan watched Job carefully because he was loved so much by God and Satan wanted to make him fall.

So, the all-knowing God asked Satan "Have you considered My servant Job?" Satan does not have to carefully watch those who do not believe in God because they just commit sins and go the way of death since Satan already controls them. But Satan carefully watches those who are acting by the truth to find something to accuse them. Likewise, Satan can work on only those who are acting in the untruth.

But nothing can be done to those who believe in God and walk in the light.

"Then Satan answered the LORD, 'Does Job fear God for nothing? Have You not made a hedge about him and his house and all that he has, on every side? You have

blessed the work of his hands, and his possessions have
increased in the land. But put forth Your hand now and
touch all that he has; he will surely curse You to Your
face'" (1:9-11).

Satan knew the cunning heart of men who give thanks to God only when they receive the blessings of wealth, health, and fame. That is why Satan brought the accusation that Job stood in awe of God only because God gave him many blessings.

There are people who give thanks to God when they receive answers from God, but when they face trials, they forget God's grace, fall into temptation, and complain against God. The biggest reason God's children have to hold Him in reverence is because God saved us and is guiding us in the way of eternal life. Therefore, it is not right to have reverent fear of God only when we are blessed.

Next, God's 'making a hedge about him and his house and all that he has, on every side' means that God protected everything Job was doing and gave him abundance.

But Satan knew the crafty heart of men and began to test Job's heart through this point of accusation.

"Then the LORD said to Satan, 'Behold, all that he has
is in your power, only do not put forth your hand on
him.' So Satan departed from the presence of the LORD"
(1:12).

Satan knows that the authority to bless or curse belongs to God, so it asked God to get rid of all Job had. Then, God allowed Job's possessions to be taken away, but did not let Satan touch his body. It's because God already knew that Satan would ask for Job's life next, so God did not allow it.

Because the authority over life and death also belongs to God, even Satan can take one's life away only by God's permission. Namely, when God allows Satan's accusations, tests or trials can come upon men. But the important thing is that Satan's accusation was not a just accusation here. Even when Satan took away all of Job's possessions and even the lives of his children, Job only praised God rather than complaining against God.

Then, why did almighty God allow Satan's accusations against Job? God praised only the good points of Job, which were that he was both blameless and upright. God did not address Job's weak points. So, Satan had a reason and some things against which it could accuse Job before God. That's why Satan could accuse Job, and God had to allow it.

If Job had no untruths in him whatsoever, God wouldn't have allowed Satan's accusations at all, no matter how much Satan accused him.

4. Job Passes the First Test of Satan

"Now on the day when his sons and his daughters were eating and drinking wine in their oldest brother's house, a messenger came to Job and said, 'The oxen were plowing and the donkeys feeding beside them, and the Sabeans attacked and took them. They also slew the servants with the edge of the sword, and I alone have escaped to tell you'" (1:13-15).

As God allowed the accusations of Satan to take place, Satan began to test Job. God allowed only Job's possessions to be taken away. 'Possessions' means all he had including his children. While Job's children were eating and drinking at a party in the first son's house, one servant who was working in the field came with bad news. The Sabeans attacked and took their oxen and donkeys, and slew the servants.

Tests come to both believers and non-believers. The believers can find their problems with the word of God and repent of their sins so that they can receive God's grace to recover again, or receive greater blessings than before.

But unbelievers have no one but themselves to rely on for help. In some cases, they may solve the problem easily, but they can also get into even more difficult situations.

Satan managed the Gentiles causing them to take away Job's possessions. Even today, around us, we can see those who claim to be believers but are not protected from disasters and are swindled out of their money and suffer from other great loss.

In these occasions, they should not complain against God saying, "Why did God not protect me?" Instead, they should find the reason in themselves as to why they had to face such problems. Then, they should repent of their wrongdoings and turn away from them and the problems will be resolved.

"While he was still speaking, another also came and said, 'The fire of God fell from heaven and burned up the sheep and the servants and consumed them, and I alone have escaped to tell you'" (1:16).

Before the servant finished his talking, another servant came and told him that fire from heaven came and burned up Job's possessions.

In the Old Testament, there were punishments of fire, and Elijah also received the answer of fire. In the days of the Old

Testament, which is the shadow of the New Testament, people were saved by their deeds. So God sometimes showed real fire. But in New Testament, Jesus Himself came down to this earth and showed many evidences through which we could believe, so God doesn't have to show fire.

This disaster of Job could be compared with some people's houses or factories being burned up completely by big fire or having great damage to their crops because of typhoons or other natural disasters.

Of course, you may think natural disasters cause damage to everybody in the same way, but those believers who walk in God's word can be protected. Because the Holy Spirit moves their hearts, they can also plant crops that will not be harmed by those specific natural disasters.

> *"While he was still speaking, another also came and said, 'The Chaldeans formed three bands and made a raid on the camels and took them and slew the servants with the edge of the sword, and I alone have escaped to tell you'" (1:17).*

Satan brought about the third situation of damage to Job's possessions. Here, if Job had known the law of the spiritual realm, he would have looked back on himself and repented of his shortcomings. If we repent and turn away, we will not face any more damage, but if we do not turn away bigger problems will be coming our way.

With detailed planning, Satan took away Job's possessions through the Gentiles. In today's sense, it can be compared with the situation where one is cheated out of his money by the very cunning planning of a swindler.

"While he was still speaking, another also came and said, 'Your sons and your daughters were eating and drinking wine in their oldest brother's house, and behold, a great wind came from across the wilderness and struck the four corners of the house, and it fell on the young people and they died, and I alone have escaped to tell you'" (1:18-19).

In three occasions, Satan took away all the property of Job, who was the greatest man in the east, and finally, Satan touched the house and his children. When Job's 7 sons and 3 daughters were eating and drinking in a party, a great wind came, and the house fell, and all of them died.

The 'corners of the house' means important positions. Striking the four corners of the house means Satan struck his children who are like pillars of his family. Job was heartbroken at having lost all his properties and even his children. In such a situation, most people would probably complain and weep against God so much. But Job, who was blameless and upright, only praised God and thanked God without any complaints.

"Then Job arose and tore his robe and shaved his head, and he fell to the ground and worshiped. He said, 'Naked I came from my mother's womb, And naked I shall return there. The LORD gave and the LORD has taken away. Blessed be the name of the LORD.' Through all this Job did not sin nor did he blame God" (1:20-22).

Tearing his robe means that Job humbled himself. He expressed his shortcomings and weaknesses. His action meant he could not do anything without God's help. He humbled himself completely, meaning, "It's not by my ability that I had my children or gained my properties. All these things were from God, and I am nothing."

He also expressed his lack of wisdom and virtue. When he tore his robe He meant to express his sorrow in his inability to raise his children properly.

If we leave evil completely and live by the truth only, our pride, our 'self,' and our 'ego' will die. Only Jesus Christ in us will live and work. If we confess that we cannot do anything but everything is possible in the Lord, and rely on God completely, we will not complain against God even if God takes away all our possessions.

Next, shaving his head means that all his belongings disappeared.

The head of the man is the Christ (1 Corinthians 11:3), and by shaving the head, he expressed all his belongings were given by God, and God took them away, so he now had nothing.

In the Old Testament, they showed their faith in God with their actions. So, Job shaved his head and fell to the ground and worshipped, saying, "Naked I came from my mother's womb, And naked I shall return there. The LORD gave and the LORD has taken away. Blessed be the name of the LORD" (v. 21). He only gave thanks to God, not complaining against Him. Through this, Satan's accusations, in which Satan said Job feared God only because God blessed him so much, were proved to be wrong.

Beginning in chapter 2, the reasons why Satan accused Job and why God had to allow that accusation are explained.

Chapter 2

Job Complains against God

"And he took a potsherd to scrape himself while he was sitting among the ashes. Then his wife said to him, 'Do you still hold fast your integrity? Curse God and die!' But he said to her, 'You speak as one of the foolish women speaks. Shall we indeed accept good from God and not accept adversity?' In all this Job did not sin with his lips." (Job 2:8-10)

1. Satan's Second Test

"Again there was a day when the sons of God came to present themselves before the LORD, and Satan also came among them to present himself before the LORD. The LORD said to Satan, 'Where have you come from?' Then Satan answered the LORD and said, 'From roaming about on the earth and walking around on it.' The LORD said to Satan, 'Have you considered My servant Job? For there is no one like him on the earth, a blameless and upright man fearing God and turning away from evil. And he still holds fast his integrity, although you incited Me against him to ruin him without cause'" (2:1-3).

Even through the sufferings, Job's faith was not shaken because he was blameless and upright as God had recognized him. Then, Satan should have departed from him. Why does Satan still accuse him again?

Usually, when somebody has something difficult to discuss, he is not so straightforward, but begins by talking about lesser matters and then he gets to the point and talks about the real matter. In the same way, Satan had already known that test of wealth would not be a problem for Job, but Satan was still around and accusing Job until there were no accusations left to bring against him.

If we do not stand firmly in the truth, we will continuously suffer from tests and trials. Because God truly loves His children, if they go the way of death due to their sins or if they do not stand on the truth, God turns His face away so that they can turn away, repent, and be more perfect. That is why Hebrews 12:5-6 says, "You have forgotten the exhortation which is addressed to you as sons, 'My son, do not regard lightly the discipline of the Lord, Nor faint when you are reproved by Him; For those whom the Lord loves He disciplines, And He scourges every son whom He receives.'"

If God's children can rejoice and give thanks in all circumstance, they can pass the tests and receive great blessings. Because Job was blameless and upright, he passed the first test. But he still had some untruths in him of which he could not escape from being accused.

Satan knew Job's heart exactly, and Satan's actual interest was not to take away Job's wealth. That is why Satan didn't stop there but continued his accusation. God of justice had to allow the accusations against Job.

"Satan answered the LORD and said, 'Skin for skin! Yes, all that a man has he will give for his life. However, put forth Your hand now, and touch his bone and his flesh; he will curse You to Your face.' So the LORD said to Satan, 'Behold, he is in your power, only spare his life.' Then Satan went out from the presence of the LORD and smote Job with sore boils from the sole of his foot to the crown of his head" (2:4-7).

Satan accused Job saying, "Skin for skin!" Namely, if his life were threatened, Job would complain against God. Satan now asks for permission from God to touch his bone and his flesh. We have life, death, fortune, and misfortune in God, but if we have something to be accused of, Satan will accuse us before God.

Because God is just, if the accusation of Satan is correct, He has to allow it to take place. Only with the permission from God can Satan bring about tests to men. Neither does God touch men at His discretion nor can Satan touch men without permission of God.

Next, 'to touch his bones and his flesh' means that if the bones are not in the proper place, the shape of men will also change, and this means a life-threatening situation. Satan was saying that Job had still revered God because his own life had not been threatened, and that if his life were threatened, he would complain against God.

Bones are like the pillars of support and the flesh makes up the shape of men. If bones and flesh are hurt, the fundamental structure is distorted, and men's structure is changed and hindered. So, this refers to a test or challenge that can threaten one's life.

Satan acknowledged that God had all the authority over life and death and blessings and curses, and it is saying something like, "Let me touch Job's bones and flesh. Let us see whether Job is really the kind of person You told me he is." If one is perfectly right in the sight of God, God will always protect him and Satan cannot bring any accusation against him.

Only by God's permission can Satan bring tests and trials to men, and therefore, if we have any test, we quickly have to repent of our wrongdoings and turn back from sins so that we can be protected by God.

When God allowed the accusation of Satan, Satan struck Job

with boils all over his body. Boils that Job had festered from the joints of the bones and came up to the skin, and they festered again on the skin to cause such great itchiness. In the beginning, it started as a small boil, but as he scratched more and more, it spread very quickly, and it spread all over his body, from the sole of his feet to the crown of his head.

2. Job Misunderstands God Gives Blessings and Curses without Reason

"And he took a potsherd to scrape himself while he was sitting among the ashes. Then his wife said to him, 'Do you still hold fast your integrity? Curse God and die!' But he said to her, 'You speak as one of the foolish women speaks. Shall we indeed accept good from God and not accept adversity?' In all this Job did not sin with his lips" (2:8-10).

Job was sitting on the ashes scratching himself with his hands, but when it got so severe, he took a potsherd to scrape himself. In the Old Testament, sitting on the ashes meant humbling oneself before God to the lowest possible extent with repentance.

Even in this situation, Job did not curse God, but his wife cursed her husband who was in pain, "Do you still believe in God who put you through this? Curse God and die! Just die!"

Actually, unlike the gentle characters of Job, his wife did not fear God. That is why Job always had worries that his children might resemble their mother and commit sins, and that's why he always gave sacrifices for them. His wife, rather than trying to comfort him, told him to curse God and die, and cursed him to fall into hell. If you curse God and die, where will you go except hell?

Job said to this wife, "You are truly foolish. We received blessings from God, and we also receive curses along with them." He didn't complain against God with his lips. But Job did misunderstand God. God is not One who gives blessings or curses without cause.

> "If you will give earnest heed to the voice of the LORD your God, and do what is right in His sight, and give ear to His commandments, and keep all His statutes, I will put none of the diseases on you which I have put on the Egyptians; for I, the LORD, am your healer" (Exodus 15:26).

> "Now it shall be, if you diligently obey the LORD your God, being careful to keep all His commandments which I command you today, the LORD your God will set you high above all the nations of the earth. All these blessings will come upon you and overtake you if you obey the LORD your God. Blessed shall you be in the city, and blessed shall you be in the country. Blessed shall be the offspring of your body and the produce of your ground and the offspring of your beasts, the increase of your herd and the young of your flock. Blessed shall be your basket and your kneading bowl. Blessed shall you be when you come in, and blessed shall you be when you go out" (Deuteronomy 28:1-6).

Since the Book of Job was written from the viewpoint of Job, we should not think that all that was spoken by Job is correct. The misunderstandings and the wrong ideas that Job had about faith are also expressed. In order for us to interpret this Book correctly, it is imperative that we understand that many things he spoke are not correctly understood by him when compared to the truth.

Then, how can we receive blessings, and how are we accused by Satan to face difficulties? God does not give disasters to men for no reason.

There is a certain reason when He gives punishment. If we live by His word and obey Him, we will receive blessings, but if we do not obey and do not keep all His decrees and commandments, curses fall on us (Deuteronomy 28:15-19).

As Jesus said in John 8:32, "You will know the truth, and the truth will make you free," if we do not know the truth, we will have something to be accused of by Satan, for we do not have freedom coming from the truth.

Job knew very well the fact that God gave the blessings, but He misunderstood that God also gives disasters without a reason, and thus, he actually let Satan work on him. He humbled himself by sitting on the ashes and shaving himself, but he misunderstood when he believed that God gave diseases or disasters without cause. So, he could not discover himself, and he was not able to find anything to repent. Job did not really understand God's word, and he believed that God is like a dictator who could do anything as He pleased.

Therefore, because of Job's wrong belief, he could not be protected, and he had to face this accusation of Satan to go through disasters. If Job had understood why he was suffering, he could have repented and turned back from it, but because he could not find it himself, he could not understand the reason. That is why he had to keep on suffering from the tests.

3. The Appearing of Job's Three Friends

"Now when Job's three friends heard of all this adversity that had come upon him, they came each one from his own place, Eliphaz the Temanite, Bildad the Shuhite and Zophar the Naamathite; and they made an appointment together to come to sympathize with him and comfort him. When they lifted up their eyes at a distance and did not recognize him, they raised their voices and wept. And each of them tore his robe and they threw dust over their heads toward the sky. Then they sat down on the ground with him for seven days and seven nights with no one speaking a word to him, for they saw that his pain was very great" (2:11-13).

Usually, Job was a very generous and virtuous man, so he had many friends. Job's friends heard the news that Job had lost all his wealth and children, and he himself had been stricken by disease. They doubted it but still came to comfort Job. Three of them were Eliphaz the Temanite, Bildad the Shuhite and Zophar the Naamathite.

Even from a distance, they could see that Job's situation was exactly the same as they had heard, and they were choked with emotion. They raised their voices and wept. And each of them tore his robe and they threw dust over their heads toward the sky. Then they sat down on the ground with him for seven days and seven nights with no one speaking a word to him.

Then, what happened? Job, who had always feared God and never cursed Him, opened his mouth and began to curse the day he was born.

Chapter 3
Job's Resentment and Lamentation

1. Job Curses the Day of His Birth
2. Job Offered a Fleshly Sacrifice

"Why did I not die at birth, Come forth from the womb and expire?
Why did the knees receive me, And why the breasts, that I should suck?" (Job 3:11-12)

1. Job Curses the Day of His Birth

"Afterward Job opened his mouth and cursed the day of his birth. And Job said, 'Let the day perish on which I was to be born, and the night which said, "A boy is conceived.' May that day be darkness; Let not God above care for it, nor light shine on it"'" (3:1-4).

From the Bible, we can understand that our body is given by God, and so, we cannot just treat it indiscriminately. But Job was cursing his own birth, and we can see that the pain he felt from the boils was so great.

In old days, people considered the seed to continue their family much more important than we do today, so they were much happier to have a son rather than a daughter. Job's parents must have been very happy about his birth, too. But because Job became diseased and lost all his possessions, he realized that being born a man was also useless and everything was meaningless.

So, Job was cursing his day of birth and lamented. The 'darkness' Job talked about refers to complete darkness and also the Grave/Sheol. It refers to a useless being which has no life and cannot do anything. He meant his entity itself which he thought was completely valueless.

Job cursed his life. He was cursing against his parents and

lamenting. "Only if that night was dark and I was not born!" "If only I had not been given life!" He was complaining that he had been born.

Because he acknowledged that God is the One who exercises control over all souls, he was complaining against God who cared for his soul. If God had not cared for his soul there wouldn't have been life in him, or if there had been no light of life, even when a baby was born, the cells wouldn't have grown up and survival would have been impossible. But because God gave the light, he could live. He was complaining about these things that had occurred.

"Let darkness and black gloom claim it; Let a cloud settle on it; Let the blackness of the day terrify it. As for that night, let darkness seize it; Let it not rejoice among the days of the year; Let it not come into the number of the months" (3:5-6).

If the darkness and black gloom claim Job's birthday, it could harm Job, so that he wouldn't have been born. Also, the 'cloud settling on it' means it is going to rain. So, Job's parents must have been busy caring for the crops and cattle, thus having no time to make love, and he wouldn't have been born.

Job continued to use comparisons even with the solar eclipse. When the solar eclipse takes place, nobody can see the sun, so it will be dark even during the day. We who are living in modern days know this fact, so we don't feel afraid, but those who lived in those times shuddered with fear when they observed a solar eclipse taking place.

Because the day was dark, those who were in fear would not make love, and even when the night was seized by the darkness, it would have been the same. Therefore, he meant he wouldn't have been born if those conditions had prevailed. "Let it not rejoice among the days of the year" or talking about the number of the months also mean that he wished he had not been born. He was complaining about his conception and resenting his own birth.

"Behold, let that night be barren; Let no joyful shout enter it. Let those curse it who curse the day, Who are prepared to rouse Leviathan. Let the stars of its twilight be darkened; Let it wait for light but have none, And let it not see the breaking dawn" (3:7-9).

Also, if the night had been barren, his parents wouldn't have made love, so he wouldn't have been born. 'Joyful shout' means that his parents made joyful shouts when they made love and they rejoiced when he was born because he was a son. So, he meant that if those joyful days had not existed, he wouldn't have been born.

Leviathan is like a big crocodile, and it looks repulsive and evil. This means the form of evil itself. If somebody has an affair with another person other than the spouse, his/her heart is dirty and repulsive like the Leviathan. One who is prepared to rouse Leviathan can do the things that cannot really be done by human beings.

Namely, Job wants somebody to take away his life. He thought anybody was OK. He wanted such an evil man to curse that night so that he wouldn't have been born. Job said all these things because he resented his birth.

God promised Abraham that He would give him as many descendants as the stars in the sky. Likewise, 'star' refers to 'man.' Also, the 'stars of twilight' symbolizes 'promised word.' The 'stars of twilight' refers to Job's parents. It means if his parents had not kept the promise to make love with each other, he wouldn't have been conceived.

If his parents had not kept the promise to make love, they wouldn't have gained any children, no matter how bright it is. Also, if there were no twilight in this world, it would have been complete darkness and the world would have fallen into destruction, so that he wouldn't have been born.

"Because it did not shut the opening of my mother's womb, or hide trouble from my eyes. Why did I not die at birth, Come forth from the womb and expire? Why did the knees receive me, and why the breasts, that I should suck?" (3:10-12).

Job is lamenting that if his mother's womb had been shut, he wouldn't have been conceived and not suffered from those trials. He also said, even if he had been conceived, if he died at birth, he wouldn't have suffered like now. He was lamenting and complaining against his parents.

Also, he was saying, even if he had been born, if his mother hadn't nursed him, he would have starved to death, but because his mother fed him, he was suffering like now. Job knew the fact that God is the One who controlled his life, but he was cursing his birth itself. Consequently, he was complaining against God.

"For now I would have lain down and been quiet; I would have slept then, I would have been at rest, with kings and with counselors of the earth, who rebuilt ruins for themselves; Or with princes who had gold, Who were filling their houses with silver. Or like a miscarriage which is discarded, I would not be, As infants that never saw light" (3:13-16).

Job was saying if he had not been born or died at birth, he would have been in the Grave, being laid down quietly resting. He was saying in that place he would have been with those counselors of the earth or those who rebuilt ruins for themselves. If he had been born dead, he wouldn't have seen the light like a miscarriage which is discarded.

What Job was saying now was not the truth in God's sight but his personal thoughts, which were words of untruths.

"There the wicked cease from raging, And there the weary are at rest. The prisoners are at ease together; They do not hear the voice of the taskmaster. The small and the great are there, And the slave is free from his master" (3:17-19).

Job began to explain about the life in the Grave, saying that if he had died at birth and went to the Grave, and there, the wicked would cease from raging and the weary are at rest. The taskmaster here means 'being controlled' or 'controlling.' It refers to everything about restriction and being under control, such as putting oneself into some kind of restriction or being restricted in the word of God.

Job was explaining about the Grave, and he was saying in that place nobody was under the control of anybody, and everybody, whether small or great, is the same there. But this was merely Job's opinion, and it was not really the truth. The beggar Lazarus, who feared God during his life on earth, went to the Upper Grave after his death, and he could be at Abraham's side. But the rich man who only enjoyed himself on earth went to the Lower Grave, which is Hades, and suffered forever (Luke 16:19-31).

It's not true that everybody is treated the same in the Grave, whether good or evil, like what Job said.

"Why is light given to him who suffers, and life to the bitter of soul, who long for death, but there is none, and dig for it more than for hidden treasures, who rejoice greatly, And exult when they find the grave? Why is light given to a man whose way is hidden, and whom God has hedged in? For my groaning comes at the sight of my food, and my cries pour out like water" (3:20-24).

Job was in such despair because he had lost all his possessions and children, and he even had boils all over his body. Job cursed that he had life, and he wanted to die, but he couldn't do as he wished. If somebody knows that there is hidden treasure in a field, he would definitely try to dig it out; Job wanted death more than this.

His only wish was death, so when he had to eat, he lamented. It's not lamenting because there is no food, but if he ate, his life was extended, and because of the pains of the boils, cries poured out like water.

By the way, there are some people who cry while taking spiritual food. Many people live in the world, in darkness, as they wish, without knowing the truth. But as they accept the Lord and come out to the light, they listen to the spiritual words. They hear, "Keep the Lord's Day holy," "Do not drink alcohol," "Do not envy or be jealous," "Cast off all forms of evil." As they eat the word of God the spiritual bread, they now have to try to cast off the old habits, and it is painful for them.

If they do not cast them away, they feel afflicted in their hearts and they lose the fullness of the Spirit. They cannot just cast those things away as they wish, and therefore, they come to lament. They still eat spiritual bread, but at the same time they lament and cry about it.

2. Job Offered a Fleshly Sacrifice

"For what I fear comes upon me, and what I dread befalls me. I am not at ease, nor am I quiet, and I am not at rest, but turmoil comes" (3:25-26).

Job had fear that God would someday punish him for no reason, and as he was under test, he was confessing from heart. He usually thought that God would strike him and he feared that God would give him a disease or something, and it actually happened in reality.

Job did not offer a spiritual sacrifice from a loving heart with which God is really pleased. It means that he did not offer his sacrifices with true love for God and with all his heart, mind, and soul, nor did he worship Him in spirit and in truth. He offered sacrifices because he had worries. He worried that if he didn't give the offerings, something bad might happen to his children or some curses might fall on his family. He was confessing that he offered fleshly sacrifices out of his fear and apprehension.

Revelation 21:8 says, "But for the cowardly and unbelieving and abominable and murderers and immoral persons and sorcerers and idolaters and all liars, their part will be in the lake that burns with fire and brimstone, which is the second death." It tells us that those who fear will not be saved.

They know the word of God, but do not have true faith to believe in God. They still befriend the world and do evil things, so they have fear. These people cannot receive salvation.

Proverbs 26:2 says, "Like a sparrow in its flitting, like a swallow in its flying, so a curse without cause does not alight." 1 John 3:21-22 also says, "Beloved, if our heart does not condemn us, we have confidence before God; and whatever we ask we receive from Him, because we keep His commandments and do the things that are pleasing in His sight."

A curse without cause does not come, but Job was afraid of God because he didn't really understand God's word. He gave his sacrifices only because he was afraid of God. He didn't give them with true love for God stemming from heart.

He spoke that, since he had lost all his possessions and his children, he now didn't have any foundation for a resting place in life. He said that, because he didn't have a resting place on earth, he had no rest. This tells us that Job was a man of flesh who did not have faith or hope for heaven.

Therefore, his lips were full of only resentment and complaint, so he could not have any peace or rest. He used to enjoy peace and rest relying on material conditions, but true peace and rest do not come from material things but are given only by God.

Those who have true faith will rely on God completely even if they get a disease. Even though they don't have any children and no place to rest, they can be at rest because they have hope for heaven.

The Old Testament is the shadow of the New Testament, but it doesn't mean God accepted only the outer deeds. Between men, they do not understand the spiritual things of each other, so God allowed the outer deeds seen with physical body. But God doesn't permit anything fleshly or physical between Himself and men. He is spirit, and He accepts only spiritual things.

The law of the Old Testament did not condemn the people even when they had adulterous minds or hatred in their heart as long as it was not shown as outer deeds. But God does not only look at the deeds, but also the inner hearts of men, so only if we have sinful things in our heart, God considers it evil. In the New Testament, just having evil thoughts is also considered as sin.

God accepted the blood sacrifice of Abel but not Cain's (Genesis 4:4-5). Blood sacrifice means giving spiritual sacrifice in spirit and in truth with all one's heart, mind, and soul.

If you worship God in spirit and in truth and have spiritual faith with which you can believe from the bottom of heart, your joy, peace, comfort, and thanks will not leave your heart. But if you lose these things from your heart, you should understand that you are only like a child in faith, not having spiritual faith.

God told Saul to destroy all Amalekites and all their possessions, but Saul used his own fleshly thoughts. He kept fat herd and sheep saying he was giving them to God. This may seem right from a fleshly viewpoint, but it was disobedience to God's word saying "To obey is better than sacrifice" (1 Samuel 15:22). After all, God did not receive the fleshly sacrifices and finally discarded him.

The Bible tells us to 'fear God' and it means that we should believe the existence of heaven and hell and God is the Judge, and we should keep His word and not commit sins with reverent fear of God.

When we obey His word and practice it, God answers us when we ask and He is with us. Thus, He is our good Father. But, if we serve Him with fear and apprehension, it is because we do not have true faith.

1 John 4:18 says, "There is no fear in love; but perfect love casts out fear, because fear involves punishment, and the one who fears is not perfected in love."

Job was so upright and honest to be acknowledged by God, but in his heart were hidden untruths. That is why God, who loved Job's uprightness and honesty, allowed those tests so that Job would remove all the evil in him and he would receive the blessings of prosperity in everything, regain his health, as his soul would prosper.

God does not give trials to His children for no reason. Because there are things to change in us, we face trials. Therefore, if we realize ourselves and turn back, we can lead a triumphant Christian life. We can receive God's answers, giving glory to Him.

Chapter 4

Eliphaz the Temanite's Rebuttal

1. Eliphaz Condemns Job as an Evil Man
2. Eliphaz' Spiritual Status and Pride

"Remember now, who ever perished being innocent?
Or where were the upright destroyed? According to what I have seen,
those who plow iniquity And those who sow trouble harvest it." (Job 4:7-8)

1. Eliphaz Judges Job as an Evil Man

"Then Eliphaz the Temanite answered, 'If one ventures a word with you, will you become impatient? But who can refrain from speaking? Behold you have admonished many, And you have strengthened weak hands. Your words have helped the tottering to stand, and you have strengthened feeble knees. But now it has come to you, and you are impatient; It touches you, and you are dismayed'" (4:1-5).

As Job was cursing the day he was born and his parents, his friend, Eliphaz, could not bear it any more and he was the first to open his mouth and speak. What we have to remember here is that the conversations among Job and his friends may be sometimes correct in the sight of God, but many parts were just their own opinions.

God let all these things be recorded because it was necessary. Now, Eliphaz was saying what he had been thinking because he got angry. In his sight Job was not the same person he used to know. He compared the actions and words of Job before and after the incidents, and he thought Job's words now were meaningless. That is why he was angry because of what Job had been saying.

According to the Bible, we can see Eliphaz' action was not

right. James 1:19 says, "This you know, my beloved brethren. But everyone must be quick to hear, slow to speak and slow to anger."

Also, Matthew 7:1-5 says, "Do not judge so that you will not be judged. For in the way you judge, you will be judged; and by your standard of measure, it will be measured to you. Why do you look at the speck that is in your brother's eye, but do not notice the log that is in your own eye? Or how can you say to your brother, 'Let me take the speck out of your eye,' and behold, the log is in your own eye? You hypocrite, first take the log out of your own eye, and then you will see clearly to take the speck out of your brother's eye."

But this friend considered only himself to be right and he was criticizing and measuring Job.

In verse 3, we can find that Job had lived an honest life and could admonish many. 'Weak hands' represents those who have lost their energy and zest for life. Job had strengthened those people and guided them.

Also, the 'tottering' refers to those who have fallen and have given up on life. For example, they are people whose business went bankrupt over night or those abandoned by their lover. They are those who lost the willpower or the motive to continue living. Job encouraged and strengthened these people.

What does 'strengthening feeble knees' mean? Men can walk only with strong knees. With weak knees, they cannot walk. Thus, 'strengthening feeble knees' refers to actions. Job helped and held those who had no abundance in life or whose actions were not sufficient. Because Job was a very rich man, he sometimes gave money to those who were in need and he gave them strength, courage, and hope. But when Job himself was in that kind of difficulty, Eliphaz was discontent and he was rebuking Job saying that Job had become like those whom he had once helped.

Why did God have all this recorded? We have to check whether we are not like Job. Suppose somebody came to consult with you while you were leading a life of faith and full of the Spirit. Then, you might have confidently said, "If there is anything wrong, you can repent and turn back. If you rely on God completely, He will solve your problem. Fast and pray. God is just and is full of love."

However, if you yourself were later faced with the same kind of problem, wouldn't you have spoken just like Job? Would you not have worried and complained like Job? Through Job's situation, God is telling us about our different attitudes that we have when we are in favorable condition and when we are in unfavorable conditions.

We can check our faith when we are faced with tests and trials. Our inner heart and actual faith will be revealed. When faced with tests, we can turn away with fasting and prayers to receive the solution to the problems. The apostle Paul was beaten, imprisoned, and suffered many things for the name of the Lord Jesus, but he never complained against God. We should also have this kind of faith.

"Is not your fear of God your confidence, And the integrity of your ways your hope? Remember now, who ever perished being innocent? Or where were the upright destroyed?" (4:6-7).

Eliphaz' anger was increasing and he was pointing out Job's shortcomings. Rather than seeing within himself by what was said, Job also began to get angry. If you advise somebody with love, the other person will feel that love and accept the advice. But advice with ill-feelings or anger will only cause ill-feelings for the other person as well. So, the person will not accept the advice.

Job feared God, and he relied on Him. To rely on God is to leave everything to Him. To fear Him is to revere and respect Him. Job respected Him but in another sense he was also afraid of Him. Also, because he believed in the almighty God, he relied on Him in his life.

But we should check whether Job really and truly feared God and relied on Him. To fear God is to keep His words (Deuteronomy chapter 28).

If we believe that God is able to do all things, we can rely on Him in everything. Job wanted his deeds to be perfect in the sight of God. He wanted to be perfect before Him. And Eliphaz, because he was Job's friend, knew very well about Job's deeds.

But as Job himself encountered problems, his words were very different from what he said before! "Job, did you not rely on God because you feared Him? But as I hear your words, how can I say you relied on God? If you truly fear Him, you cannot say such things!"

"Didn't you want your deeds to be perfect in the sight of God? Just think to yourself! Everybody comes to destruction because of his sins. If you were an honest man, wouldn't God give you prosperity?" In verse 7, Eliphaz asked Job, "Who ever perished being innocent?"

Then, can an innocent person perish? Romans 6:23 says that wages of sin is death. Death comes from sin. Men perish because of sins. Since Enoch and Elijah lived holy lives without any blemish or blame, they were caught up to heaven alive without having to see physical death.

God's word certainly tells us that God is with a person who is honest and righteous. He will also guide such a person to prosperity. So, when Eliphaz said, "Where were the upright destroyed?" it was the word of truth. But it's not true that Eliphaz said this because he knew the truth very well. He was sometimes saying the truth because he also believed in God, but at other times he spoke many untruths.

"According to what I have seen, those who plow iniquity and those who sow trouble harvest it. By the breath of God they perish, and by the blast of His anger they come to an end" (4: 8-9).

If you plow iniquity and sow trouble, the fruit turns out nothing but trouble. The field that is plowed here spiritually refers to a man's heart. God wants our heart to be a field of good soil. These fields of the heart are all different for different men.

People have heart-fields like a pathway, rocky soil, thorny fields, or fields of good soil. Job's heart was good soil. Up to the point Eliphaz said, "Those who plow iniquity and those who sow trouble harvest it," what he said was correct.

But actually, Eliphaz was judging Job with his own thoughts. He believed that because Job was suffering from boils, he must have sown evil, and that is why he was harvesting evil. "In my opinion, you plowed evil and sowed trouble, so it must be that you are harvesting the fruit of trouble now!"

Therefore, by saying "By the breath of God they perish, and by the blast of His anger they come to an end," Eliphaz was now condemning Job as a sinner. However, Job was not the kind of sinner Eliphaz was talking about. On the contrary, Job was upright and honest.

Job did not plow evil. He plowed goodness and he did not sow troubles. The reason why Job complained and lamented was not because his heart was evil but because he didn't really know the truth and he had no experience of meeting God.

Therefore, the viewpoint of Job's friend and that of God concerning the heart of Job were completely different. Eliphaz kept on saying evil words with his evil.

"The roaring of the lion and the voice of the fierce lion, and the teeth of the young lions are broken. The lion perishes for lack of prey, And the whelps of the lioness are scattered" (4: 10-11).

If the voice of the lion, which is the king of beasts, ends, it means everything is finished. If the young lion's teeth are broken and they cannot catch and eat their prey, then they would be useless. Old lions do not have the strength or speed to catch other animals.

"Even the king of beasts, the lions, would be useless if their teeth are broken. If they get old, they don't have strength to catch prey, so even the whelps are scattered. Lions are strong at one point, but they also get old. Likewise, men have good times and bad times. It is one's fate, and we cannot do anything about it."

Eliphaz was now talking about the principles in this world. He was saying men had ups and downs in life. But this is just the principle for this world; it is not correct according to the word of God.

God says in Exodus 15:26, "If you will give earnest heed to the voice of the LORD your God, and do what is right in His sight, and give ear to His commandments, and keep all His statutes, I will put none of the diseases on you which I have put on the Egyptians; for I, the LORD, am your healer."

It tells us that if we live by God's word, He will keep us from all diseases. If we fear God and live with faith, the word of Mark 9:23, saying, "'If You can?' All things are possible to him who believes" will be realized in our life. It is the law of God to reap what we sow (Galatians 6:7-8).

Therefore, saying there are ups and downs and good times and bad times in life is just the principle of this world, not the will of God. So, we should know that Eliphaz' words were not true. It is not the word of God. It was just his personal opinion.

In the Book of Job, we should clearly discern which parts are God's words and which parts came from personal opinions. But some people quote the verses that were written with human thoughts as if they were the word of God, and this cannot be right.

2. Eliphaz' Spiritual Status and Pride

"Now a word was brought to me stealthily, And my ear received a whisper of it. Amid disquieting thoughts from the visions of the night, When deep sleep falls on men, Dread came upon me, and trembling, And made all my bones shake" (4:12-14).

'When deep sleep falls on men' means 'in the middle of the night.' Eliphaz saw some kind of vision. He had a spiritual experience, but he did not fully understand it, so he had disquieting thoughts.

Though he had not had experience of meeting God, he

studied the law, and he also knew about Abraham and Moses. Have you walked deep in the woods alone in the middle of the night? If you do not have complete trust in God who is with you, you may tremble with fear. You may feel your bones shake. Eliphaz felt his bones shake.

"Then a spirit passed by my face; The hair of my flesh bristled up. It stood still, but I could not discern its appearance; A form was before my eyes; There was silence, then I heard a voice: 'Can mankind be just before God? Can a man be pure before his Maker? He puts no trust even in His servants; And against His angels He charges error'" (4:15-18).

A certain spirit passed by Eliphaz. He didn't see it very clearly, but he felt the spirit as it passed by him. So, the hair of his flesh bristled up. When you have spiritual experience for the first time, you may have this kind of phenomenon.

Spirit is not seen in eyes, but even new believers can feel that a spirit passed by or the enemy devil is working.

When I was a deacon, I sometimes prayed all-night in the church. There were some elderly senior deaconesses who came to pray, too. But after about 30 minutes from the time they started praying, I couldn't hear their prayers any more. When I saw them they were dozing.

At that time, I had a spiritual experience. The enemy devil and Satan were making the senior deaconesses tired and were making them fall asleep. When I strongly prayed in other tongue, "Enemy devil and Satan, go away! The devil of tiredness and slumber, go away!" Then, the senior deaconesses suddenly woke up and I could hear them praying.

When I strongly prayed to drive away the enemy devil, I could feel the demons passing by my side. After I prayed, "God, protect us with the fiery walls of the Holy Spirit so that no devil can be at work," I could see the senior deaconesses praying fervently.

Whenever they told me, "We can pray so fervently when we pray with you!" I could just laugh inside. Even though we do not have the gift of visions, those with clear spirits can feel something. Many people can discern whether the spirit is moving or disturbing.

We Should Clearly Discern the Spirits

Verse 16 says, "It stood still, but I could not discern its appearance; A form was before my eyes." There was a spirit in front of Eliphaz, but he could not discern whether it was Satan or spirit sent by God. If he could discern it properly, he didn't have to fear at all. Because Eliphaz believed in God, he tried to hear His voice.

"Can mankind be just before God? Can a man be pure before his Maker? He puts no trust even in His servants; And against His angels He charges error." Before, Eliphaz listened to the teachings of Job, who feared God, and he also studied the Law, but like Job, he had no experience in actually meeting God.

He was not at the level to discern the spirits, so with his minimal spiritual experience, he was saying something as if it were given by God, along with his own thoughts.

We are justified before God by faith, and we can become more righteous and sanctified to the extent that we find out our evil in us, cast it off, and practice the word of God. But we can never be 100% righteous and holy like God Himself. It's so obvious that mankind cannot be more righteous or more pure than God. It is true that men can never be like God, and they cannot be more just and purer than God.

But verse 18 says, "He puts no trust even in His servants; And against His angels He charges error." This is not right.

God trusted Abraham, and He appointed him as the Father of Faith. Moses, David, and Paul all had trust from God and were used by Him. If God appoints His messengers or servants, He doesn't charge error against them, but He gives them strength to accomplish their ministries.

Just think about who God is! Also, how can angels managed by God do anything foolish? Especially, God Himself is using them, and would He say, "Why are you so foolish?" God who knows everything has His plans even since before time began, and He trusts and uses appropriate servants according to their vessels. Now, Eliphaz at one moment was quoting from the word of God, but in the next moment, he was saying something against the truth.

It's the same today. Among those who pray a lot, some of them say they heard many kinds of the voice of the Holy Spirit, but many times, they were not really the voice of the Holy Spirit. Also, many people misquote the words of God

Eliphaz Is Proud of His Spiritual Experience

"How much more those who dwell in houses of clay, whose foundation is in the dust, who are crushed before the moth! Between morning and evening they are broken in pieces; unobserved, they perish forever. Is not their tent-cord plucked up within them? They die, yet without wisdom" (4:19-21).

Eliphaz likened Job with those who dwell in houses of clay, whose foundation is in the dust, who are crushed before the moth. He was expressing the status of Job who used to be the richest man in the east but lost everything. But it was too much to say men are to be crushed before the moth.

In Eliphaz' opinion, Job was completely destroyed forever. There seemed to be no possibility for Job to rise again. Eliphaz was judging and concluding that nobody would remember Job, who was completely destroyed, without strength to even rise again.

If the tent-cord is plucked up, it means the foundation itself has disappeared. Eliphaz was being cynical by saying, "They die, yet without wisdom." "Job! You used to advise and counsel people for you had much wisdom, but where is your wisdom now? If you had real wisdom, would you have been in this kind of situation today?"

Eliphaz used to listen to the teachings of Job and respected him, but as Job had nothing left, Eliphaz was trampling on Job, making him feel more miserable. This act of Eliphaz is like the Pharisees and scribes at the time of Jesus, who taught the law but did not practice it themselves.

Now, Eliphaz was very proud saying, "I heard this in vision. I also received inspiration." He was judging and criticizing Job just by looking at the outward appearances. He was spiritually arrogant thinking he heard the voice of God, but in fact, he was receiving Satan's work.

Chapter 5

The Anger and Jealousy of Foolish Men

1. Through Spiritual Arrogance
   Eliphaz Wrongfully Discusses the Word of God
2. Difference between Fleshly Viewpoint and Spiritual Viewpoint
3. Eliphaz' Different Words and Actions

"For anger slays the foolish man, And jealousy kills the simple." (Job 5:2)

1. Through Spiritual Arrogance Eliphaz Wrongfully Discusses the Word of God

"Call now, is there anyone who will answer you? And to which of the holy ones will you turn? For anger slays the foolish man, And jealousy kills the simple" (5:1-2).

In chapter 4, it was explained that Eliphaz had some spiritual experience, but didn't know the truth completely, and so he used his own thoughts as if he had heard the voice of God. He thought he experienced the spiritual realm, and he became arrogant because of it.

In his spiritual arrogance, he spoke the following that was not the word of God as if it were the word of God saying, "Call now, is there anyone who will answer you? God has forsaken you, and will there be an answer even if you cry out? If you are among the holy ones, you will only be ashamed of yourself, and you will not dare stand before them!"

Eliphaz concluded no matter how much Job prayed and cried out to God, God wouldn't answer him. In his arrogance he denied the word of God. The Bible says, "Call upon Me in the day of trouble; I shall rescue you, and you will honor Me" (Psalm 50:15), and "Call to Me and I will answer you, and I will tell you great and mighty things, which you do not know" (Jeremiah 33:3).

Therefore, it is the will of God to call on Him in the days of trials. But, Eliphaz came to a mistaken conclusion by saying there would be no answer from God no matter how much Job might pray and cry out.

Jesus did not come for the righteous, but for sinners. Because of his misunderstandings concerning God's word, Eliphaz, just like the Pharisees, blamed Job for his uncleanliness and he also denied the truth of the word of God. Because of his misunderstanding of God's word, Eliphaz wrongfully criticized Job. He didn't realize his own evil but rather he was rebuking a righteous man.

However, in verse 2, what he said was correct, that anger slays the foolish man. Proverbs 12:16 says, "A fool's anger is known at once, But a prudent man conceals dishonor." There are many people who easily get angry. It happens between parents and children, between friends and between husbands and wives.

Furthermore, some mothers get angry at such little children who do not really know anything, and this is also something foolish. Anger, jealousy, or envy comes from Satan, and they lead men to the way of destruction. They are evil that we have to remove.

2. Difference between Fleshly Viewpoint and Spiritual Viewpoint

"I have seen the foolish taking root, And I cursed his abode immediately. His sons are far from safety, they are even oppressed in the gate, and there is no deliverer. His harvest the hungry devour and take it to a place of

*thorns, and the schemer is eager for their wealth" (5:3-
5).*

Eliphaz thought Job was so foolish because he could not
control his feelings, but instead he poured out his complaints
and resentments against God. And now, Eliphaz was cursing the
foolishness of Job and his family. Before Job had troubles, his
children were also well-off, but since their father was in agony,
they could not have any peace.

In verse 4 is 'to keep the gate.' 'They are even oppressed
in the gate' means that they are oppressed by some form
of authority. Eliphaz was saying Job and his children were
oppressed by the authority of God to be put into that kind of
disaster. He also concluded that because God was doing it, there
was no deliverer either.

What does "His harvest the hungry devour and take it to
a place of thorns, and the schemer is eager for their wealth"
mean? The hungry means the invaders. Because invaders lack
something, they invade other countries to fill their needs.

The thorns can be compared with barbed wire that is strung
on the walls of the rich people's houses. We can say that Job had
the barbed-wire to keep his harvest, but it would be taken by the
invaders. Eliphaz intended to say that the evil words coming out
from Job's mouth would become a trap for him and that he was
oppressed by authority and all his possessions were taken away.

Proverbs 18:21 says, "Death and life are in the power of the
tongue, And those who love it will eat its fruit." Even when we
speak jokingly, if it is against the truth, it will become a thorn to
us and a trap for bringing accusation by Satan. Many of us do
not realize this fact while we are living on the earth.

"For affliction does not come from the dust, Nor does trouble sprout from the ground, For man is born for trouble, As sparks fly upward" (5:6-7).

This word seems to be right, but we have to realize that Eliphaz still misunderstood. Of course, it is right that affliction does not come from the dust and trouble does not sprout from the ground. But all afflictions and trials, or blessings actually do come from the ground. Men can eat from the ground by sowing in it and harvesting from it.

Now, Eliphaz was lecturing Job. Is man born for trouble as Eliphaz said? Unbelievers would say men are born for trouble and we only live to eat and survive.

Also, they think everything comes to an end by physical death, so they seek only their benefit while living on this earth. They maintain the fleshly viewpoint toward life as being only to enjoy the most of fame, authority, and wealth possible. Therefore, they are actually just going towards their graves day by day. Rather than living happy and joyful days, they have increasing tears, pains, and sighs in their lives.

So, in the viewpoint of the people who have hope of only this world, the life is a continuum of sufferings, and they feel man is born for troubles. Therefore, not only unbelievers but also those believers who aren't able to really have true faith and have no hope of heaven will have the fleshly viewpoint like Eliphaz. So they will eventually become tired of their daily lives.

On the other hand, those who have a spiritual outlook have hope for the heavenly kingdom where they will live happily forever. They can rejoice always, give thanks in all circumstances, and pray continually. Also, they have a clear view of the purpose of life that is to live for God's glory. Whether they eat or drink or whatever they do, their lives on earth are joyous and happy.

Therefore, those who have spiritual viewpoints think men are not born for trouble but for God's glory and to enjoy happiness.

3. Eliphaz' Different Words and Actions

"But as for me, I would seek God, And I would place my cause before God; Who does great and unsearchable things, Wonders without number. He gives rain on the earth And sends water on the fields, So that He sets on high those who are lowly, And those who mourn are lifted to safety" (5:8-11).

We can see how untruthful Eliphaz is through these verses. He completely forgot what he had just said. He said that no matter how much Job might cry out to God, there was no way for God to answer Job. And now, Eliphaz is advising Job to ask God and receive the answer from Him.

Eliphaz was advising Job with the truth, but he himself was a hypocrite who spoke the words but did not act according to them, just like the Pharisees. The almighty God moves all the things in heaven and earth and all nature. He does wondrous things and lifts up those who humble themselves.

Then, what does "And those who mourn are lifted to safety" mean? Here, 'those who mourn' are those who mourn not for fleshly things but in spirit with their love for God. 'Being lifted' means their spirit will be lifted and rise.

We should be able to mourn for God's kingdom and for those

poor souls who are going the way of death. If we observe any blasphemy and actions disturbing to God, our spirits ought to have righteous indignation sometimes, but fleshly righteousness with anger will only disgrace God.

"He frustrates the plotting of the shrewd, So that their hands cannot attain success. He captures the wise by their own shrewdness, And the advice of the cunning is quickly thwarted. By day they meet with darkness, And grope at noon as in the night" (5:12-14).

The Webster's Revised Unabridged Dictionary defines 'shrewd' as 'to be able or clever in practical affairs; sharp in business; sharp-witted; sagacious; keen.' But its spiritual meaning is to swindle others with unrighteous methods and making oneself more of that kind of person. Judas Iscariot who sold out Jesus, and Ananias and Sapphira who cheated a powerful servant of God belong to this kind of spiritual definition of 'shrewd'.

Plotting is to prearrange something secretly or deviously. With plotting they may feel things will go as they want, but after some time, they will fall by tests and trials. The wise will honestly follow the right way.

The Bible says that those who do not live in the truth are foolish. Because men think and plan things that are not right according to the truth, they are caught in their schemes and fall. God protects those who live in the truth. The Bible prohibits us from being guarantors for debts. If we have become guarantors for debts, it means we have violated the truth (Proverbs 22:26).

Because men are foolish, they plot, and because people plot things, others are cheated. But if we live in the truth, God gives us a way out, and works for the good of everything. Also, even if we love God and are loved by Him, if we make schemes before God, He will not accept us. Because God punishes those whom He loves, He will destroy the plots.

Being cunning is a level higher evil than being shrewd. When faced with tests and trials, these people do not have a way to solve the problem, so they face darkness.

But those who live in the truth will not face a situation like darkness because they rule over the enemy devil. Even if they were to meet with darkness, God works for the good in everything.

"But He saves from the sword of their mouth, And the poor from the hand of the mighty. So the helpless has hope, And unrighteousness must shut its mouth" (5:15-16).

The poor here does not just mean those who are sorrowful and distressed, but those who are spiritually poor. Namely, they are the ones who are hungry and thirsty for righteousness and who have poor hearts. Those who have poor hearts have hope for heaven and earnestly seek God, so they will gain faith.

In Luke, chapter 16, the beggar Lazarus was poor, but he could be at the side of Abraham. He was saved and he went to heaven. But the rich man enjoyed himself on this earth and did not seek God. So, he fell to the eternal death. That is why the poor have hope and unrighteousness must shut its mouth.

If we are hungry and thirsty for righteousness and rely on God, He saves from the sword of their mouth, and the poor from the hand of the mighty. Those who are poor in heart will have hope for heaven and naturally, they will depart from unrighteousness.

"Behold, how happy is the man whom God reproves, So do not despise the discipline of the Almighty. For He inflicts pain, and gives relief; He wounds, and His hands also heal. From six troubles He will deliver you, even in seven evil will not touch you" (5:17-19).

When we accept Jesus Christ as our Savior and repent of our sins, we will receive the gift of the Holy Spirit. If we receive the Holy Spirit, our names are written in the book of life in heaven, and we gain the rights of the children of God. That is why, if God's children violate the word of God and go the wrong way, God allows punishment.

If there is no punishment even when we do not even keep the Lord's Day holy and do not live according to the truth, we should check whether we are illegitimate sons (Hebrews 12:5-8). Eliphaz was counseling Job saying, "You are punished because of your sins, and why are you complaining? Receive the punishment of the almighty God with joy."

Then why did Eliphaz say in verse 18, "For He inflicts pain, and gives relief; He wounds, and His hands also heal"? He heard a lot from his predecessors about the law beginning with the Book of Genesis, and he also studied the word of God.

But he didn't have any spiritual understanding of the knowledge he had. He was just trying to teach Job with only the knowledge he had gained (Job 5:27). Though Job heard his words he was not able to clearly understand or turn away from sins and change. God's word is written by the inspiration of the Holy Spirit, so only when we understand the spiritual meaning can our heart change. Just teaching the literal word of God cannot give true life.

Here, what is the spiritual meaning of "He inflicts pain, and gives relief"? When Satan accused Job, God allowed trial. It was because there was a reason that God had to allow it. It is not God Himself that punishes Job and gives him disease, but Satan accuses him according to how much he has violated the law of the spiritual realm and brings on him disasters or diseases.

Because God commanded the serpent to eat dust, Satan brings about disasters to men to the extent that they commit sins. But if they turn back and repent, God heals them and makes them perfect.

Next, what does 'six troubles' and 'seven evil' mean? The 'six troubles' refer to the six thousand years of time in which mankind lives on this earth since Adam and Eve were driven out from the Garden of Eden. But Eliphaz did not use this expression knowing this spiritual meaning.

"He will deliver you from six troubles" means that just as God created the heavens and earth for six days and rested on the seventh day, those who fear God and live in the truth during the six thousand years in which mankind is under the rule of the enemy devil will receive salvation by the name of Jesus Christ.

Also, 'Even in seven evil will not touch you' refers to the providence of God. The number "7" is the number of perfection in the Bible. After the six thousand years of human history, the Millennium Kingdom will take place on this earth, and after the seven thousand years of history, the eternal kingdom of heaven and hell will be revealed through the Great White Throne Judgment.

Therefore, 'in seven evil' symbolizes the perfect providence and will of God who planned the seven thousand years of history. Even in trials, the Bible promises that those who rely on God completely and ask Him will be delivered from those trials.

"In famine He will redeem you from death, And in war from the power of the sword. You will be hidden from the scourge of the tongue, And you will not be afraid of violence when it comes. You will laugh at violence and famine, And you will not be afraid of wild beasts" (5:20-22).

In famine everybody is affected, and how can God redeem us? In 1 Kings chapter 17, there was a famine for three and a half years at the time of Ahab's reign in Israel, because of severe idolatry that brought about God's anger.

But the prophet Elijah was loved by God, and God guided him to the brook Cherith and fed him with bread and meat through a crow. Also, when the brook also dried, God guided him to the widow in Zarephath. Those who do not doubt God, and cast off sins and rely on Him will receive God's help.

Next, it says, "And in war from the power of the sword." The prophets were also redeemed from the sword. Jeremiah was taken as a captive but was always protected by God. Even when the Jezebel the queen tried to kill Elijah, he was always protected.

Likewise, if we trust and rely on God completely, we can be recognized and loved by God, and no sword can harm us.

It also says, "You will be hidden from the scourge of the tongue," and what is the scourge of the tongue? Scourge of the tongue is to show the words of one's mouth in action.

For example, when somebody says, "I will kill you!" and then he really kills another person, it is the words in action.

In Daniel chapter 6, there was a decree issued that if anybody prayed to any other god or man except the king himself, he would be put into lion's den.

Daniel, knowing this fact, went back home, and following his habit, prayed to God three times a day facing Jerusalem. So he was thrown into the lion's den. But not one hair on him was hurt. The angel of God shut the mouths of the lions.

Next, 'violence' is the destruction caused by wars and diseases in family and business fields. Even if trials come upon families or fields of business, and even if somebody is dying of a disease, if he repents and turns away, he can experience the healing work and answers of God.

It says, "You will laugh at violence and famine." This means that if Job trusted and relied on God and left everything in His hands, he would not have been cursing and lamenting like now, but he would be laughing in the face of violence and famine. Namely, 'to laugh at' means that the person is confident and brave.

It says, "And you will not be afraid of wild beasts." God created Adam and made him rule over all wild beasts, birds, and fish. But since he disobeyed God and was cursed, wild beasts are afraid of people, or they attack men.

"For you will be in league with the stones of the field,
And the beasts of the field will be at peace with you"
(5:23).

"Job! If you really trusted and relied on God, you wouldn't have foolish lips cursing God, yourself, and your parents. Even if you have violence and famine, you must be confident and bold. You will not fear wild beasts, and the stones of the field and the beasts of the field will be at peace with you!"

Here what do 'field' and 'stone' spiritually symbolize? Field is the heart of man, and the stone is Jesus Christ who is the Rock. When we open our heart and accept Jesus Christ, the Holy Spirit comes into our heart. As we listen to the truth, the word comes into us so that we gain realization and begin to change our heart. This truth is the word of God and Jesus Christ Himself who is the Rock.

Thus, to the extent that our heart changes into good soil, our soul will prosper, everything will go well with us, and we will be healthy. 1 John 3:21-22 says, *"Beloved, if our heart does not condemn us, we have confidence before God; and whatever we ask we receive from Him, because we keep His commandments and do the things that are pleasing in His sight."* In many parts of the Bible God promises His blessings to be given to those whose souls prosper through His word.

Likewise, the truth of Jesus Christ changes us into men of spirit and men of God, and God protects us with the fiery walls of the Holy Spirit and the light of glory, so that the enemy devil and Satan cannot work on us.

If our faith grows up and our souls prosper, disasters cannot come upon us, and the devil, which is symbolized by the 'wild beasts of the field,' cannot harm us, so that even our enemies will be at peace with us.

"You will know that your tent is secure, For you will visit your abode and fear no loss. You will know also that your descendants will be many, And your offspring as the grass of the earth. You will come to the grave in full vigor, Like the stacking of grain in its season. Behold this; we have investigated it, and so it is. Hear it, and

Eliphaz was instructing Job that if he relied on God and asked Him, his family would have peace, and he would receive all blessings of life including the blessings of wealth, children, and long life. But Eliphaz said it was what they had made a study of, but not something he had experienced or believed.

What we have to remember is that even though we may study the word of God and teach it, but with only the knowledge, the listener cannot gain faith. If you accumulate more and more knowledge of truth without practicing it, it is very likely that you will only become arrogant. You will not have any faith with which you can believe from heart, so it is difficult for you to live within the word.

As Jesus said in John 3:6, "That which is born of the Spirit is spirit," so we have to deliver a spiritual message so that the Holy Spirit will work together with the word. This way, the hearts will be opened, and they will understand the truth and gain faith.

Eliphaz proudly counseled Job concerning what he had investigated, but rather than coming to repentance, Job had only increasingly greater ill-feelings.

Chapter 6

Job's Debate

1. Job Expresses His Feelings in Twisted Sarcasm

2. Job Misunderstands that God Is a Fearful God

3. Job Disappoints God with His Words

4. Job Becomes Weaker

5. Fleshly Love Changes

6. Let's Not Argue

7. Job's Evils He Did Not Know of Are Revealed

"Oh that my grief were actually weighed And laid in the balances together
with my calamity! For then it would be heavier than the sand of the seas;
Therefore my words have been rash." (Job 6:2-3)

1. Job Expresses His Feelings in Twisted Sarcasm

"Then Job answered, 'Oh that my grief were actually weighed And laid in the balances together with my calamity! For then it would be heavier than the sand of the seas; Therefore my words have been rash'" (6:1-3).

Job was very angry and resentful, so he is saying his grief is heavier than the sand of the seas. There is a reason for his anger to be extremely fierce.

First, it's because he thinks that the almighty God took away all his children and possessions. Because Job was a righteous man, he did not complain against God initially. But as he was suffering from boils all over his body, he could not bear it any more; he began to complain against God and his parents.

Also, his friends came to him, and yet they did not comfort him but only rebuked him with the words of God, so his anger was fierce.

God tells us not to keep our anger until the sunset, but to love our enemies, to rejoice always and give thanks in all circumstances. But Job did not even realize his anger was not proper in the sight of God while he was debating his side of the argument. Job thought that he was suffering without any reason.

Here, when he said, "My words have been rash," it does not mean that he realized his shortcomings and repented, but he was being cynical. Because his friends did not accept his words but rather criticized them, he regretted that he had spoken them.

On the other side of the argument, Job's friends thought they were right and they rebuked Job. At the same time, Job also thought he was right, and he was saying his friends were bad. Both sides are arguing that they are right, but according to the word of God, both parties do not really understand the truth.

If we have faith, we will cry out to God in prayer in a situation like Job's, and if friends come and rebuke us with the truth, we will accept it with thanks.

2. Job Misunderstands that God Is a Fearful God

"For the arrows of the Almighty are within me, Their poison my spirit drinks; The terrors of God are arrayed against me" (6:4).

Job is misunderstanding that God preplanned to punish him by saying he was shot by the arrow of God, and so his spirit, namely his heart drank the poison. It means he believed that God cursed him and struck him. He believed God's force hit him.

Job was usually afraid of God (Job 3:25). The God whom Job heard about through the law was the God of punishment who parted the Red Sea and gave the Ten Plagues. Job offered God sacrifices out of fear because he wanted to receive salvation.

God is righteous judge and also God of love, but Job did not realize that fact. So, how could his offerings be pleasing in God's sight? So, how could God just leave this upright and honest Job as he was?

God allowed the trials for Job so that he would deny himself and realize that God was love and that He was just. This way,

Job could love God from the bottom of his heart and be loved by Him. Through this process, Job could cast away untruths from within him one by one and became sanctified. Likewise, it is important that once we realize ourselves, we have to cast off what is not right within us according to the truth.

"Does the wild donkey bray over his grass, Or does the ox low over his fodder? Can something tasteless be eaten without salt, Or is there any taste in the white of an egg? My soul refuses to touch them; They are like loathsome food to me" (6:5-7).

A wild donkey brays because it is hungry. If there were food for it, it wouldn't bray. In the same way, Job is saying that he is crying because he has unbearable pain. Also, he is being cynical about the words of his friends saying that just as food without salt and only the white of the egg have no taste, their words without meaning were so bad that he couldn't accept them.

Job said, "My soul refuses to touch them," and this tells us that Job was arrogant. Because what his friends said was of no benefit to him it was no help at all. He was only irritated by them and since he couldn't accept what was said, it only hurt his feelings.

His friends thought they were giving Job a lesson in the word of the truth, but actually they were beating him with their own ill-feelings. And Job was also taking it personally from his friends. He was thinking, "Are you God? I also have much wisdom and knowledge. How much do you know?" He closed the door to his heart with arrogance of his mind, so that even the words of truth from his friends could not give him any lesson. No matter how much truth was in the words of his friends, he was unable to realize it and accept it.

God told us not to throw pearls to the dogs and pigs. If they do not accept it, we should not speak the word of God, even if it's the truth. But Eliphaz did not realize that Job closed the door of his heart and continued to argue with him to teach Job a lesson.

Job could not just accept advice of Eliphaz, but he was irritated by it. That is why he said it was like undercooked and tasteless food to him.

3. Job Disappoints God with His Words

"Oh that my request might come to pass, And that God would grant my longing! Would that God were willing to crush me, That He would loose His hand and cut me off! But it is still my consolation, And I rejoice in unsparing pain, That I have not denied the words of the Holy One" (6:8-10).

Job was praying to God to take his life. We can understand his pains, but we should never ask such a thing of God, for it is disappointing to God. We should not even think about this.

Man's life is given by God, and we cannot treat it as though it were something at our disposal. Furthermore, if we believe in God and ask God to take our life away, it proves that we do not have any faith and it is such a great disappointment to God. But Job was not able to realize this fact.

Daniel had known that he would be thrown into the lion's den because of the schemes of other ministers who were jealous of him, but he did not compromise. He still followed his habit and gave thanks to God in his prayers as he faced towards Jerusalem

(Daniel 6:10).

He was thrown into the lion's den, but God was with him and protected Him through His angel, so not even a hair of Daniel's was hurt. Through this, he could testify the living God to the king and the people of that nation and gave great glory to God.

Even in great pain, when we give thanks to God, hoping that God would work for the good of everything, God can work seeing that faith.

But Job did not understand the truth properly and had no hope for the life to come. That is why he complained before God and disappointed God. Job was not acting by the truth, but he was rather bold before God insisting that he was right.

Job thought the almighty God did not show mercy to him but pitilessly gave him only pain. Job is saying that the almighty One punished him harshly, even though he did not violate His word, which means, Job lived within the truth.

Job was saying all these words of untruthfulness because he didn't have a proper understanding about God. And yet, he kept insisting that he lived in the truth, and he wouldn't have any regret even if God should take his life.

4. Job Becomes Weaker

"What is my strength, that I should wait? And what is my end, that I should endure? Is my strength the strength of stones, Or is my flesh bronze?" (6:11-12).

Job thought it was impossible for him to recover and he had no choice but to return to a handful of dust. It seemed impossible to him because he did not have faith. He was tired of asking God to heal him, and he was completely exhausted.

That is why he was saying he could not endure any more. He felt miserable about his body, which was struck by boils from the head to toes. Since he had no hope of recovery and he didn't expect it, he just hoped for God to take his life away.

"Is it that my help is not within me, And that deliverance is driven from me? For the despairing man there should be kindness from his friend; So that he does not forsake the fear of the Almighty. My brothers have acted deceitfully like a wadi, Like the torrents of wadis which vanish" (6:13-15).

Job thought that he once had wealth, and he could help many people, but now he could do nothing. He was once famous for his knowledge and wisdom, but he had nothing now.

God is almighty and He could even raise Lazarus, who had been dead for four days. But Job had no spiritual faith to believe in God who creates things out of nothing. Because he could not rely on God and had no faith, he became weaker and weaker. Finally, he lost all his strength and will. Because he did not rely on God, he had no wisdom and he was left with only foolishness. We can see that when Job departed from the truth, his evil came out.

"Friends, you are heartless people. When I was rich and healthy and my family seemed happy, you loved and respected me, but when I am left with nothing, where is your love? Without rain, the streams dry up, and isn't it just like you people?"

Job expected warm comfort from his friends, but they were

only giving him harsh advice to rely on God with their ill-feelings. Job did not like it. When we are in tests and trial, we may expect somebody's consolation, but it will only make us weaker; it doesn't help us at all.

When Peter was walking on the sea, he saw the waves of the sea, his own thoughts began to come in, and he sank into the water. Jesus did not comfort him saying something like, "Peter! You almost drowned! How nice it is that you didn't drown. How dangerous it was!" Instead He only rebuked him saying that Peter had little faith.

In the same way, we should plant faith in those who are suffering from trials with the word of God, and guide them to pray so that they will realize and become conscious of themselves and turn away from wrongdoings. We should let them receive the strength to drive away the enemy devil and Satan. This is true and spiritual love. Namely, we should not give advice with our ill-feelings like Job's friends. Only when we give the advice or rebuke with love, can the listener receive strength to stand upright before God.

If we just give simple consolation to those who are experiencing failure or who are in despair, they may say you are the one who understands them, but they will not receive strength from above. They will become even weaker and speak words void of faith before God. Thus, they disappoint God and make the enemy devil happy.

5. Fleshly Love Changes

"Which are turbid because of ice And into which the snow melts. When they become waterless, they are silent, When it is hot, they vanish from their place" (6:16-17).

Snow itself is pure, but as it melts to water, it becomes dirty. If the sun shines, even this water will evaporate. Job was saying that his friends' hearts were like snow. Why did God let this be recorded through Job?

It's because the heart of man is as crafty and as changeable as melting snow. Job's friends advised and rebuked Job using the word of God in their thoughts, but because those words were not words of love, they could not touch or move Job's heart. That is why their conversation only became arguments between Job and his friends.

In the world, when a person is wealthy, many people follow him. But if he goes bankrupt in one day, it's very difficult to find a person who loves him until the end.

Furthermore, fleshly love urges one to seek his/her own advantage or benefit. Spiritual love, however, seeks the benefit of the other person and is the sacrificial and unchanging love. Job's friends also had fleshly love, and Job pointed out their changing hearts.

> "The paths of their course wind along, They go up into nothing and perish. The caravans of Tema looked, The travelers of Sheba hoped for them. They were disappointed for they had trusted, They came there and were confounded" (6:18-20).

In the desert, people move in a group to look for water. If they do not get water, they cannot help but go back to the wilderness and die. "The caravans of Tema looked and the travelers of Sheba hoped for them" means that our hearts are the same.

Before, they had love and affection with one anther, but when they could not gain anything from Job, their original nature was revealed and they were confounded.

6. Let's Not Argue

"Indeed, you have now become such, You see a terror and are afraid. Have I said, 'Give me something,' Or, 'Offer a bribe for me from your wealth,' Or, 'Deliver me from the hand of the adversary,' Or, 'Redeem me from the hand of the tyrants'?" (6:21-23)

As Job continued arguing, his feelings got even more intense. He was feeling that his friends ought to be comforting him having compassion on him, but they were only rebuking him. So he thought they had misunderstood him, that is, Job reasoned that his friends must have thought he wanted to rely on them.

Job said that he would never have asked them to give him something or deliver him from the hand of the adversary. That is why he asked them why they were afraid and treated him the way they did.

In this situation, how dumbfounded his friends must have been! They tried to teach a lesson to Job with what they had studied, but Job shut the door of his heart and didn't listen at all. He rather had more and more anger and argued with them. When many people have arguments, this kind of thing happens.

That is why the word of God tells us not to argue. In 1 Corinthians 6:7, God tells us not to bring any lawsuits against one another but rather accept having been cheated.

If we argue, the enemy devil and Satan will certainly find a way to enter. Satan works through the feelings of peoples to cause them to have ill feelings toward one another developing into the hatred that exists between enemies. That is why we have to cast off all ill-feelings. If we have ill-feelings, even the best advice will not work.

"Teach me, and I will be silent; And show me how I have erred. How painful are honest words! But what does your argument prove?" (6:24-25)

Job's friends had been pointing out the shortcomings of Job, but he did not understand any of it. That is why he said, "If you show me how I have erred, I will be quiet."

7. Job's Evils He Did Not Know of Are Revealed

"Do you intend to reprove my words, When the words of one in despair belong to the wind? You would even cast lots for the orphans And barter over your friend. Now please look at me, And see if I lie to your face. Desist now, let there be no injustice; Even desist, my righteousness is yet in it" (6:26-29).

In other words Job was saying, "Are you all trying to dispute what I have said? My words are out of my despair, and they are like the wind." The expression 'Belonging to the wind' means that it was not truthful and had no value.

When he said, "Are you trying to dispute the words of the one in despair?" Job was continuously reproaching his friends asking how their actions could be reasonable and appropriate. As in verse 27, casting lots for orphans and bartering over friends are things that are totally unacceptable. And in Job's sight, his friends looked as bad as those who are doing these things.

In effect this was what Job was saying, "Now, judge for yourself and if you are confident that you are right without any doubt, then you can look at me straight in the eye and say so! My words are the truth and the facts. You are the ones who have to look back on yourself and turn away. I am right."

Job did not have an evil heart and wouldn't tell a lie. But because he did not understand the truth properly, he could not see his iniquity in himself. Job's friends spoke for Job's own good, but Job himself got mad about it because of what they said. They were hurting Job instead of helping him.

Therefore, when we give advice to others, even though our advice is absolutely correct, we have to say what we do without any personal emotion but only with a manner that is kind and gentle in nature. It is important to give advice with a warm heart and love.

Here, we can find why Job had to go through the trials. Because he did not really understand the truth, Job thought his friends were all wrong and only he was right. This was arrogance. Being arrogant means one's ego and self-importance are standing in contempt or disregard for others. Job thought he was the best in everything, and God punished him for no reason. That is why he could not come to any self-realization in understanding himself. Even when his friends tried to make him realize, he did not want to listen. Rather he reproached his friends believing that they were wrong.

Up to this point we have been able to discover that Job had many mistakes in what he said as fact. He was speaking words that could bind him spiritually. With his words, he was offering chances to Satan to bring accusations against him.

God tells us, "Therefore let him who thinks he stands take heed that he does not fall" (1 Corinthians 10:12). It's dangerous when we think, "I've done this much, it is enough." Like the confession of the apostle Paul, we have to die in the truth every day (1 Corinthians 15:31). Job thought he was standing, and that is why he was falling and suffering.

Another reason why Job could not come to any self-realization in understanding himself was that he believed he tried his best to live a good and righteous life, so he thought he could never have any kind of evil in him.

"Is there injustice on my tongue? Cannot my palate discern calamities?" (6:30)

It clearly reveals to us why Job had to go through the trials. Among the things that Job said, there were many things that were not consistent with the truth. There were also words of unrighteousness. But Job concluded that all his words were righteous and appropriate, but his friends' words were all evil and wrong. How ridiculous and mistaken what Job said really was!

Chapter *7*

Throw Off the Worms of Heart

"As a slave who pants for the shade,
And as a hired man who eagerly waits for his wages." (Job 7:2)

1. Job's Tedious and Painful Daily Life

"Is not man forced to labor on earth, And are not his days like the days of a hired man? As a slave who pants for the shade, And as a hired man who eagerly waits for his wages, So am I allotted months of vanity, And nights of trouble are appointed me. When I lie down I say, 'When shall I arise?' But the night continues, And I am continually tossing until dawn" (7:1-4).

As Job suffered through the trials, he felt that life was miserable because he had lost everything. He was just waiting for death, but he couldn't even die. Rather than comforting Job, his friends showed only contempt for him. He saw no hope.

A hired man's only hope is to receive his daily wages. When the sun rises, he works. After the sun sets he returns home and sleeps. Also, a servant does only what his master tells him to do. He hopes only for night to come so that he is able to rest.

Since Job had been suffering for several months, he felt he was just like a hired servant who was spending meaningless and hopeless days only hoping for the sun to go down. He couldn't get to sleep and he kept on tossing and turning until dawn due to his pain. Since Job had lost his dream and vision, he lamented in despair.

But even a laborer who was hired on a daily basis should

not have the kind of attitude that Job had. A man who knows God and knows about the heavenly kingdom has life in him, so what kind of life should he lead? He should give glory to God in everything, whether eating, drinking, or whatever he does.

In Luke chapter 16, the rich man did not believe in God but enjoyed his life on this earth, and after he died he went down to the Lower Grave which belongs to hell. But Lazarus, who had eaten what fell from the table of the rich man, lived in reverent awe of God and went into the bosom of Abraham in the Upper Grave belonging to heaven. We must have a dream.

We must have hope and dreams to go into New Jerusalem, the best dwelling place in heavenly kingdom. We have to have the dream of receiving the Crown of Gold and Crown of Righteousness by working faithfully for God's kingdom on this earth and by struggling against sins to make ourselves sanctified. The wealth on this earth can be taken away by thieves and it all disappears with the passage of time. But if we store treasure in heaven, we will never have to worry about anything like that. It's because God gives back to us 30, 60, or 100 times more.

Those who fear God and have hope can live with the dream and a vision, so even if they are merely hired men or slaves, they can lead a joyful and happy life. They don't have to lament, complain, or argue like Job did.

2. A Heart Dirty with Worms

"My flesh is clothed with worms and a crust of dirt, My skin hardens and runs" (7:5).

Job had been rich. At one time he was able to live his life in a clean environment and in abundance of all things, including his clothing and everything else. But now, worms and crusts of dirt were all over his body. Even if a person knows God, if he does not have any experience in meeting God or in having spiritual faith, he will naturally lament and speak in words of resentment during a trial like this.

Then, what is the spiritual meaning of this verse? If we look into what Job had said up until this time, we realize that what he said was neither good nor truthful. He had spoken words that were not right or appropriate in the sight of God. What was in his heart was coming out through his lips. It means what was in Job's heart was coming out like filthy worms.

Originally, Job had a good heart that was like rich fertile soil. He was upright and honest in the sight of God. But if we leave even good soil unattended for 10 years, good soil will later have many kinds of weeds and may become like the hardened field.

In this case, we have to plow it, pull out the weeds, and break up the hardened soil to make it good soil again. Of course, just by removing the weeds, we cannot make it completely good soil, because each of the good and bad soils has its own characters.

Job could become like very good soil if he just pulled out the untruth that was like weeds in his heart. That is why God recognized him as being blameless and upright (Job 1:1). But because he had not experienced meeting God nor did he know the truth in the word of God very well, he had spoken out worm-like filthy words.

Since Job was lamenting and complaining, speaking out worm-like filth, the enemy devil and Satan would obviously seize the opportunity to accuse him of it. So God allowed the accusations of Satan to take place.

Job also said, "My skin hardens and runs." When his skin hardened, it meant that new skin grew over a boil or cut and the skin closed. His skin was decaying and festering all over his body. As time went by his skin hardened from the repeated closing, festering and oozing again and again. So, what is the spiritual meaning of this?

When people are full of the Spirit, it seems they have great faith. No matter what the test or trial they may face they feel confident of achieving their victory. This is like when their skin is hardened. But when they actually do face trials and they cannot overcome them, they break down; they show their resentment; and they complain. This complaining and lamenting corresponds in meaning to the 'running skin'. In this kind of situation, how painful and unsettled the heart must be!

In the same way, Job had the kind of heart that was repeatedly hardened and then running. That is why we have to stand on the rock of faith. Those who are armed with the truth have nothing with which Satan can bring his accusations against them, because they stand on the Rock and have already cast off untruthful feelings.

Therefore, we have to quickly kill all the worms of our hearts. If we have such filthy things in our hearts, we have to clean them completely. God looks at our inner heart, so our heart must be clean. Being clean on the outside alone is of no value. If we have any dirt or filth on our clothes or skin, we should quickly wash it off right away.

If we have worm like things in our hearts, can you imagine just how filthy and unsettling it would be! The things of the flesh, which are sinful natures in our heart; the works of the flesh, which are the actions of sins; and all evil things such as ill-feelings, envy, jealousy, and hatred, these are all like worms in the sight of God. Even men hate filthy worms, and how much more would God dislike what is represented by them?

This is reason why Job was suffering from worms all over his body.

3. Job Gives Up on Himself

"My days are swifter than a weaver's shuttle, And come to an end without hope" (7:6).

Job was tossing and turning until dawn not being able to get to sleep. He only hoped for the morning to come quickly, and the day to pass quickly. Job felt one day was as long as several months.

Then, does "My days are swifter than a weaver's shuttle" mean that his days are passing quickly? Long ago, people made cloth material using a loom and made clothes of it at home. When you weave, the shuttle passes very quickly.

What Job meant was not that his time was going fast as the weaver's shuttle, but he wanted to mention the value of time. He was lamenting that time was passing while accomplishing nothing. He had done many valuable things before, but now time was passing by without any hope. He was lamenting this fact.

"Remember that my life is but breath; My eye will not again see good. The eye of him who sees me will behold me no longer; Your eyes will be on me, but I will not be" (7:7-8).

It takes only a couple of seconds for a man to breathe once. It may be a minute or two at the longest. Saying that his life was but breath is about the value of life. Job never knew when he would die, and he could not anticipate anything more in his life.

Before the trials came, Job lived a noble life. He lacked nothing, lived a blessed life, and gained respect and recognition form others. But Job did not have true faith, so he was saying he would not be able to see anything good again.

In no matter what kind of situation we find ourselves, we should never give up like he did. Lazarus had been dead in the tomb for four days, but still he was revived.

Job concluded that people would not see him any more. But in reality, at the end, Job's glorious life returned to him. How did that happen? It was because Job finally met God and repented. Through that he removed the 'worms of his heart.'

When Satan accuses us of something, the problem can be solved only if we remove the thing that was the point of Satan's accusation against us. In the same way, even if we are in a situation like Job's, or even worse, if we are able to stand upright before God, the circumstances are actually nothing. If God meets us, any kind of problem can be resolved.

4. Concerning Sheol (the Grave) in the Bible

"When a cloud vanishes, it is gone, So he who goes down to Sheol does not come up. He will not return again to his house, Nor will his place know him anymore. Therefore I will not restrain my mouth; I will speak in the anguish of my spirit, I will complain in the bitterness of my soul" (7:9-11).

Clouds do not stay in one place, but move about. Even after a long time, they never come back to the original place. Other clouds may come to the same place, but the same cloud will never come back. Because Job had no hope of heaven, he thought man's life ends like moving clouds, and when one dies his spirit goes down to Sheol.

Because he thought life on earth is everything, he was complaining as he so desired. He spoke of complaining 'in bitterness of my soul.' How painful his heart must have been that he lost his children and all possessions!

He did not complain up to that point, but when he had boils all over his body and his skin continually hardened and festered repeatedly, he could not bear any more and spoke words of resentment and complained. It was because Job never really knew about the heavenly kingdom.

If he had known about the kingdom of heaven, he wouldn't have done as he did. But, because he had pain in his heart, he said whatever he wanted to say. He didn't feel the necessity to have righteous lips. But those who have hope for heaven obey the word of God and try to bear and understand everything even when they have pains in their heart. They don't recklessly speak out words of evil just because their heart is broken.

The word 'Sheol' is found both in the Old and New Testament. But the terms 'kingdom of heaven' and 'Paradise' are recorded only in the New Testament.

Genesis 37:35 says, "Then all his sons and all his daughters arose to comfort him, but he refused to be comforted. And he said, 'Surely I will go down to Sheol in mourning for my son.' So his father wept for him." Jacob heard his son Joseph was killed by an animal, and he was saying if Joseph died, he must have gone down to Sheol, and he also wanted to follow his son. When people died in the Old Testament times, they went down to Sheol or otherwise called the Grave.

Also, 1 Samuel 2:6 says, "The LORD kills and makes alive; He brings down to Sheol and raises up." But Job did not know the fact that even after men died and went down to Sheol, they could come up again.

The Structure of Sheol (the Grave)

Proverbs 9:18 says, "But he does not know that the dead are there, That her guests are in the depths of Sheol." It talks about the 'depths of Sheol.'

Isaiah 14:9 says, "Sheol from beneath is excited over you to meet you when you come; It arouses for you the spirits of the dead, all the leaders of the earth; It raises all the kings of the nations from their thrones," and we know that there is Sheol from beneath, which means there is also Sheol above.

Isaiah 14:14-15 says, "'I will ascend above the heights of the clouds; I will make myself like the Most High.' Nevertheless you will be thrust down to Sheol, To the recesses of the pit." Lucifer who betrayed God will fall into the deepest recesses of Sheol.

Luke 16:19-26 talks about the beggar Lazarus and the rich man. The beggar Lazarus who feared God went to the Upper Grave and was put into the side of Abraham, and the rich man went down to the Lower Grave, or Hades, and was suffering from unbearable pain in fire.

The rich man asked Abraham to cool his tongue with just a drop of water, but Abraham told him that there was a big chasm between the Upper Grave and the Hades, so he could not go there.

Namely, the parts of Sheol, the Two Graves are differentiated. One is the Lower Grave that is often called 'Hades' which belongs to hell and the other is the Upper Grave that belongs to heaven. The role of the Upper Grave in Old Testament and the

New Testament is different.

During the Old Testament times, Sheol above was a waiting place for those who were saved. But since the Lord resurrected and ascended into heaven, people who are saved will not go to the bosom of Abraham in the Upper Grave but they will go into Paradise to be at the side of the Lord.

So, when one criminal who was on one side of Jesus repented and accepted Him as the Savior, Jesus said to him, "Truly I say to you, today you shall be with Me in Paradise" (Luke 23:43).

But the Bible tells us that Jesus did not go to Paradise right after He died on the cross. Jesus said, "For just as Jonah was three days and three nights in the belly of the sea monster, so will the Son of Man be three days and three nights in the heart of the earth" (Matthew 12:40). Namely, He went down to the Grave.

5. What Is the Judgment of Conscience?

What did the Lord do in the Grave?

1 Peter 3:18-20 says, "For Christ also died for sins once for all, the just for the unjust, so that He might bring us to God, having been put to death in the flesh, but made alive in the spirit; in which also He went and made proclamation to the spirits now in prison, who once were disobedient, when the patience of God kept waiting in the days of Noah, during the construction of the ark, in which a few, that is, eight persons, were brought safely through the water."

As said, Jesus' spirit preached to the spirits in prison. Here, 'prison' refers to the Grave. Jesus went to the Upper Grave where saved souls were waiting, and preached the gospel.

In the Old Testament times, there must have been many

people who lived lives that were morally and spiritually better than now. Then, is it true that all of them were judged and then went to the way of death? There must have been people who sought God and lived in goodness, too. That is why God allowed all those who were eligible to be saved to enter into the Upper Grave.

Korea has the history of thousands of years, but it is only about 120 years since Christianity was introduced. Then, did everybody who died before the introduction of the gospel to Korea go to hell? It cannot be! If so, God cannot be a just judge. Therefore, among those who lived before Jesus Christ, those who acknowledged God and lived according to their conscience could be saved and went to the Upper Grave. Then, Jesus died on the cross and went to the Upper Grave to preach to the souls for 3 days, so they could be saved by the name of Jesus Christ.

Then, does that mean the souls are still in the Upper Grave? It's not really so. After those in the Upper Grave accepted Jesus Christ as their Savior, they went to Paradise. Also, those who believe in Jesus Christ and die go down to the Upper Grave and adapt themselves there for three days, and then go up to Paradise. This is the reason why we cannot find the vocabulary for the word 'Paradise' or 'Heavenly Kingdom' not even once in the Old Testament.

Romans 2:12-15 says, "For all who have sinned without the law will also perish without the Law, and all who have sinned under the law will be judged by the Law; for it is not the hearers of the law who are just before God, but the doers of the law will be justified. For when Gentiles who do not have the law do instinctively the things of the Law, these, not having the Law, are a law to themselves, in that they show the work of the law written in their hearts, their conscience bearing witness and their thoughts alternately accusing or else defending them."

When Gentiles who do not know the law do the things of the law with their nature, namely with their conscience, that conscience bears witness. If somebody wants to steal something that belongs to somebody else, his conscience will judge that it is sin, but because his conscience is weak, he may go ahead and steal it anyway.

In men's hearts, there is the heart of spirit, which is given by God and which is the truth, and the heart of untruth, and lastly the conscience, which is formed by each individual. God gave people the law in the Old Testament times, and decided the status of salvation according to their deeds of observing the law.

But this law was given only to the people of Israel, the chosen ones of God. The Gentiles did not have the law. So, people born on this earth who lived before Jesus lived according to their consciences. Likewise, the conscience becomes the standard of action of the law. So, those who are good will listen to their conscience even in difficult situations and not act with evil. But those who are evil do evil things for their own benefits or for personal advantage.

Since the Gentiles did not receive the law, God considered the conscience of the Gentiles as their law and decided the status of salvation according to their deeds done by their conscience. This is called the Judgment of Conscience. Since Jesus Christ came to this earth, people who hear the gospel but do not open their heart and not accept it cannot say, "I could not believe because I did not know."

But even today, those who have never heard the gospel will be judged by their conscience. Job did not know about the kingdom of heaven, so he thought our citizenship was in the

Grave, not in heaven. He thought, once he went down to Sheol, he would never be able to come back up. That is why he felt so hopeless.

6. Job Misunderstands that It Is God Who Tortures Him

"Am I the sea, or the sea monster, That You set a guard over me?" (7:12)

Job knew the greatness of sea, and also that the sea monster was very fearful. Some people think if they see a sea monster or dragon in their dreams, it's a very good dream.

But if believers dream of a dragon or a serpent, it symbolizes they will face a great test. Dreaming of pigs also symbolizes they will face tests and difficulties.

Here, Job was complaining to God that he was such a weak man, and why God inflicted him with unbearable pains. He was misunderstanding that God had preplanned everything to punish him. Job had the wisdom to understand the laws of nature. Just by looking at the laws of the nature, we can acknowledge the fact that Creator God exists. Job made sacrificial offerings to God, but it was only out of his fear.

"If I say, 'My bed will comfort me, My couch will ease my complaint,' Then You frighten me with dreams And terrify me by visions" (7:13-14).

If he could sleep well, Job could have forgotten about his pain for a moment, but he could not even sleep well. He was also complaining that when he fell asleep God frightened him.

When the people of the world have some problems that are difficult to solve and feel painful due to them, they may say, "Let's just forget about everything and get some sleep." But because they have so many worries, their sleep is not really restful or relaxing, and their dreams are not comfortable, either. This was the case with Job, too.

Then, if we have faith, how should we act? We can leave everything to God the Almighty so that He can solve the problem. If we are faced with tests and trials, we first have to realize what kind of walls of sin we have against God and repent thoroughly with tears. If we just worry about them and complain against God, it means we do not have true faith. We must show our faith so that God can solve the problem.

Job was frightened in his dreams, and he misunderstood that God did it. But God does not frighten people in their dreams. Job misunderstood God thinking that God would not give him even a moment's rest, but tortured him even in his dreams.

In dreams, there are spiritual dreams and fleshly dreams. Spiritual dreams come to one's spirit. Through dreams, God shows us what will happen in the future, and the Holy Spirit tells us something.

There is also a dream of the soul. This is the dream that we have with our own thoughts. Those who do not live in the truth cannot help but live in their own thoughts, so they dream within their thoughts and desires.

For example, if somebody wants to go to the United States, he may go to the United States in his dream. If he has some kind of fear, then he may be chased by a robber. This kind of dream does not agree with the reality later.

But to the extent that we cast off our thoughts and live in the truth, which means, to the extent that we become men of spirit, we have more of the spiritual dreams, so they also come true in reality.

"So that my soul would choose suffocation, Death rather than my pains. I waste away; I will not live forever. Leave me alone, for my days are but a breath. What is man that You magnify him, And that You are concerned about him, That You examine him every morning And try him every moment?" (7:15-18)

When a man suffocates, he dies. Because Job thought God was giving him hard times even in his dreams, he wanted to die from his heart. That is why he said, 'Death rather than my pains.' How painful it was for him!

Then, how should we act when we suffer from pains? As God said in Psalm 50:15, "Call upon Me in the day of trouble; I shall rescue you, and you will honor Me," so we have to seek Him and cling to Him. We have to give thanks whether we may have a disease or our business goes bankrupt or it goes well. We have to give thanks even in tests. If we follow the will of God for us to give thanks in all circumstances, God will work for the good of everything, and there will surely be something to be joyful for in actuality.

Next, Job said, "I waste away; I will not live forever." Just as a man without faith has no hope for heaven, there was nothing else left for Job but hating his life. Even if Job was healed, he had already lost all his possessions and children, so what kind of hope did he have? Could he have understood the value of life?

But those who have faith have hope for heaven, so even if God takes their children away, they can give thanks to God because their children are with the Lord.

Job knew that God controls life and death. So, he was complaining that God did not take away his life though he wanted to die so much.

Job said God magnifies man, and this is truth. In Genesis chapter 1, when God created man, He made him after His own image and set him as the lord of all creation. Because God deems man great, He gave even His one and only Son Jesus to be crucified. Also, God watches us every second and every minute with His blazing eyes.

It also says, "You examine him every morning." By examining, God encourages us to do good and allows punishments for evil things we do. For us not to fall into ways of destruction, God sometimes allows trials and tests when we do not live in the truth, so that we can realize what we are doing wrong. Because we are not illegitimate sons but true sons, if we befriend the world and sin, God allows us to repent and come back to the light.

So, if we face any kind of problem or trials, we should give thanks to God and find why we are facing such a problem. Then, we have to repent of our wrongdoing.

"Will You never turn Your gaze away from me, Nor let me alone until I swallow my spittle? Have I sinned? What have I done to You, O watcher of men? Why have You set me as Your target, So that I am a burden to myself?" (7:19-20)

It takes such a short time to swallow spittle. Job was complaining that God wouldn't leave him alone even when he swallowed his spittle. God watches us every second, not forsaking us for a moment, because He loves us.

God was watching him and allowed trials to him to sanctify him and to bless him. But Job did not understand the truth. He knew about God only as knowledge without having any real experience with Him.

So, God had to allow trials to Job so that he could realize what was not right according to the truth, repent, and become a true child of God who loves Him with true heart and perfect faith. Even when His creature, man, was speaking such evil words and complaints, God just heard them and bore with them.

He endured just to change even one more soul and to guide him to the way of salvation and blessings. We should be able to read this heart of God.

God searches our heart and thoughts. If His children commit sins, He suffers a lot. If we commit sins, it's same as spitting on God's face. It's same as spitting on God's church and His servants.

Job was asking what harm it would do to God even if he committed sin. Then, what harm was there?

First, by committing sins, the relationship between the Father and the children is broken. Secondly, God's heart is broken because He knows His children are going the way of destruction. Thirdly, those children who committed sins cannot go into the kingdom of God, and so, there will be no relation between God and His children. Therefore, God cannot help but suffer from pain in heart.

Fourthly, the precious blood of the Lord becomes meaningless. Fifthly, God suffers because things are going as the devil wants. The will of the devil is to make God's children stand against God and to prevent God's kingdom from being established.

Let us say the father in a household is telling his son to study hard. After hearing his father, what if this son argues saying, "Even if I do not study well, what harm would it do to you, father? What's the matter whether I excel in academics or not?" Then, how heartbroken his father must be! It's the same with God here.

"God, why have You set me as Your target, so that I am a burden to myself?" Job was now going beyond just complaints and resentment. He was being sarcastic to God. He was even mocking God with his twisted heart. But God did not feel the pain of it just because of the words.

Because He waits for us to change with joy, it is not really a burden.

"Why then do You not pardon my transgression, And take away my iniquity? For now I will lie down in the dust, And You will seek me diligently, But I will no longer be" (7:21).

Job now had two different minds. One is that he wanted God to take away his life and the other was he wanted to be healed. But there was no answer, and Job says that it was because God did not forgive his transgression and iniquity.

When we realize our sin and repent and turn away, God forgives us. However, though Job had many transgressions and iniquities, he didn't repent. He was just saying, "God, how come You are not forgiving my transgressions and iniquities? Why don't You just take it easy?" He was speaking nonsense, so how could his problem be solved?

Job offered sacrifices out of his fear of God before the trials came. But when he was suffering from boils, he had no fear. He was only lamenting and wishing that he could die quickly because once he went down to Sheol, he thought, it would be the end, whether God forgave his sins or not.

Chapter 8

The Wise Counsel of Bildad the Shuhite

1. Bildad Explains Retribution for Sin
2. How to Solve the Problems and Receive Answers
3. Bildad Tries to Use Parables to Make Job Understand
4. Bildad Advises Job to Recover by Living in the Truth

"Though your beginning was insignificant, Yet your end will increase greatly."
(Job 8:7)

1. Bildad Explains Retribution for Sin

"Then Bildad the Shuhite answered and said: How long will you speak these things, And the words of your mouth be like a strong wind?" (8:1-2)

Now, the second friend appears. He is Bildad the Shuhite. He has been quietly listening until now, and he gently begins to give his advice to Job to make him understand with the word of God. Bildad was not talking in heated temperament like Eliphaz, but was trying to make his friend, Job, understand with gentleness of heart.

He was trying to find a way to teach Job the truth that he knew, thinking of ways to make Job realize and repent. Bildad could not deal with Job's complaints and lamentation any more and asked him, "How long will you speak these things, And the words of your mouth be like a strong wind?"

What Are Words That Are Like a Strong Wind?

Let us first look at the spiritual meaning of 'strong wind.' When hurricane comes, houses fall, ships are wrecked, and people die due to landslides; it causes great damage.

Likewise, if believers do not live in the truth but speak words of untruth like Job, God says it is like 'strong wind.' If we speak words of untruth, it is something that Satan can accuse of, so trials and difficulties come upon us. If we hurt other's feelings, complain, lament, or curse, it is like strong winds. Just like hurricanes and tornadoes do not benefit us at all, if we let such strong words out from our mouths, it benefits neither others nor ourselves.

Why should we let Satan accuse us of the words of our lips? We should always be awake to pray and check ourselves so that we will not have lips like strong winds. With merely one word, on one hand, we can plant faith, grace, and life in another person, and on the other hand, we may cause him to fall. Words of strong winds hurt others' heart and cause pains.

"Does God subvert judgment? Or does the Almighty pervert justice? If your sons have sinned against Him, He has cast them away for their transgression" (8:3-4).

God does not subvert judgment or pervert justice. God always pays us back according to what we have done.

Revelation 22:11-12 says, "He who is unjust, let him be unjust still; he who is filthy, let him be filthy still; he who is righteous, let him be righteous still; he who is holy, let him be holy still. And behold, I am coming quickly, and My reward is with Me, to give to every one according to his work." As said, God never subverts judgment.

Job offered sacrifices on behalf of his children. Job 1:5 says, "It may be that my sons have sinned and cursed God in their hearts." Because Job feared that his children's misdoings would bring disaster to them, he offered the sacrifices on behalf of them. But because it was not his children who repented, he always feared some kind of disaster might come upon them, and he was uncomfortable all the time. Job was afraid of God (Job 3:25).

Job's friends knew that Job's children were not as righteous as Job. That is why they were saying that God took Job's children because of their sins. And they were asking, "Why was Job complaining against God because of it?"

If God's children try to live by the word of God, pray, and keep His commandments and love Him, God is always with them and protects them. So, if there are some kinds of trials or tests, it means they are cheating God in some areas or there must be something untruthful in their deeds.

When David committed the sin of murder by letting one of his most loyal subjects be killed by the Gentiles, God sent Prophet Nathan to rebuke him. David, as soon as he received the rebuke, repented and was forgiven of his sins, but still, he had to go through trials through the accusation of Satan.

2 Samuel 12:14 says, "However, because by this deed you have given great occasion to the enemies of the LORD to blaspheme, the child also who is born to you shall surely die." David committed a sin that allowed the devil to bring accusations against him, and God had to allow it according to the rules of the spiritual realm. David held on to God with fasting, but his son finally died.

In John chapter 5, we can see a man who had been sick for 38 years was healed by Jesus. Then, Jesus met him again later.

John 5:14 says, "Afterward Jesus found him in the temple and said to him, 'Behold, you have become well; do not sin anymore, so that nothing worse happens to you.'" If we commit sins again, something worse will reoccur, but if we do not sin, we will be healed completely.

God controls even the enemy devil and Satan. Thus, if we live in the truth, we will be protected by God, and our lives will be prosperous.

2. How to Solve the Problems and Receive Answers

"If you would earnestly seek God And make your supplication to the Almighty, If you were pure and upright, Surely now He would awake for you, And prosper your rightful dwelling place. Though your beginning was small, Yet your latter end would increase abundantly" (8:5-7).

Bildad the Shuhite was advising Job to earnestly seek God, to pray to Him and repent before Him. Here, we can see that the opinions among Job's friends were different.

Eilpaz was saying something untruthful. He said in Job 5:1, "Call out now; Is there anyone who will answer you?" But Bildad was telling Job the truth of seeking God and praying to Him.

For Job to repent before God and turn away, he first has to earnestly seek Him. "God, I had strong winds in my mouth because of the evil in my heart. Please forgive me of speaking these evil words." He must show his deeds of repentance with this kind of prayer.

If we just confess with lips, that is not all that needs to be done. We have to circumcise our heart and cleanse it. We have to repent of sins, turn away, and cleanse our heart.

"[God will] prosper your rightful dwelling place" means that if we do not lie and have proper deeds, God will consider us as in the rightful dwelling place.

God looks at our inner heart, so if our heart is not clean, He does not say we are right. Men may say one is honest and upright just by looking at one's deeds, but God looks at the inner heart. Thus, our heart must be clean. Only then will God cause us to prosper so that though our beginning may be small, in the end we will be increased abundantly.

Job had to start from the bottom now. He doesn't have children or wealth, but if he repents of his words like strong winds and earnestly seeks God and prays, God will allow him to prosper. This is not the word of Bildad, but of God.

Our workplace cannot just be managed by itself. Above all, we need faith. Without faith, we can neither repent nor turn, neither can we be cleansed. When we keep the word of God by praying, we can receive faith from above. We start with the faith as small as a mustard seed, but it will continue to grow.

God works according to this faith. If we earnestly seek God, pray to him and if we are clean and upright, our soul prospers. If our soul prospers, God gives us blessings in our family, workplaces, and businesses. He also gives us health.

"For inquire, please, of the former age, And consider the things discovered by their fathers; For we were born yesterday, and know nothing, Because our days on earth are a shadow" (8:8-9).

Bidad was telling Job not to insist that he alone was right, but inquire of the former age and consider the things discovered by their fathers. In order for us to realize ourselves, we have to self-reflect on ourselves with the word of God. The Bible teaches us how the beloved servants of God acted and how they loved God.

'Knowing nothing' means they didn't have much wisdom compared to the former age. It says, "Our days on earth are a shadow." Shadow disappears, and it is different in the morning and evening. It changes often. Likewise, our life is only momentary, not eternal. So, Bildad was urging Job that they should learn from the fathers and realize the wrongdoings in them.

Then, from whom should we learn? First, we have to learn from God. We should not say that only our knowledge and opinions are right, and instead we must kneel down humbly and learn from God. God gave us the never-changing truth in the 66 Books of the Bible.

The Bible also writes about those fathers of faith who loved God and were loved by Him. We can learn how Noah prepared the ark, how Moses guided so many people, how David loved God, and how Daniel did not compromise with the world.

"Will they not teach you and tell you, And utter words from their heart?" (8:10)

All the words and deeds of the fathers of faith, and everything concerning them will be compared with us in judgment. When we reflect on ourselves looking in the mirror of the patriarchs of faith who were deemed right in the sight of God, we can discern whether we are really right or wrong. We can see whether we have sin or not.

The word of God contains everything including what is right and wrong, what is good and evil, and what is righteous or unrighteous. It also contains what faith is, what salvation is, what heavenly kingdom and hell are, and what good and evil are.

3. Bildad Tries to Use Parables to Make Job Understand

"Can the papyrus grow up without a marsh? Can the reeds flourish without water? While it is yet green and not cut down, It withers before any other plant. So are the paths of all who forget God; And the hope of the hypocrite shall perish, Whose confidence shall be cut off, And whose trust is a spider's web. He leans on his

house, but it does not stand. He holds it fast, but it does not endure" (8:11-15).

Bildad was explaining the relativity of things with the examples of the papyrus and the reed. Bildad, with all the love in his heart for Job, used all his wisdom to speak in high metaphorical parables to let Job understand his wrongdoing. Job was a very knowledgeable man.

Papyrus is a tall water plant that grows annually and is used to weave mats. Every one knows that papyrus grows in muddy marshes, and reeds need to grow in water. Just as papyrus needs to grow in marshes and reeds need to grow in water, there is relativity of things in everything.

People plant papyrus into a marsh in which unclean water has permeated and decayed, and then it takes the root in the ground that is not solid. So, it withers earlier than other plants or is easily rooted when men pull it out.

Reeds also flourish in the ground that is beside waters or seashores. Their roots are not stable, either. Papyrus and reeds are green but wither and turn yellowish under the scorching sunlight. In a moment, they become nothing and useless.

Then, what was it that Bildad really wanted to say?

"Job, you are speaking words like strong winds, and it's because you do not revere or fear God! When you were healthy, you offered sacrifices for your children and served God with your reverence. But because your heart is evil, you are speaking these words like strong winds."

Papyrus can grow in marshes, but if the sunlight is too strong, it dies. Likewise, because Job stayed away from God, Bildad was saying that if he didn't repent and turn away, Job would perish like those plants. He is saying those who forget God have the same destiny.

The complaints, grudges, resentment, curses, and lamentation do not come from some special place. It comes from the heart. Bildad was trying to let Job realize with parables that Job was speaking those words of grumbling because the field of his heart was evil, just as the seeds will grow and bear fruit.

Bildad understood that if one speaks candidly and straightforwardly when the other's feelings are hurt, it will only cause more problems. So he was implementing a more of gentle method using parables.

Next, it says, *"And the hope of the hypocrite shall perish."* By saying this, Bildad was indirectly trying to make Job realize that Job was a kind of hypocrite, rather than directly saying Job's heart was evil. If we truly believe in God, we shouldn't be hypocrites. We have to make our hearts good, righteous, and holy.

Bildad was saying *"And whose trust is a spider's web. He leans on his house, but it does not stand. He holds it fast, but it does not endure."* Then, what had Job trusted? Job had trusted his children, his wealth, and many other things. Just as a spider web will break just by touching and a blowing wind, those who do not fear or trust God will break like spider web.

As if Job had relied on a spider web, he had nothing in his hand. Just as plants will dry by scorching sunshine, when the light shines on the evil heart of man, he will be judged and fall into the punishment in the dark. In other words, this was what Bildad was advising Job:

"Job, just as papyrus grows in marsh and reeds can grow with waters, you can speak words like strong winds because you have evil in your heart. God turned His face away from you because you have evil. But if you earnestly seek God, repent, and make your heart clean, He will recover you. Your beginning will be small, but in time you will increase abundantly."

4. Bildad Advises Job to Recover by Living in the Truth

"He grows green in the sun, And his branches spread out in his garden. His roots wrap around the rock heap, And look for a place in the stones. If he is destroyed from his place, Then it will deny him, saying, 'I have not seen you.' Behold, this is the joy of His way, And out of the earth others will grow" (8:16-19).

What is the spiritual meaning of the 'green in the sun'? Sun is the light and light refers to the truth, the word of God. Jesus is the true light, the way, the truth, and the life. Just as plants grow with the sunshine, we have to live in the word of God for our faith to grow, so that we can stand on the rock of faith.

Then, what does it mean that the plant grows green with the sun but is destroyed? Even though a plant grows well with the sunshine, if it is pulled out for some reason, it is useless. Namely, even though one may stand on the rock of faith, if he looks at the world, leaves God, and lives in sins again, his life is of no value anymore.

If we leave the truth, God has to turn His face away, and we cannot be protected by Him. In the process of our faith growing up, if arrogance comes into our way, we have to drive it away immediately. If we accept it, then little by little we will be captured by Satan.

Then, we will be pulled away from God, so our lives will be

worthless. If the root of the plant is pulled out, it dries and its life ends. A life that has left God will fall into hell, so how tragic it is! Therefore, just as plants keep their green as they receive the sunshine, we have to live in the word of God and place our roots on the rock to keep on growing until our Lord comes back again.

When Job had much wealth, he lived in joy, but when it was uprooted, only suffering was waiting for him, and he only wanted to die.

"Behold, God will not cast away the blameless, Nor will He uphold the evildoers. He will yet fill your mouth with laughing, And your lips with rejoicing. Those who hate you will be clothed with shame, And the dwelling place of the wicked will come to nothing" (8:20-22).

God will not cast away the blameless, nor will He uphold the evildoers. For an evil man, even if his business is going very well, how many worries will he have? Even though it seems that he is prosperous, we can see finally it fails in the end.

More important thing is that his soul will finally fall into hell, which is eternal death, so what value does his life have? If we stand on the word of truth of Jesus Christ who is the Rock, and love God and receive His love, then we can be prosperous in everything in our lives.

This kind of person will rejoice always, pray continually, and give thanks in all circumstances, being full of the Holy Spirit. If we live in the truth and become sanctified like this, we will not lack anything. Even if someone hates us, he will be put to shame.

If some people curse a child of God whom God loves, that curse will fall on them. After all, the dwelling place of an evil man will disappear, and he will go the way of death.

Chapter 9

Job's Ignorance

1. Job Misunderstands that
   Whatever God Wants to Do He Does
2. Job Misunderstands that God Predestines Everything
3. Helpers of Rahab and Spiritual Blessings
4. Job Misunderstands God as a Fearful Judge
5. Double Mindedness
6. The Reason Why God Said Job Was Upright
7. Job Blames God as Being a Bad God

"Were He to pass by me, I would not see Him;
Were He to move past me, I would not perceive Him." (Job 9:11)

1. Job Misunderstands that Whatever God Wants to Do He Does

"Then Job answered, In truth I know that this is so; but how can a man be in the right before God? If one wished to dispute with Him, He could not answer Him once in a thousand times. Wise in heart and mighty in strength, who has defied Him without harm?" (9:1-4)

Job agreed to what his friend Bildad was saying. But Job said, "I know that this is so," which means that when he was in such a difficult situation, he could not help speaking out words like strong wind and words of resentment and complaints against God.

Job said in Job 6:29-30, "Desist now, let there be no injustice; even desist, my righteousness is yet in it. Is there injustice on my tongue? Cannot my palate discern calamities?"

This means that Job could say that he did not commit sins and was righteous compared with other people. But here he said, "How can a man be in the right before God?" It tells us that he had a tinge of conscience. He considered himself to be upright compared to other people, but since his friends were pointing out only his shortcomings, his feelings were hurt.

"If one wished to dispute with Him, He could not answer Him once in a thousand times." It is something obvious. But, we should understand what Job meant by it. We should never dare to dispute anything with God, and we should only obey and have reverent respect towards Him.

God is just, blameless, and spotless, so what is there that we could argue with Him about? It is so obvious that if one wished to disagree and argue with Him, he would be able to respond to Him once in a thousand times.

Job thought he was wise, but he also knew that he was not wise before God. Job thought that in God's wisdom and mighty power He just took back all his children and possessions that He had given him and then gave him the pains of disease as well.

Job knew about God only in a fleshly way. Job could not understand God's wisdom in guiding us to the kingdom of heaven with His providence that has been hidden since before time began. It is God's wisdom and mighty power that destroys the camps of the enemy devil, Satan.

As Job said, those who defy God and do not live by His word cannot receive blessings from God. But he did not realize that he was defying God and not keeping God's word. Because he defied God, he did not listen to his friends and he did not want to repent even when they advised him with the truth.

If everything that Job said in his confession had been heartfelt and truthful, namely if Job had really feared God, he would have repented, and turned, and God would have healed his disease completely. But he was in all talk and no action. His confession had no substance, so what is the use of all his words?

2. Job Misunderstands that God Predestines Everything

"It is God who removes the mountains, they know not

how, When He overturns them in His anger; Who shakes the earth out of its place, And its pillars tremble; Who commands the sun not to shine, And sets a seal upon the stars; Who alone stretches out the heavens And tramples down the waves of the sea; Who makes the Bear, Orion and the Pleiades, And the chambers of the south; Who does great things, unfathomable, And wondrous works without number" (9:5-10).

God does not remove or overturn mountains in His anger. Job had the misconception that God preplans everything and does everything absolutely according to His plan. Job meant that he was righteous and had no faults, but God destroyed him according to the plan that He had made anyway.

In verse 7 is recorded, "Who commands the sun not to shine, and sets a seal upon the stars." But God does not overturn mountains or shake the earth just at His own discretion. He once stopped the sun and moon from moving through Joshua, but He never commanded the sun not to rise. There are also many stars and constellations, and each of them has its own position. This is what "[God] sets a seal upon the stars" actually means.

As Job said, God stretched out the heavens by Himself. When He did that, it's not that He stretches out heavens without any reason. God is the Owner of not only all things in the universe but also the spiritual realm, which is the 4th dimensional world. As recorded in Genesis chapter 1, God made the sun, the moon, stars, and earth in accordance with the law of the spiritual realm, and spread the universe according to the exact necessity of space.

He did not just stretch it out as He wanted within His sovereignty. He created the sun, the moon, and the stars for us men, so that we can be cultivated on this earth in God's providence. Unlike what Job said, God did not just create everything indiscriminately.

Here, the 'Bear, Orion, and Pleiades' have no special spiritual meaning. When Job mentioned 'chambers of the south' he thought there could be chambers in the south because warm wind blows from the south. In the Bible, we can see many extraordinary works of God such as the parting of the Red Sea, the destruction of the city of Jericho, and the Ten Plagues on Egypt.

We can also understand the many wondrous things God has been doing for thousands of years. Even today, God is showing us so many signs and wonders and extraordinary things through Manmin Central Church.

Therefore, we should not misunderstand that God does everything just as He had preplanned. Job misunderstood that he was suffering because God had preplanned everything that way. That is why he could not find his fault or repent.

"Were He to pass by me, I would not see Him; Were He to move past me, I would not perceive Him. Were He to snatch away, who could restrain Him? Who could say to Him, 'What are You doing?'" (9:11-12)

Job was saying that even if God were to pass by in front of him he wouldn't know it. He wouldn't see Him and would not be able to sense His presence. But, if God were to pass by us, don't you think we would realize it? If we have received the Holy Spirit, we can feel that God is with us. We also believe that God is keeping us with His blazing eyes. We know that He counts each and every hair on our head.

When we open our heart and accept Jesus Christ as our Savior, we receive the Holy Spirit as the gift. Because we keep on praying with this experience and assurance, the hope and joy of heavenly kingdom come into our heart. We gain peace to the extent that we cast off evil and live by the word of God, and we can hear the voice of the Holy Spirit.

We can also discern between the truth and untruth to the extent that we live in the word of God. Therefore, if God were to pass by, namely, if the Holy Spirit works, we can feel and realize it.

Job is complaining that God is bad because God took away his children, possessions, and health. He complains that he cannot even ask God, "What are You doing? How can you snatch away my possessions like this?" God does not take away the possessions of His children. When we ask, He gives us, when we seek, He lets us find, and when we knock, He opens the door. But Job is saying something completely opposite to this.

In the Bible, we can see some scenes where God talked to His beloved servants such as Abraham, Moses, and David. God also foretells the things that He is going to do to His servants (Amos 3:7). He gives His children dreams, visions, and the voice of the Holy Spirit in communication with them.

But Job is saying that God will not answer to his question nor will He allow him to ask a question. Job thinks God is like a dictator who does everything at His discretion, thus revealing his ignorance about God.

3. Helpers of Rahab and Spiritual Blessings

"God will not turn back His anger; beneath Him crouch the helpers of Rahab. How then can I answer Him, And choose my words before Him?" (9:13-14)

God is not a person who will not turn back from His wrath.

If we repent and turn, He will turn back from His wrath. During the time of the Old Testament when the people of Israel worshipped idols and left God, they were attacked by their neighbor countries and were taken as captives. But when they repented and turned back seeking God, God forgave them and allowed them to recover their lost nation.

If we repent, God removes our transgressions away from us as the east is far from the west (Psalm 103:12), and He will not remember our sins (Hebrew 8:12).

Then, Job says, "Beneath Him crouch the helpers of Rahab." Here, what does 'Rahab' refer to?

Isaiah 30:7 says, "Even Egypt, whose help is vain and empty. Therefore, I have called her 'Rahab who has been exterminated.'" Isaiah 51:9 says, "Awake, awake, put on strength, O arm of the LORD; Awake as in the days of old, the generations of long ago. Was it not You who cut Rahab in pieces, Who pierced the dragon?"

Namely, Rahab refers to Egypt. Then, who helped Egypt in the Bible? In the history of Israel, we can see that, of Jacob's 12 sons, it was Joseph, the eleventh son, who helped Egypt.

Had Joseph not been there, Egypt must have collapsed due to the seven years of famine. Egypt was saved thanks to Israel, and as time passed, Egypt made the descendants of Joseph, namely the people of Israel, their slaves. They trampled on those who had saved them. This is the heart of man. We should not have this kind of heart.

Here, the 'helpers of Rahab' refers to Joseph, his brothers, and their descendants. Job is saying that just as the people of Israel helped Egypt but later God allowed them to become the slaves of Egypt and receive trials, God also gave Job miserable consequences even if he had faithfully offered God sacrifices.

Job is saying that because God is not just and fair as said above, he cannot argue with God.

Here, there is one thing you should not misunderstand. Why did God allow the people of Israel to become slaves of Egypt? It was for their benefit: for them to receive blessings.

God accepted the sacrifice of Abraham joyfully, but promised him that his descendants would be strangers, enslaved and oppressed for 400 years. And then, they would come out of there with treasures (Genesis 15:13-14).

Seeing this, one may think God is a little strange and gives a strange kind of blessing. How can the slavery in a foreign country be a blessing?

If we do not understand the will of God, some may misunderstand Him. People may have doubts thinking, "I prayed. I served God diligently, and why have I failed to receive blessings and answers, yet?"

Then, what is the most important blessing in life? We can receive salvation and go into heavenly kingdom only when we have faith, but faith cannot be seen with the eyes. So, if God gives us this important gift of faith, what could be a greater blessing than this?

If our faith grows up and our souls are prosperous, then, everything will go well with us, and we will be healthy. If we receive material blessings while we do not have faith and our soul is not prosperous, it is not from God. Those blessings may collapse any time. The heart of man is crafty and cunning. That is why many people seem to diligently lead Christian lives, but they abandon God, and fall back into the world again because they have a desire for the material things of life.

That is why Genesis 15:16-17 tells us that trials are a blessing.

"Then in the fourth generation they will return here, for the iniquity of the Amorite is not yet complete. It came about when the sun had set, that it was very dark, and behold, there appeared a smoking oven and a flaming torch which passed between these pieces."

Some people say Abraham offered an improper sacrifice and God was angry, and that is why his descendants had to suffer as slaves for 400 years. But this is not correct.

Abraham obeyed the word of God completely. He did not offer sacrifices just once or twice and he offered proper sacrifices. God accepted them joyfully and answered with fire.

Now then, God could bring judgment on the Amorites, who were living in Canaan, only when their sins were filled. Because God is just, He could not simply give Abraham the land of Canaan since it was the land of Amorites. When their sins prevailed enough for them to be punished, God would take their land and give it to Abraham's descendants.

That is why God sent Joseph down to Egypt to raise up a nation and let them come out of Egypt with great wealth and possessions. By the miracles of parting the Red Sea and Ten Plagues on Egypt, it was made known to all nations that Israel was the chosen people of God. How great blessing this was!

Also, just as weeds grown in the fields have more strength to survive than those grown in a greenhouse, Israelites became stronger while they were slaves. That is why they could conquer the land of Canaan and became a strong nation. There were many plans and providences of God in Abraham's descendants being enslaved in Egypt.

But, Job is saying here how he could expect God to work justly toward him since he had offered such small sacrifices, because God is a God who had allowed the Israelites to be the slaves of Egypt even though Joseph had saved that great country.

4. Job Misunderstands God as a Fearful Judge

"For though I were right, I could not answer; I would have to implore the mercy of my judge. If I called and He answered me, I could not believe that He was listening to my voice" (9:15-16).

Why does Job use the word, 'if'? Job had conflict in his mind. He thought he was righteous, but his friends were accusing him of being unrighteous and that he was a sinner.

But also, standing before God, he knew he was not very righteous. Namely, on the one hand, he considered himself to be righteous, but on the other hand, he felt he was not righteous in the sight of God. This was the conflict in his mind.

Right now, Job's mind is twisted and he is speaking against God. Now, what kind of ideas do you have while reading the Book of Job?

Don't you sometimes think to yourself, "Job troubled God's heart so much; I am not a person like him!" Through the Book of Job, God is revealing and scrutinizing each of man's characters and the evils of his mind. Through this, we might be able to realize our true hearts.

Job questioned God in various ways, but there was no answer. He almost gave up on himself and he expressed his broken heart.

He is saying that even if God answered when he called Him, he wouldn't believe that God did listen to his voice. We can see that Job's mind is becoming more twisted and more distorted.

"For He bruises me with a tempest and multiplies my wounds without cause. He will not allow me to get my breath, But saturates me with bitterness" (9:17-18).

Just by looking at the words coming out from Job's mouth we can see that he is committing great sins against God. Because he had these evils, Satan accused him, and God accepted the accusation.

Let's read Exodus 15:26.

"And He said, "If you will give earnest heed to the voice of the LORD your God, and do what is right in His sight, and give ear to His commandments, and keep all His statutes, I will put none of the diseases on you which I have put on the Egyptians; for I, the LORD, am your healer.""

It's not that God bruised Job with a tempest and gave him disease without cause. Since Job had the filthy and foul smelling boils, the evils in his heart also came out. That is why God had to refine Job.

Job is complaining that God does not even let him get his breath. God is not a person to fill us with bitterness. He only wants to give blessings to His children and receive glory through them.

"If it is a matter of power, behold, He is the strong one! And if it is a matter of justice, who can summon Him?"

God is strong. But when Job says that God is strong, he does not mean that power belongs to God. His word is different from many other believers' confession. Job thought God is a fearful God who took away everything from him, and that is what he meant by 'the strong one.'

But we should understand the mighty strength of God correctly. God loves us and He sent His one and only Son Jesus Christ to this earth to break the authority of the enemy devil. The strength of God is the might to overcome the authority of death. It is the might of resurrection. Also, God is the strong one as the Judge who repays us according to what we have done.

Job said that God is a fearful Judge who uses His sovereignty at His will and does everything according to His preplanning. But we should understand that the just judgment would take place through Jesus Christ who is the Rock and the Truth itself. John chapter 1 says that God created everything in heavens and earth through the name of Jesus Christ. We can be saved and receive answers by the name of Jesus Christ.

God is the righteous Judge who judges everything according to the unchanging word of truth and the rules of the spiritual realm. Job didn't understand this, and he is saying something completely different, which is that God uses His authority at His discretion.

5. Double Mindedness

"Though I am righteous, my mouth will condemn me;
Though I am guiltless, He will declare me guilty. I am

guiltless; I do not take notice of myself; I despise my life" (9:20-21).

Here, we can find Job's double-mindedness. Job was pleading for himself and also making excuses. The condemnation refers to the price for one's sinful acts, and the guilt means being destroyed.

Job thought he lived an upright, righteous, and guiltless life. But his friends kept on accusing him of being unrighteous and being a sinner. So, he reluctantly expressed the other view that God would declare him guilty although he was guiltless.

We should cast off this kind of double-mindedness. 1 John 3:18 says, "Little children, let us not love with word or with tongue, but in deed and truth."

Job concluded that he was guiltless, and he didn't do anything wrong, but his life was corrupted because of the almighty One, and he cannot help but despise his life. We should not have double-mindedness like Job here. If something is not right in us by the truth, we should boldly accept it so that we can realize ourselves.

"It is all one; therefore I say, 'He destroys the guiltless and the wicked.' If the scourge kills suddenly, He mocks the despair of the innocent" (9:22-23).

Job is saying that because God does everything just as He pleases and according to His plans that He has pre-conceived, there is no meaning in living a righteous life, and that living an evil life will make no difference in the final result. Namely, Job is saying that even though he lived a righteous life God made him suffer in such a way, and thus God treats good men and evil men in the same manner and He is a God of predestination who has no justice.

But God is the just Judge who judges between good and evil. God lets evil men receive evil rewards and He gives upright and good things to those who are good (Malachi 4:1-3, Deuteronomy chapter 28).

Job has misunderstood in thinking that God mocks the sufferings of sinless men. He says, "If the scourge kills suddenly," because he thought scourge was killing him suddenly.

Job had more and more ill feelings and became increasingly cynical about God. In his mistaken understanding of God, Job was saying that he was wrongfully punished. Job was the one who kept on speaking out evil words, but he was saying God was evil.

6. The Reason Why God Said Job Was Upright

"The earth is given into the hand of the wicked; He covers the faces of its judges. If it is not He, then who is it?" (9:24)

Men have very deep inner hearts of which they themselves are not aware. They have life-energy, or life-force sometimes called chi that is inherited from their parents. They also form the frameworks of their hearts based on what they have seen, heard, and learned in their lives.

When Job began to suffer from hardships and trials, his inner heart was revealed. We can find filthy and evil things coming out from him. God looks at our inner heart and searches the very deep parts of it. Before Job faced the trial, he was recognized as an upright man, but God knew the evil things that were deep inside his heart. Satan was also aware of this. That is why Satan brought accusation against Job and God allowed it to proceed.

Job is rationalizing that God is making judgments that are unjust since He let such an upright man as himself live in such great pains.

If somebody pays bribes to a judge to receive favorable judgment in a trial and the judge is bribed, his conscience becomes increasingly numb as he makes unjust judgment. As a result, justice is covered over and ignored. Job concluded that God is no different from a judge who is bribed and ignores justice.

But God is a just God as said in Psalm 9:8, "And He will judge the world in righteousness; He will execute judgment for the peoples with equity." At first, Job's hidden evil was being revealed little by little, but now, it is coming out without any constraints. It was evil that Job had not been aware of before.

Why, then, did God say Job was upright and blameless? God said it considering Job's situation at that time.

"Now my days are swifter than a runner; They flee away, they see no good. They slip by like reed boats, Like an eagle that swoops on its prey" (9:25-26).

Before the test came, Job had faith as knowledge from hearing about God, and so, he could overcome the primary tests within the boundaries of the knowledge and faith that he had. He had a boundary to his thinking such as, "If I give thanks to God and pray, He will answer me," and he could endure within that framework.

But the second test went beyond his boundary, and as he began to suffer from boils, his evil began to be revealed.

"Now my days are swifter than a runner; They flee away, they see no good. My soul is meaningless as there is no trace after a boat passes by, and is hungry as an eagle that swoops on its prey."

When he said, "My days are swifter than a runner," it refers to something that is beyond his boundaries and also to the flow of time. Also, just as there is no trace left after a boat passes by on a sea, he was presenting a parable to explain that his life was passing by without any meaning.

Also, he is pleading that his heart is earnest and hungry just like an eagle that sees its prey from the sky and quickly comes down to the ground to swoop on its prey.

If Job's friends could read this painful heart of Job, they could have advised him with love according to the state of his heart. They would not have directly blamed and accused him for his current condition, but understood his painful and broken heart and with their love let him realize himself so that he could have repented and turned back.

7. Job Blames God as Being a Bad God

"Though I say, 'I will forget my complaint, I will leave off my sad countenance and be cheerful,' I am afraid of all my pains, I know that You will not acquit me. I am accounted wicked, Why then should I toil in vain?" (9:27-29)

Because Job thought that he was receiving his punishment from God without cause, he also felt like he had been falsely accused. Furthermore, he is saying everything would be meaningless even though he may forget his chagrin, try to change his outlook and have a joyful heart as his friends kept on advising him.

Here, what does it mean that 'I am afraid of all my pains'? Job meant that even if he had been healed, God would strike him again without cause, so he would have to live in pain again.

If we repent and turn away in our deeds, God removes our transgressions as far as the east is from the west and He does not remember it. Psalm 103:12-13; 18 say, "As far as the east is from the west, So far has He removed our transgressions from us. Just as a father has compassion on his children, So the LORD has compassion on those who fear Him…To those who keep His covenant And remember His precepts to do them."

This verse presents to us a condition in which God's forgiveness and compassion apply to us only when we fear God. If we fear God and keep His statutes, we will repent of our sins and turn about in our actions. If we do then God will forgive us and cleanse us with the blood of the Lord Jesus so we can be justified and called children of God.

But Job did not accept the advice of his friends. He only kept on saying that, because God would still consider him as a sinner, he would have to live in pains. After all, he meant that there was no point in him repenting of his sins and turning back. If we have this kind of heart, we must repent.

We can find Job's evilness in these words. We can see some new-believers try to set some conditions before God. We should only be thankful for the grace that we are forgiven of our sins and are saved. But beginners try to make a deal with God.

"God, if you solve this problem, I will serve the church."

"God, since there is no answer even though I fasted and prayed all night, I am going to leave church."

Also, if they are faced with tests, they soon doubt God and live in worries. If we begin to give conditions to God, it is not faith at all. Job is suggesting some conditions to God like them.

When professing our faith in God, if we are faced with a problem and we do not pray to God and leave it to God, but instead we worry and try to solve the problem for ourselves, it means that we do not really have faith and believe in God completely.

"If I should wash myself with snow And cleanse my hands with lye, Yet You would plunge me into the pit, And my own clothes would abhor me" (9:30-31).

'Washing himself with snow' means that water is very scarce. Also, if he is 'cleansing his hands with lye,' how difficult it is! And Job is saying that even if he washes himself cleanly despite so much difficulty, God will just put him into another pit.

So, even his clothes that have no life would spite him. We can see that Job is blaming God as a very evil and bad God.

"For He is not a man as I am that I may answer Him, That we may go to court together. There is no umpire between us, Who may lay his hand upon us both" (9:32-33).

Job knew about God by hearing from his fathers. Abraham, Moses, and other prophets communicated with God, but Job is saying he would not even answer Him.

Job only had faith as knowledge that he gained from hearing. Because he didn't have faith with which he believed in his heart, he could not confess anything with faith. God is not a God who does not answer us, but He meets us when we earnestly seek Him.

Furthermore, Job is saying that, because God gave him the disease, God is the prosecutor and he is the defendant. He is lamenting that there is no judge to judge between the prosecutor and the defendant. He is saying that he was wrongfully accused, and is asking a question as to who can be his unbiased judge.

We can understand that Job was speaking such foolish and ridiculous words, but that Job was not foolish from the beginning. We should understand that the different kinds of hearts of our lives are revealed in these words.

While we are living in this world, we may face tests. Some lose all their fortunes and meet with problems that they cannot solve by themselves. Because there is no helper, they are in despair, and they put themselves more into wretched states. They blame and curse themselves.

But those who believe in and rely on God will give thanks to God and show their faith with rejoicing, having hope of heavenly kingdom, even if they have become beggars. They will not become like Job here.

"Let Him remove His rod from me, And let not dread of Him terrify me. Then I would speak and not fear Him; But I am not like that in myself" (9:34-35).

'His rod' refers to God's sovereignty. As revealed through Moses' staff that performed ten plagues and Aaron's rod that sprouted, put forth buds, produced blossoms and bore ripe almonds in the Old Testament, 'rod' refers to the power of God. Job is saying that, because God is striking him with His rod, he could not do anything.

He meant that if God would take away His rod that stands for His sovereign power against him, he would curse God as much as he wanted because he could not bear the feeling of being wrongfully accused. How unrighteous are such words as these? He was controlling himself because he was afraid of God, and otherwise, he would speak out even more evil. And yet, he is giving the excuse that he was not such a person before.

Now you can understand why God allowed all those things happen to Job and let everything be recorded in the Bible. Job who thought he knew God and thought of himself as a righteous man acted this way, and how much more evil those who do not know God at all would be!

Chapter 10

Job's Evil in His Deep Heart Is Revealed

1. Arrogance
2. Mistaking God for the One Who Loves Evil Men
3. Mistaking God for a Hunter of the Righteous
4. Self-abandonment of Job

"I loathe my own life; I will give full vent to my complaint;
I will speak in the bitterness of my soul." (Job 10:1)

1. Arrogance

"I loathe my own life; I will give full vent to my complaint; I will speak in the bitterness of my soul. I will say to God, 'Do not condemn me; Let me know why You contend with me'" (10:1-2).

Job says he loathes his life. It means that he was so tired. He felt too tired to live. In the beginning, he didn't complain against God though he lost his children and possessions. But as he began to suffer from boils, he began to complain against God, and through the conversation with his friends, his evil that had been hidden deep inside his heart was being revealed.

Job thought he had not done anything wrong and lived only in righteousness. Yet his friends kept on telling him that he was a sinner who was speaking out words like strong wind and that he had to repent. This increased his pain because he could not accept their advice.

His soul was too tired and troubled to endure any more. He said that he had more things to say but he was controlling himself (Job 9:35). But he forgot what he said and he is now saying he will give full vent to his complaining. His evil is exposed even more.

Job had the arrogance of mind to think that he was better than his friends. That's why he could not find how untruthful he was. One of his friends taught him with the word of truth, but Job would not accept it. Because he thought he was better than his friends, he would not accept their advice.

Job was asking his friends in his mind, "I am in this situation now, but I had more possessions and more knowledge than you, and I had beautiful family, and I was giving advice to others. Why do you look at only the present situation to try to teach me a lesson? I don't want to deal with you."

Job heard a lot of advice from his friends, but he did not accept any of it. His heart became even more hardened and he ignored his friends and would not talk to them. He now talks directly to God with what his friends had said to him.

2. Mistaking God for the One Who Loves Evil Men

"Is it right for You indeed to oppress, To reject the labor of Your hands, And to look favorably on the schemes of the wicked? Have You eyes of flesh? Or do You see as a man sees? Are Your days as the days of a mortal, Or Your years as man's years, That You should seek for my guilt And search after my sin?" (10:3-6)

Is God somebody who oppresses and rejects the labor of His hands? Job is saying that God created him to make him suffer from diseases and trials. Also, he says that God looks favorably on the schemes of the wicked.

Because his heart is so twisted, he is saying that God is a bad God. He is arguing that God makes a good person like him suffer from trials, and thus God persecutes and despises the righteous and loves the wicked.

Verse 4 says that God does not have the eyes of men. Actually, men look at the outward appearances, but God looks at the inner heart.

Job meant the following: "God, You look at inner heart, but why would You look at me with the eyes of men? My friends look at my wretched appearance and condemn me as if I were sinful and evil. But You look at the inner heart, so You must know that I am righteous and upright. Now why are You not giving me blessings?"

Then, what does it mean that "Are Your days as the days of a mortal, or Your years as man's years, that You should seek for my guilt and search after my sin?"

Job said that God is eternal, having no beginning and no end, and thus God is everlasting, but men live but for a moment. Job said that God is eternal, but his life is but a moment, so how could God consider Job as Himself and give such great pain to him as what he was receiving?

Job was thinking, "How can the magnified God the Creator and this wretched life be the same? How can Your years be man's years that You admit that I am guilty? Isn't it God's love to forgive man, even if he has sin, for his life is so short compared to the glory of God? And how can You do this to me who is not even a sinner?"

It seemed in the beginning that Job is raising up God, but actually, he was being sarcastic toward God, saying that He is not generous.

"According to Your knowledge I am indeed not guilty,
Yet there is no deliverance from Your hand" (10:7).

Job says that God knows he is not guilty. Until now, Job has been saying that God is such a bad God. But here he is saying God knows that he is not guilty. So, we can see how inconsistent and ridiculous this is!

Then, why is Job saying this? It's because he is thinking

about himself before this trial began. At that time, as God knew, Job helped the poor with his money. He also helped the orphans and widows, and encouraged others to stand on one's own. Even when God took away his possessions and children, he did not complain but only gave thanks to God. With all this, Job is saying that he is such a good person.

Because Job could not find any evil in himself, he is thinking of himself in the past when he controlled his heart with his education, knowledge, and manners. But because God saw the evil deep in Job's heart, He allowed the accusations of Satan to take place so that Job's evil could be revealed.

In the passage, Job says nobody can deliver him from God's hand. Actually, nobody can flee away from God's hand. Everybody has to face the judgment after this life, even kings and others of nobility.

Those who did the good deeds will have resurrection of life, and those who committed the evil deeds will have resurrection of judgment.

3. Mistaking God for a Hunter of the Righteous

"Your hands fashioned and made me altogether; And would You destroy me? Remember now, that You have made me as clay; And would You turn me into dust again? Did You not pour me out like milk And curdle me like cheese; Clothe me with skin and flesh, And knit me together with bones and sinews? You have granted me life and lovingkindness; And Your care has preserved my spirit" (10:8-12).

Job knew that he was a creature made by God. Not only eyes, nose, mouth, bones, and blood of men, but also the invisible spirit and soul were all created by God. Here, 'made me altogether' refers to all of spirit, soul, and body of man.

Job asked God a question, "You have made me altogether, and now, why would you destroy me?" But in the next verse, he is asking a question of opposite meaning. It's because Job was feeling that God was treating him so unkindly. So he expressed his disappointment.

In effect Job was saying, "When You made me, You just made me as if You had only put some clay together. That's why You are discarding me like dust, aren't You? Just as a mother would throw out useless milk, You made me not only like useless milk but curdled me like cheese."

To put some clay together is very easy. Job said God fashioned him so beautifully, and then He was destroying him. But now Job changes his words by saying God discarded him so easily because He made him as if He had just put together a lump of clay.

Milk for a new-born baby is crucial. But a mother will throw out the remaining milk after the baby has been nursed. If there is much milk remaining after nursing the baby, the mother will have pain in her breast. Also, milk that is already squeezed will have bad odor and curdle, so we cannot keep it. Job likened himself to useless milk. It is good metaphorical expression because his body was covered with boils all over and they kept on festering and drying.

God gave men life and everything for their living. Namely, He made our spirit, soul, and body, and also created everything including the sun and air, so we can therewith keep our lives.

Job had a lot of knowledge and wisdom. Though he did not understand very deeply about spirit, he at least knew there is a master in a man's body.

When Job said 'my spirit' in the passage, it refers to his heart. 'To keep his heart' means that he did not commit sins, but helped the widows and orphans and lived a life in goodness, for he had known God.

"Yet these things You have concealed in Your heart; I know that this is within You: If I sin, then You would take note of me, And would not acquit me of my guilt. If I am wicked, woe to me! And if I am righteous, I dare not lift up my head. I am sated with disgrace and conscious of my misery" (10:13-15).

When Job said, "If I sin, then You would take note of me," this is true. But when he said, "And would not acquit me of my guilt," it's not true. If we repent and turn, God promises us that He will forgive us and remove our transgression as the east is far from the west (Psalm 103:12; Hebrew 10:17).

Job also said, "If I am wicked, woe to me!" and this is something obvious. It says, "And if I am righteous," and it means he is a righteous man. But he also says, "I dare not lift up my head. I am sated with disgrace." Why is he saying this?

Those who keep the commandments of God have the confidence and can boldly dare to ask God and receive the answer. What Job is saying is that he is a righteous and good man, but because he was in such a wretched situation where he lost all his possessions and children and was suffering from boils all over his body, and on top of that, his friends were despising him telling him only to repent, so he was so ashamed of this kind of reality.

But even in this kind of situation, if we are confident before God, we don't have to be ashamed in front of anybody.

"Should my head be lifted up, You would hunt me like a lion; And again You would show Your power against me" (10:16).

'To lift up one's head' spiritually means arrogance. Of course, Job didn't mean that he was arrogant here. He means that if he argued a little bit and insisted that he was right, God would hunt him like a lion. Job was testifying that he believed in a fearful God likening God to a lion. Job is saying that just as a lion hunts the prey when it's hungry, God is hunting him down, even if he is a man who has been living a good life.

Job is now talking about what he has experienced. He means he is righteous, but if he lifts up his head and argues with God that he is right, his whole body will bleed and fester along with greater pain, just as the prey that is being hunted by a lion.

If we act according to the truth and follow the will of God, God Himself will work for us so that even the most serious problem can be resolved. But if we respond in evil and argue just because the other person acts in evil, God cannot help us. Only when we completely follow the will of God, will He begin to work and the enemy devil and Satan go away.

"You renew Your witnesses against me And increase Your anger toward me; Hardship after hardship is with me. Why then have You brought me out of the womb? Would that I had died and no eye had seen me! I should have been as though I had not been, Carried from womb to tomb" (10:17-19).

'Your witnesses' refers to the angels of God. "You renew Your witnesses against me" means that God is training His angels, targeting on Job, and showing him more and more anger.

"God, why did you bring me out of the womb? If you had not let me be born, I would have died and been buried. Why did you give me life so I have to live in this pain?"

Job misunderstands that God brought him out of the womb

and gave him birth. In His providence God gave humans the original seed of life through which life is conceived, but the decision of conception is completely up to the parents.

God controls life and death, but only within the boundary of the law of the spiritual realm. Some people complain against God if things go wrong for them in marriage, business, or in family. These problems rise because of men's faults. They are not caused by God, so we should never take the name of God in vain.

4. Self-abandonment of Job

"Would He not let my few days alone? Withdraw from me that I may have a little cheer Before I go and I shall not return To the land of darkness and deep shadow, The land of utter gloom as darkness itself, Of deep shadow without order, And which shines as the darkness" (10:20-22).

By saying 'few days,' Job means life is only 70 or 80 years, and how longer he might live.

Job is saying, "God, I am already old and not so far away from the day of my death. So please do not be so cruel to me. Change Your mind and give me happiness while I live on this earth. The land I am going next is dark and hopeless, so before I go into that land, please let me live without pains. Please leave me alone."

Job is talking about the life to come, as if he knows about it very well, saying he will go to the land of darkness and deep shadow. We can understand that Job does not even know about heaven and hell.

That is why Job had no hope of heaven or the fear of hell, which is a place for eternal punishment.

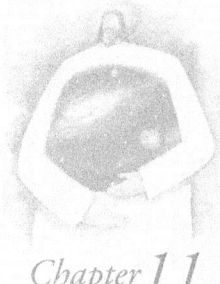

Chapter 11

Zophar the Naamathite's Opening Argument - Zophar Scolds Job

"Can you discover the depths of God? Can you discover the limits of the Almighty? They are high as the heavens, what can you do? Deeper than Sheol, what can you know?" (Job 11:7-8)

1. The Importance of Words

"Then Zophar the Naamathite answered, 'Shall a multitude of words go unanswered, and a talkative man be acquitted? Shall your boasts silence men? And shall you scoff and none rebuke?'" (11:1-3)

Zophar is pointing out that because Job's words are many and he is talkative, he is not right. When a person has ill-feelings and his anger wells up, he will naturally become talkative, and not be able to speak words of truth.

"Job! Because you are talking so much, how can I not have a word to answer you? Those who are talkative make many mistakes, and how can you say you are right? How can your boastings silence others, and if you scoff, how can there be nobody to rebuke you?"

Proverbs 10:19 says, "When there are many words, transgression is unavoidable, But he who restrains his lips is wise." It means those who speak a lot make many mistakes and they are not wise.

Proverbs 18:21 also says, "Death and life are in the power of the tongue, and those who love it will eat its fruit." It tells us about the importance of words.

We believers in God should always have positive lips no matter how many sufferings and hardships we have. If we speak negative words such as, "It's difficult. I am tired of it. I can't bear it any more," more of difficult things will occur and we will be tired even more. Even in the most difficult situations, God can begin to work for us only when we confess positively with faith like, "I believe You, Lord, that You will do it."

Verse 3 days, "Shall your boasts silence men? And shall you scoff and none rebuke?" What does this mean?

Job has been saying that he is righteous and good, and ignored and looked down upon his friends saying that he is better than they are. And Zophar is asking how Job's friends can continue to keep quiet hearing such words from Job.

1 Corinthians 13:4 says, "Love does not brag," and 1:31 says, "Just as it is written, "Let him who boasts, boast in the Lord."

The worldly people brag about their children, husbands, and so many other things. But those others who hear it become actually jealous, even though they seem to be amazed. Especially, believers do not need that kind of boasting.

But if we have received an answer to a certain problem through prayer, we can boast of it. It is to plant faith in the other person and to plant life by letting him believe in the living God, so it is good to boast in the Lord as much as possible.

Job scoffed at his friends and God. He spoke many words of mocking God. If we boast, mock, and rebuke just because the other person is doing so, we will not be any different kind of person.

Therefore, we should be able to understand and embrace the others with love and generous virtue. Even though we may see somebody's transgressions, we should not reveal it to others but keep it confidential while praising his good points.

2. Rebuking Job by Explaining the Truth

"For you have said, 'My teaching is pure, And I am innocent in your eyes.' But would that God might speak, And open His lips against you, And show you the secrets of wisdom! For sound wisdom has two sides. Know then that God forgets a part of your iniquity" (11:4-6).

We cannot dare say we are righteous in the sight of God, but Job is insisting he is righteous in God's sight. When his friends were hearing him, they were dumbfounded.

"Job! You are not trying to repent and turn away but only insisting that you are right and pure. If you truly have no sin, how could God hear the accusations of Satan and allow you such great trials? Then, does it mean that you are right and God is wrong?"

God created the heavens and the earth and everything in them by His word, and He gave us the Bible. In the Bible is contained the rules of the spiritual realm. It tells us about the beginning and the end, how we can receive blessings and salvation, and in what kind of situations we receive curses.

The Bible contains the endless wonders and wisdom of God. We as men can never fathom how great God's knowledge is.

In Zophar's opinion, God's power is limitless, so He should have taken Job's life away because Job was speaking against God so much. But God was just watching him. That's why Zophar is saying that if God were not as generous as He is, Job would have already died. But since He let Job live to that moment, His mercy is far greater than the weight of Job's sin. Zophar is telling Job to realize this fact.

"Can you discover the depths of God? Can you discover the limits of the Almighty? They are high as the heavens, what can you do? Deeper than Sheol, what can you know? Its measure is longer than the earth And broader than the sea" (11:7-9).

Because Job did not understand the wonders and might of God, he complained against God and cursed his own parents. If we understand the wonders and might of God, we will not give up even in trials and tests, but receive the answer through our prayers and give glory to God.

Of course, even Zophar who is saying this did not clearly understand about God. We come to know and understand God to the extent that our faith grows. The Holy Spirit searches even the deep things of God. Because the Holy Spirit reveals to us what is in us, we can clearly understand about God.

According to the extent that the word of truth of God fills our heart and works in it, and according to how great our faith is, we can understand God.

Also, Zophar says that God is as high as heavens and deeper than Sheol. He thought Sheol is the place for those who are dead, where they are asleep forever, and which is like a dark valley of death. That is why Zophar is saying it's a very deep place. He means just as they don't know the height of heavens and the depth of Sheol, God is higher and deeper.

Concerning God's measure, Zophar is saying that His generosity is longer than the earth and wider than the sea. Namely, Zophar means, "Job, you cannot understand the heart and thoughts of God who embraces the whole universe, and why do you pretend to know all those things?"

3. Let Us Not Become False Men

*"If He passes by or shuts up, Or calls an assembly, who
can restrain Him? For He knows false men, And He
sees iniquity without investigating. An idiot will become
intelligent When the foal of a wild donkey is born a
man" (11:10-12).*

'Calling an assembly' means opening a court trial. Namely,
if God begins a court trial, who can stop it? Here, 'assembly'
symbolizes the sovereignty of God.

But God is a just God who rules over people according to
the law of the spiritual realm. If those children of God who have
received the Holy Spirit commit sins or act in unrighteousness,
God allows tests and trials to refine them. This is to let them turn
away and lead them to the way of salvation.

In verse 11, Zophar says, "For He knows false men." A
false man refers to one who has much falsehood and absurdity,
worships idols, is unreliable and breaks his promises.

If the people around us cannot trust us, it means we are
untruthful men. Those who change their mind very often are also
false and unreliable. These people will someday regret that they
have lived meaningless lives.

Job had no dream and no hope. He only complained and
wanted to die quickly. That is why Zophar is saying that Job was
a false man.

Of course, Job was going through the trials to receive more
perfect blessings, but his friends did not know this. They just
thought that God was punishing him because he was evil, and
they just condemned him.

Now, let us look into false men in this world and false men by the truth.

False men in the world are those who have no dream. Everything is destroyed in their lives, so they have given up on themselves. They just live their lives recklessly. From their mouths will come out the words of falsehoods, absurdity, untruth and vanity.

Then, what kind of person is a false man according to the truth?

First, a false man refers to those who do not cast off the things of the world even though they understand what eternal life and true life are. Knowing the true things, they still cling to the meaningless things of the world. In the end what they get is only death.

Secondly, it's those who disgrace God although they are believers in God, because they do not properly understand the will of God. These people do not practice the will of God properly, so they cannot receive salvation. Because they also cling to meaningless things, they will finally go the way of death (Matthew 7:21).

Thirdly, it's those who say they believe in God but are very stubborn or give out evil. Those who act evil are all false men. Even though they believe in God, it's difficult for them to receive salvation.

God looks at our heart. He keeps us under watchful eyes and counts even a single hair on our head. When Jonah disobeyed Him and went into the bottom of the ship, God was still watching him. Even though we steal something in the deep darkness of the night, God sees us.

Verse 12 says, "An idiot will become intelligent When the foal of a wild donkey is born a man."

'Being intelligent' means having the capacity for thought and reason especially to a high degree. Its spiritual meaning is 'complete understanding and knowledge that has been accumulated in one's life.'

If we are intelligent, we cannot be false men. People worship idols because they are false men. If we have intelligence, we know God the Father who has given birth to us. Those who have any sense will not bow their heads before idols. Will you bow down to a pig if somebody tells you to? If you have any sense, you won't.

The foal of a wild donkey will jump around here and there if not tied. It may be caught in a trap or be eaten by ferocious animals. We should not act like this unintelligent foal of donkey, but obey the word of God and fear Him according to the law of the spiritual realm.

4. Blessings of Leaving Unrighteousness and Obeying the Word of God

"If you would direct your heart right And spread out your hand to Him, If iniquity is in your hand, put it far away, And do not let wickedness dwell in your tents" (11:13-14).

Zophar is telling Job to direct his heart right and spread out his hand to the LORD. Job has been telling so many things that are not right according to the truth. Here, 'spreading out one's hand' means surrender before God, namely denying oneself.

Zophar is telling Job to direct his heart. For example, if he is going to the west while God is telling him to go to the east, he has to change his direction and go to the east. Zophar is advising Job to leave all iniquity that is in his hands.

Why does Zophar say iniquity in the hands, not iniquity of the heart? During the Old Testament times, they were saved by deeds. How many sins do men commit with their hands? What is in heart comes out to the hands.

Also, "do not let wickedness dwell in your tents" means that we should cast away all the untruthful things from our heart, family, workplace, and business fields.

Zophar is also explaining what kinds of blessings will come if Job would turn his heart, surrender before God, and leave all the iniquity in his hands.

> *"Then, indeed, you could lift up your face without moral defect, And you would be steadfast and not fear. For you would forget your trouble, As waters that have passed by, you would remember it. Your life would be brighter than noonday; Darkness would be like the morning" (11:15-17).*

"You could lift up your face without moral defect" means that he can lift up his head boldly before God without any shame. Men feel ashamed and are not confident before God because of their sins and guilty feelings.

Why did Job lose all his possessions and children and why did he suffer from boils? This was for him to realize the evil in his heart and cast it off, so that he could receive greater blessings.

But Zophar did not understand this providence hidden in

God's love. So, he misunderstood that Job was suffering so much because he must have committed sins and because he must not have lived by the word of God.

Psalm 66:18 says, "If I regard wickedness in my heart, The LORD will not hear." Isaiah 59:1-3 says that if our sins make up a wall against God, God will not hear us even if we pray to Him.

Zophar heard the truth and he is trying to make Job realize what the truth is. If we live by the word of God, we don't have to be ashamed, so we will have no fear and be confident (1 John 3:21-22). Men are afraid, nervous, and afflicted because of their sins.

Furthermore, verse 16 says, "you would forget your trouble." If the river flows and goes into the sea, we cannot bring the water back because new water keeps on coming. Namely, this is about the flow of time.

Suppose you had disease or problems in family or workplace, but after some time those trials went away. If you are living a new life now, you will not be sad because of the past. If you have good times now, you will rather be happy to remember the past.

Zophar continues to say, "Your life would be brighter than noonday; Darkness would be like the morning." What does this mean?

In Job 11:14, the iniquity in hands is something that we can cast away by repenting and turning away when the word of truth of God comes into us. So, we can cast off the iniquity of the hands, and there will be no unrighteousness in our family, workplace, and in business fields. Therefore, "Your life would be brighter than noonday" means that when the light of life of truth comes in, the dark past of befriending the world and living in darkness will pass away, and we can now walk in the truth and live in noonday.

"Darkness would be like the morning" spiritually means that when we accept Jesus as the Savior and the light of life comes into us, even though there remain some trials and tests and darkness, it will be like morning. Morning symbolizes new life and new hope to have the new day.

Also, it means that when a person who had no hope meets God his trials and tests will leave, he receive new strength, and new days come upon him.

"Then you would trust, because there is hope; And you would look around and rest securely. You would lie down and none would disturb you, And many would entreat your favor. But the eyes of the wicked will fail, And there will be no escape for them; And their hope is to breathe their last" (11:18-20).

"You would trust, because there is hope" means that as the difficult problems are solved and you are able to begin a new day, you have hope. Suppose a person who once had such difficulties of finance was able to open a shop. Then, he could work with much hope. Because there is hope, we can also stand more firmly in the truth. Spiritually, to stand firm is to stand on the rock of the word of God.

"And you would look around and rest securely" means that if all the wickedness disappears from our family, workplace, and business fields by casting away the iniquity in the hands, God keeps us with His blazing eyes, heavenly host and angels, and with the fiery walls of the Holy Spirit, so we will have rest and peace of mind. Trials and tests will have nothing to do with us, and we will only have peace.

If we live in the truth completely, namely if we stand on the rock of faith, we will commit everything into God's hands, so we gain the rest of the heart.

Verse 19 says, "You would lie down and none would disturb you, And many would entreat your favor." If we stand on the rock of faith, all worries and concerns will leave us. This rock is strong and unbreakable. It refers to Jesus Christ in the spiritual sense.

In our Christian life, if there is any problem, we have to realize that we are not standing on the rock of faith yet.

"You would lie down and none would disturb you" means that if we stand on the rock of faith, the enemy devil and Satan cannot work on us, so in any kind of situation, we will be free and at peace even at sleeping.

"Many would entreat your favor" means that we will gain respect, love, wealth, and many other things from many people.

It also says, "But the eyes of the wicked will fail, And there will be no escape for them." The eyes of those who are not living in the truth will fail, and here, it means spiritual eyes.

Namely, because the heart is evil, they do not accept the word of God or try to believe it. So, they do not understand any truth. Finally, because they are spiritually blind, they cannot find escape.

Then, where do we have to escape to? We have to escape from the swamp of death to the way of life that leads to eternal life.

We have to run not to trials and tests, but to the light, but when our spiritual eyes fail, we cannot find the way to escape. If we do not live in the truth and not cast off sins, our spiritual eyes will fail.

That is why it says, "their hope is to breathe their last." Evil men will accumulate evil upon evil, and at last, they lose all the strength and collapse. They cannot help but go to death, namely hell.

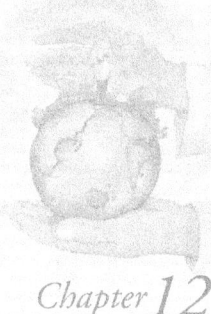

Chapter 12

The Emotionally Scarred Job's Response

1. Job's Sarcastic Rebuttals to His Friends
2. Making God Out to Be a God who Blesses Evil Men
3. Job Lifts up God's Greatness
4. What Is It that Job Really Wants to Say?

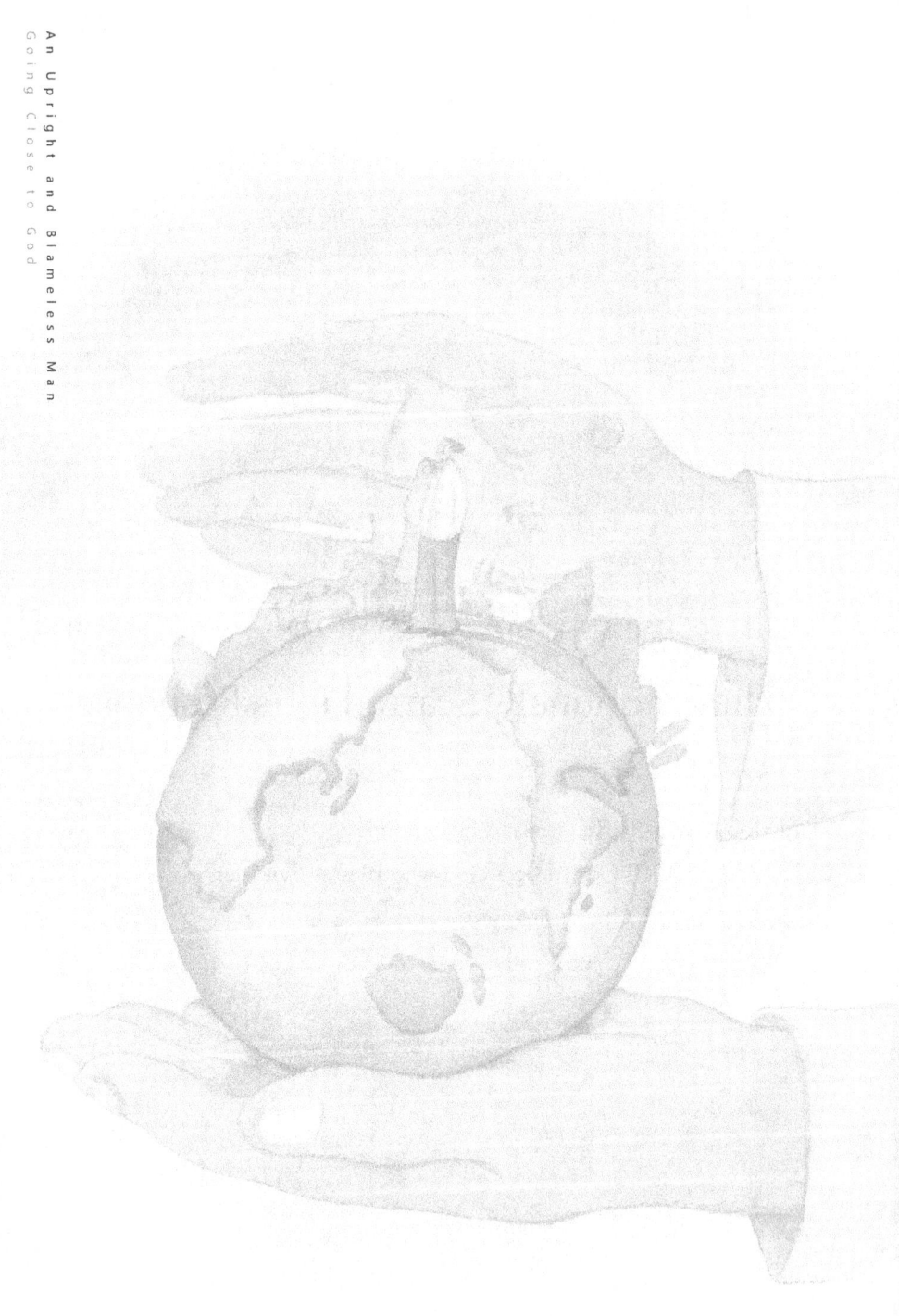

"In whose hand is the life of every living thing,
And the breath of all mankind?" (Job 12:10)

1. Job's Sarcastic Rebuttals to His Friends

"Then Job responded, 'Truly then you are the people, and with you wisdom will die! But I have intelligence as well as you; I am not inferior to you. And who does not know such things as these?'" (12:1-3)

In the previous chapter, Zophar was reproaching Job, and in chapter 12, Job is arguing back at his friends. Both parties are arguing that they are right.

You should not think it's just the conversation between Job and his friends, so that you can realize and become aware of the nature of your heart. You should put yourself in the shoes of Job and his friends. When you find out that you have a heart like Job and a heart like his friends, you can repent and turn away to receive the same blessings as Job received.

Job's friends had as great knowledge and wisdom as Job, but Job could not accept what they said. Job felt his friends were very ridiculous. They were only trying to blame Job, saying that they were right and Job was wrong, so he became more and more upset.

Job didn't like the fact that his friends were trying to teach him anything. So he was speaking sarcastically when he said that his friends' words were right and his words were wrong, and that he was not even a man. And, he said very sarcastically that if they died wisdom would die too.

What is the real meaning when Job said, "Truly then you are the people"?

Have you argued with someone, and when you could not persuade the other person to accept your point of view or if you could not win the argument, haven't you just ended the conversation by saying, "OK then, you're right!"? Because you felt any reasonable two-way-conversation was impossible, you just ended the conversation. Here, Job felt the same way.

Job thought his friends were pretending to have knowledge and wisdom, and they were looking down on him and trying to lecture him. That is why Job was upset. So, he was speaking cynically saying, "You have so much wisdom! If you die, the wisdom will die, too!"

Before, Job's friend said Job had lips like raging winds. Violent winds can destroy houses, trees, and people, and Job, who had lips like raging winds could not keep quiet here. If he really had acknowledged that his friends were truly "the" people, he would have had to keep quiet, but he kept on arguing.

What he really meant was that he also had knowledge and understanding, and he was not any worse than his friends. He meant, "I am also wise, so what do I lack compared to you? Do you think that I don't already know what you have told me?"

"I am a joke to my friends, the one who called on God and He answered him; the just and blameless man is a joke. He who is at ease holds calamity in contempt, as prepared for those whose feet slip" (12:4-5).

Why does Job bring God into the argument here? We also do the same kind of thing. When we argue with somebody, we quarrel and get upset, and suddenly we bring in a third-party.

We say that a certain pastor or a certain deacon said this or that or we might even quote the word of God. God tells us not to argue, but we argue so fiercely and then get so angry that our faces turn red, and say, "Well, God's word says this. . ."

Therefore, those who are arguing should not say, "God's word says this." The truth is telling us not to argue, and we are violating the truth if we argue with others. If we mention the word of God while we are violating the truth, it is not persuasive at all.

Verse 4 says, "The one who called on God and He answered him." It doesn't mean that Job communicated with God. Job knew about God by hearing about Him from his forefathers. He heard that there is God and that He is the almighty One through his ancestors. So when he did something wrong, he gave sacrifices, and also gave sacrifices on behalf of his children as well.

Therefore, 'calling on God and He answering him' means that Job offered sacrifices. Job is lamenting that he, who is just and blameless, offered sacrifices and he now became a joke to neighbors. He was looked down upon by his wife and also despised by his friends. We should know that these words of Job were not quite right.

If you worship in spirit and in truth and communicate with God, will you become point of ridicule by your neighbors? Those patriarchs who served God very well were recognized and praised by their neighbors. They were never mocked or ridiculed. Because they loved God and also received love from God, even the Gentiles respected them.

The Pharaoh of Egypt even lowered his head before Moses, and when the people of Israel complained against Moses, God was at Moses' side.

There may be momentary persecutions for righteous men to

accomplish the will of God, but even those who are persecuting them cannot really hold them in disrespect and mock them from the heart. A just and blameless man can never be disrespectfully and contemptuously mocked.

Next, it says, "He who is at ease holds calamity in contempt, as prepared for those whose feet slip."

Those who have knowledge, fame, authority and wealth have peace of mind. So, even when they see somebody else suffering calamity, they probably think they have nothing to do with it and remain at peace without worrying about anything.

Job thought that he had fallen into disastrous consequences and was suffering, yet his friends were still living peacefully without any worries. Here Job meant that his friends who continued living at ease were neglecting him and treating him badly.

On the other hand, he said, "As prepared for those whose feet slip." Job is the one whose feet slipped now. Namely, he meant that he was just and blameless, and calamity was waiting for him. This is a misuse of the word of the truth.

Not everything his friends said was true, but there were many truthful things, too. If Job had just said 'Amen' to that and obeyed, his calamities would have left him. But Job only insisted that he was right and looked down upon his friends even while they were explaining with the truth. So, he could not help but keep on suffering from the disasters.

2. Making God Out to Be a God who Blesses Evil Men

"The tents of the destroyers prosper, and those who provoke God are secure, Whom God brings into their

power" (12:6).

Worldly people who do not know the truth sometimes say, "Good men are not prosperous. Rather evil men are more prosperous."

But the God of justice will obviously love good men and righteous men, not evil men. God will not make evil men prosperous.

But how did Job judge God as an evil God? He said, "The tents of the destroyers prosper, and those who provoke God are secure, whom God brings into their power."

He is saying that God brought disaster on him though he was such a righteous man. Of course, Job did not show his evil from the beginning. Because his feelings got more twisted, it had led him this far.

The same happens to some believers. In the beginning they confess that they love God and lead a diligent Christian life. But at one point, if they don't receive answer to their prayers, they stop praying. If others try to give them advice about faith, they respond to it with the words that are not right in the sight of God.

In this kind of case, they have to quickly repent and turn so that the enemy devil and Satan will leave. Otherwise, they will develop more and more ill-feelings through their thoughts, and eventually they cannot control themselves.

Then, even if they want to repent, they cannot. So, they speak words like strong winds that are against the truth like Job did. If they keep on disappointing God, they will not be protected by God any more and disasters will come.

Some say, "Pastor, just look at the world. How prosperous robbers, swindlers and unrighteous people are!"

But the rich man fell to hell and the beggar Lazarus who had feared God went to heaven after they died. Of course, it is blessing to live by the word of God and go to heaven, even if one may have to live as a beggar. We cannot afford to fall into hell just because of some material things for this momentary life.

Of course, if they swindle others and collect money with unrighteous ways, how can they have peace of their mind? They always have worries. Also, if their evil is too much, they will suddenly face disasters.

3. Job Lifts up God's Greatness

"But now ask the beasts, and let them teach you; And the birds of the heavens, and let them tell you. Or speak to the earth, and let it teach you; And let the fish of the sea declare to you. Who among all these does not know That the hand of the LORD has done this." (12:7-9)

God showed His divinity with His power and created everything. That is why nobody can give excuse on the Judgment Day saying that he didn't believe in God because he didn't know there is God. His invisible attributes and His eternal power and divine nature have been clearly seen in everything (Romans 1:20).

Just by seeing animals we can understand there is God. Because strong animals eat weak animals, the weak animals then should become extinct. But it's not so. It's because strong animals do not reproduce large numbers of off-spring. Weaker animals have high birth rates, so we see many of the off-spring.

Why don't you ask sparrows how they can fly? How can flies fly? Mankind's civilization has developed so much and made airplanes. There are so many parts to the airplane, but without fuel, they cannot fly.

Mankind cannot create even a single fly. What kind of equipment do sparrows and flies have so they can fly? We can feel a sense of divinity from this. We can understand that God is living.

Job recognizes this power of God. If you could ask a fly, "How can you fly?" then, the fly would answer, "God made me this way."

If you are unable to believe in God, why don't you talk to the earth? "Hey earth, what kind of power do you have that when we sow seeds, the seeds can bud, grow up, bloom, and bear fruits in you? How is it that when we dig we can get gold, coal, and oil from you?"

If the earth could respond, it would say, "God gave me the power." If the ground could answer you, it would say that God made it that way.

Also, there are so many kinds of fish in the sea. Even big whales and sharks can swim very quickly and move around easily. Even though mankind has great technology, we cannot live underwater. All these things were done by the power of God in His providence.

"In whose hand is the life of every living thing, and the breath of all mankind? Does not the ear test words, As the palate tastes its food? Wisdom is with aged men, With long life is understanding. With Him are wisdom and might; To Him belong counsel and understanding. Behold, He tears down, and it cannot be rebuilt; He imprisons a man, and there can be no release" (12:10-14).

'Living thing' refers to everything that has life including all plants and animals. The 'life' that Job talks about here is the ability to think. It's the power to reason and think.

The 'breath' is said to express understanding of all things and the principles of natural law. This is what Job meant: Animals do not have the ability to understand and realize the principles of all things. God gave living things a soul, so they have the ability to think, but God also gave men a spirit to let them understand natural law and principles of all things. All these things were in providence of God.

Next, just as we have the tongue to discern different tastes, we have the hearing ability of the ear so we can discern sound. Saying 'with long life is understanding' means people gain more wisdom through more experiences as they become older.

'Aged men' refers to the flow of time, and 'With long life' means a person who lived long with good health. 'Wisdom and might' means one who is bright and clear about principles of things. Namely, it means one has the ability to discern between things, and he is accomplishing himself completely within that ability through the years of his life.

'Counsel' is all the wisdom and ideas to fulfill certain things. Here, Job says God has wisdom and might, and also counsel and understanding. Up to this part, what Job is saying is reasonable and true.

4. What Is It that Job Really Wants to Say?

But soon, he reveals what he really wants to say. Verse 14 says, "Behold, He tears down, and it cannot be rebuilt; He imprisons a man, and there can be no release." And what does this mean?

God does not tear down or imprison men. But when people violate the law of the spiritual realm, God has to turn His face away from them, and then the enemy devil and Satan begin to bring trials and tests to make them suffer.

Even if men have committed sins or fallen, if they repent and turn away, God will stand them up again. Even though Peter denied the Lord Jesus three times, it was not from his heart that he made the denials. So, when he repented, he was forgiven and reborn, and he became a powerful apostle.

"Behold, He restrains the waters, and they dry up; And He sends them out, and they inundate the earth. With Him are strength and sound wisdom, The misled and the misleader belong to Him. He makes counselors walk barefoot And makes fools of judges" (12:15-17).

Job knew that God also stopped the flow of Jordan River. Job is saying that just as the Jordan River stopped flowing and the people of Israel could cross it, God can restrain or dry up the waters.

"And He sends them out, and they inundate the earth" means that when there is flood, there will be landslides and other calamities to inundate the earth. Job is saying that God is a fearful God and if He once destroys like this, we cannot restore it. Job means that it is God who also causes people to be misled, or causes people to mislead others, and it is because of God that Job himself is also suffering from mockery and contempt.

In effect Job is saying to his friends, "Friends, don't you know this God? After hearing my explanations don't you realize who is really bad? Isn't God bad? If you are really wise, you can make your own judgment."

From here, Job's true heart is being revealed. Job's twisted mind is trying to make his friends think that God is bad. Job lifted up God so much and now he begins to bring Him down.

Now, what does it mean that "He makes counselors walk barefoot and makes fools of judges"?

'Counseling' is to make plans. Counselors must have wisdom.

Job heard about Israel's history from his ancestors. When God removed wisdom, no matter what kind of plans the Gentile counselors made, their armies were all captured at one moment. Job knew about the battles where hundreds of thousands of soldiers attacked Israel, but when God opposed them, the Gentiles fought among themselves and ran away.

Therefore, even though counselors devise good strategies, if God removes the wisdom, they will lose the battle.

Also, Job is arguing that God makes fools of judges. Judges have to assess and make decisions in accordance with justice. And Job means that God lets the judges make foolish judgments.

What does Job really want to say here?

Job is trying to make his friends realize that, because God is not just, He was making him suffer so much even though Job was righteous and blameless. He is implying that because God leads judges to make foolish judgments, He is also a foolish judge.

"He loosens the bond of kings and binds their loins with a girdle. He makes priests walk barefoot And overthrows the secure ones. He deprives the trusted ones of speech and takes away the discernment of the elders. He pours contempt on nobles and loosens the belt of the strong.

He reveals mysteries from the darkness and brings the
deep darkness into light" (12:18-22).

"He loosens the bond of kings And binds their loins with a girdle" is to break the authority of kings. If God removes the authority, the king cannot but be bound.

For example, when kings are captured by rebels or the enemy, they lose their authority. Their arms are placed on their side and are tied that way. If their arms are tied at their sides, they cannot use their strength.

Also, Job heard about righteous priests who were also captured or killed throughout history. He also saw a man with authority fall in one day. Job is saying that all these things were done by God.

Verse 20 says, "He deprives the trusted ones of speech." What does it mean?

Job thought that he was faithful before God, but God forsook him. But God does not deprive the trusted of their words.

When Saul attacked the Amelekites, God told him to destroy everything, including the people and animals. But Saul disobeyed the word of God and captured and brought back the enemy king and choice animals. When Samuel asked him what happened, he said that he brought them to give sacrifices to God. With human thoughts, we may think Saul did something good. But there is a spiritual meaning in whatever God commands, and Saul disobeyed God with his own thoughts.

It says, "And takes away the discernment of the elders." God does not take away the discernments of the elders. He wants them to be healthy and He wants to add wisdom and knowledge to them. Why would God like to take away the discernments of the elders?

When men get old, they lose their memory power or discernment. Job is saying that God makes them lose memory, but it's actually that men are making themselves that way.

Now, what does it mean that "He pours contempt on nobles And loosens the belt of the strong"?

The nobles are leaders. God will not pour contempt on nobles. Here, the 'belt' also has symbolism. For example, the belt of Samson was his hair. When his hair was shaved, he lost his power, and he had to suffer mockery and contempt.

Then, what is the strong belt of Job? It was his knowledge, wisdom, and wealth with which he could teach others.

Job is saying God loosened this belt of the strong. Here, Job knows that if he directly says it is him, his friends will argue back immediately, so he is explaining it indirectly. Namely, he means that "God is this kind of God, and so He loosened my belt."

Verse 22 says, "He reveals mysteries from the darkness." What does it mean?

'Being in darkness' means that something is hidden. Job actually had faint knowledge about God just by hearing from his forefathers.

With that faint knowledge, Job believed and obeyed God as best he could, and believed now a secret in God's preplanning had been revealed. And severe trials and sufferings came upon him. This is what Job means. He is criticizing God as a God who predestines everything.

Also it says, "And brings the deep darkness into light." This means that Job used to live in light, in the bright world, but in a moment death came upon him. He wants to say that he used to live in light, but a situation like death came upon him.

Then, what is the thing that God reveals from darkness? God reveals our sins that are in darkness.

By doing so, God lets us discover our sins hidden in the darkness, and leads us to throw them away and to be renewed. God does not bring death into light, but He gives life to darkness to lighten it.

Before we came to know God, we used to live in darkness of the world. But since God began to shine the light from above, we open the gate of our heart and accept the word of God. That way, we come out of darkness into the world of light, and we gain life and go the way of eternal life. God is this good God, but Job's understanding about God is the opposite.

"He makes the nations great, then destroys them; He enlarges the nations, then leads them away. He deprives of intelligence the chiefs of the earth's people And makes them wander in a pathless waste. They grope in darkness with no light, And He makes them stagger like a drunken man" (12:23-25).

"He makes the nations great, then destroys them; He enlarges the nations, then leads them away." We can clearly see this throughout the history.

When people of Israel went into the land of Canaan, they were a minor power, but at the time of King David, they became so strong that they received tributes from other countries. But sometimes, this Israel worshipped idols, and became captives or were nearly destroyed.

Even the Roman Empire fell. Also, Germany, Japan, and Italy tried to conquer the world at the World War II but all collapsed in a moment.

It's not God who makes a nation prosper or fall, or dictators rule certain countries. But Job says that everything is done according to God's predestination. If so, God will not be able to make any judgment on the Judgment Day. Those who are falling into hell will argue with God saying, "God, You made me evil and made me commit sins!" Then, what will God be able to say?

If somebody failed in his business, it is he who caused it. There shouldn't be any foolish people who say God made their businesses fail.

Lastly, let us look into the verses, "He deprives of intelligence the chiefs of the earth's people and makes them wander in a pathless waste. They grope in darkness with no light, and He makes them stagger like a drunken man."

To become a chief, one has to gain wisdom. He has to be quick in thinking, and yet he has to think deeply. He should be good in all things without making mistakes. If a leader has no such intelligence, he won't be able to function as a leader for long.

Job is explaining with a parable that he used to be a teacher of everything but is now nothing since God took away his intelligence.

He means that God made him wander in the valley of death, the dark place, and made him stagger like a drunken man.

In the beginning, Job was recognizing the almightiness of God and saying the right things, but he began to say what is not right. When a drunken man walks, he staggers, but he himself doesn't think that he is staggering, because he feels he is walking straight to the goal.

If somebody next to him says, "Why are you so drunk?

Walk straight!" he will probably say, "I am not drunk and I am walking straight. So, why are you telling me I'm staggering?"

Job was in the same situation as a staggering man. When his friends were saying, "You are a sinner and evil," Job replied, "I am not a sinner. I am upright and blameless. You are evil, and God put me in this situation."

Job is concluding that God is a bad God thinking that God predestines everything, even by using the comparison of a drunken man.

Chapter *13*

Job Argues before God

"Behold, my eye has seen all this, My ear has heard and understood it. What you know I also know; I am not inferior to you. But I would speak to the Almighty, And I desire to argue with God." (Job 13:1-3)

1. Job's Arrogance

"Behold, my eye has seen all this, my ear has heard and understood it. What you know I also know; I am not inferior to you. But I would speak to the Almighty, and I desire to argue with God" (13:1-3).

"My eye has seen all this, my ear has heard and understood it" means that Job knows not only what his friends have told him but also what he has said. What does this mean?

Suppose there is a person who is tested in trial, and you advise him with the word of God. But, he doesn't accept it. Rather, he says, "I know everything you are saying. I have heard and seen everything and read the Bible scores of times. So, I know." If he does so it means he is arrogant.

Now, Job is answering this way.

He is saying, "I know what you know. I am not any lesser than you. I don't even want to deal with you. I don't want to hear you. I will speak to the almighty God and argue with Him."

Job is saying that he is better than his friends. His friends, with their love for him, were trying to make Job come to a self-realization and let him walk properly in the sight of God.

But Job is not listening to his friends at all. He is removing himself farther away from them. It's because his friends did not advise him with perfect soundness but with their heated emotions. Job could not trust his friends. Those who keep the word of God will accept any advice with an 'Amen' if it is the truth.

2. Cunning Heart that Frequently Changes

Job said even if he cried to God, He wouldn't listen (Job 5:1), and even if God answered him, he wouldn't believe Him (Job 9:16). He also forgot that he had once said that it was impossible to argue with God, but now, he is saying he wants to argue with God (Job 9:14-16).

This is because Job is speaking freely without realizing his heart as the words come out of his mouth. It is the cunning heart that runs about in complete confusion.

Many people do not remember what they have said. You may have forgotten what you said, or you misheard something that was said.

Also, when you say something, you have to say what you have in your heart, but because you just speak out your instant thoughts, later you cannot remember what you have said. Those who speak out of their thoughts cannot fulfill what they say. It's because they don't even remember what they said. But rather, they insist on what is not right and argue with others.

We have to be honest and truthful. We have to say only what we can do and what is the truth. If we say something, we have to fulfill it. We can understand how obstinate Job is becoming. If we have perfect, unchanging, and truthful hearts we will not act like that.

"But you smear with lies; you are all worthless

*physicians. O that you would be completely silent, and
that it would become your wisdom!" (13:4-5)*

Job knew his friends very well. Because they were not completely truthful and sometimes lied, he didn't want to listen to them.

1 John 1:6 says, "If we say that we have fellowship with Him and yet walk in the darkness, we lie and do not practice the truth." If we profess our faith in God but commit sins and live in darkness, the Bible says that we are liars.

Job didn't listen to the advice of his friends. He looked down upon them. He now is also saying they were full of nonsense. Job knew that his friends were hypocrites and so their words and deeds were different.

Job is now rather advising them to be quiet. If you talk a lot, you make mistakes, and if you make many mistakes, you cannot earn trust from others.

As we have learned, Job was excellent in wisdom and knowledge, and he also had a good education, so who would be bold enough to stand up to him and change him? Unless God had worked through the severe boils, he wouldn't have surrendered before God.

Let us put ourselves into the shoes of Job now. Suppose we are in difficulties and trials, and other people give us advice with the word of God. What kind of heart would we have? Would you accept them with an 'Amen,' or would your pride be hurt, and you look down upon them?

Let us say a certain deacon is suffering some difficulties, and somebody advised him with the truth. If this deacon thinks, "You are no better than I am, and how dare you tell me what to do!"

Then, this deacon should realize how evil he is. No matter whose mouth it comes from, if it's the word of the truth, we should be able to accept it humbly.

3. Giving Excuses

"Please hear my argument and listen to the contentions of my lips. Will you speak what is unjust for God, And speak what is deceitful for Him? Will you show partiality for Him? Will you contend for God? Will it be well when He examines you? Or will you deceive Him as one deceives a man?" (13:6-9)

'Argument' is a discussion in which reasons are advanced for and against some proposition or proposal. 1 Timothy 6:20 says, "O Timothy, guard what has been entrusted to you, avoiding worldly and empty chatter and the opposing arguments of what is falsely called 'knowledge.'"

God tells us not to argue, but Job is saying that he wants to argue with God, and telling his friends to listen to his contentions.

'Contention' is the idea or opinion that they are expressing in an argument or discussion. Here, Job means that he has nothing that is wrong in him. To argue is not right according to the truth.

If we understand the truth and can discern truth from untruth then we can understand that those who are not really right try to argue and give their contention and reasons to support their opinion. Those who live in the truth, even if they are criticized by others, they just look up to God who is the True Judge and endure it. They just keep the word of God. They don't try to argue back or justify themselves. They just commit everything into God's hands so that God Himself could do the things.

Jesus just left everything to God and prayed when He was very wrongfully accused. He never gave contentions or argued back.

Next, Job says, "Will you speak what is unjust for God, and speak what is deceitful for Him?" Being deceitful is being dishonest.

Job was saying, "You are saying I am unrighteous. But you yourselves are not acting by the truth, and you are rebuking me. Therefore, aren't you liars? Will you speak what is unjust for God? Are you trying to cheat God craftily? God knows your heart."

Then, what does it mean that "Will you show partiality for Him?" To show partiality is to be inclined to favor one party more than the other.

So, in other words it is saying, "How can you, who are liars, act like you have partiality with God? How can you stand in the place of God and argue with me with the word of God?"

"God looks at your heart. Even though you may cheat people, how can you cheat God who searches your heart?"

Job is giving a sarcastic twist at his friends' weak points. Job is trying to make them quit talking. Job had a log in his eyes but he could not find it, and he was pointing out the speck in his brother's eyes.

4. Job Listens to the Truth as if It Were a Proverb

"He will surely reprove you If you secretly show

*partiality. Will not His majesty terrify you, And the
dread of Him fall on you? Your memorable sayings are
proverbs of ashes, your defenses are defenses of clay. Be
silent before me so that I may speak; Then let come on
me what may" (13:10-13).*

Not to secretly show partiality, we have to remove hypocrisy
and look up to God humbly and truthfully. If we kneel before
God humbly, we will hear the voice of God. If we are arrogant,
we cannot hear His voice.

"Your deeds are not right, and how dare you try to blame me?
If you humbly kneel before God and look up to Him, you will be
able to hear His rebukes for you!"

Job thought God is so noble and also fearful. He knew about
God's dignity. Job didn't know the God of love. He was afraid
of God knowing Him only as a God who predestines everything.

Next, Job says, "Your memorable sayings are proverbs of
ashes, your defenses are defenses of clay." Job's friends tried
their best to get Job to realize something with the word of God.
But Job did not accept what they said as the truth, but only as
some proverbs or sayings. So, how could he gain self-realization
and change?

Until now, Job and his friends were arguing and quarreling
against each other. When Job attacked, his friends defended.
When his friends attacked, Job defended himself and then
attacked again.

"Your words are not even words of God. They are only some
proverbs. What will you do to me? You should stop saying
unnecessary things and listen to me quietly. If anything happens
to me, it happens to me."

A wall made of rocks is strong, but wall of clay will easily fall. Job concluded that his friends' defense was just like a clay wall that would fall quickly. If we become arrogant, we will not be able to listen to the word of God. Also, even though it is the word of God, we may think it's just a saying of a man.

If arrogance comes first like in this case of Job, even though we hear advice or rebuke with the word of God, we can understand them only as some proverbs of men.

5. Job Defends Himself

"Why should I take my flesh in my teeth and put my life in my hands? Though He slay me, I will hope in Him. Nevertheless I will argue my ways before Him, this also will be my salvation, for a godless man may not come before His presence" (13:14-16).

Job is now defending himself. He is saying, "Who would cause pain to himself by biting his own flesh, and who would try to kill himself?" 'Put my life in my hands' means that he is trying to take his own life.

Job is saying, "Why would I try to suffer? Why would I consider my life feeble? It's not so. I didn't do anything wrong but God is trying to take my life away, so I feel hopeless. I will argue before Him about my deeds to prove what is right and what is wrong."

"A godless man may not come before His presence" means that those who are perverse and capricious cannot come near God. And Job is saying that this will be his salvation. Namely, he means that because he is not a wicked man but a righteous man, he will have salvation before God. He is insisting that he is right.

"Listen carefully to my speech, And let my declaration fill your ears. Behold now, I have prepared my case; I know that I will be vindicated. Who will contend with me? For then I would be silent and die" (13:17-19).

Job is saying that he will explain and his friends should listen and gain understanding. In verse 18, Job says he has prepared his case. Then what kind of case did he prepare?

He explained that he is righteous and has never committed sin or done anything evil. He always offered sacrifices before God not to have any blemish; he feared God, helped others and served them.

Here, he says that he knows he is righteous, because, first of all, he didn't do anything evil but acted in righteousness. Secondly, he says that he is righteous because he was really righteous when he considered his deeds.

In verse 19, he is asking, "Who will contend with me?" For there to be anybody to argue with him, that person must be more righteous than Job himself, and he is asking who that person can be. Job is saying that if there is anybody who is more righteous than he is, then he will be silent and die. Namely, he will surrender before that person.

Job thinks he didn't do anything wrong, so he has no sin. Namely, he thought it was not really sin to fight back if the other person hits him first and to curse back if the other person curses at him first. But what does the word of God teach us?

Matthew 5:39-42 tell us in detail. It says, "But I say to you, do not resist an evil person; but whoever slaps you on your right cheek, turn the other to him also. If anyone wants to sue you and take your shirt, let him have your coat also. Whoever forces you to go one mile, go with him two. Give to him who asks of you, and do not turn away from him who wants to borrow from you."

Job's friends didn't ask Job to either give his cloak or go with them a mile. They only tried to let Job realize something through the word of God. Job did not turn the other cheek; he rather was hitting them back two or three times more.

"Only two things do not do to me, Then I will not hide from Your face: Remove Your hand from me, And let not the dread of You terrify me. Then call, and I will answer; Or let me speak, then reply to me" (13:20-22).

Job is trying to argue with God because there is nobody who is better than he is. But because he was still afraid of God, he couldn't pour out all that he wanted to say. Now, he is asking God not to do two things so that he can argue with Him freely.

He is saying that God's hand is on him, and so, if He removes His hand from him, and if God's dread should not terrify him, he has so many things to argue about.

Why was Job afraid of God? It's because of his mistaken concept and understanding of God. Because he thought of himself as a righteous man and he also had incorrect knowledge about the truth, he misunderstood God as a fearful God. He means that if God would not terrify him and then if He calls him, he would answer, so God can say what He wants after that.

"How many are my iniquities and sins? Make known to me my rebellion and my sin. Why do You hide Your face and consider me Your enemy? Will You cause a driven leaf to tremble? Or will You pursue the dry chaff?"

When Job says, "How many are my iniquities and sins? Make known to me my rebellion and my sin," we may think he wants to find out his sins. His real intention is to bring his complaint against God.

He is arguing against God saying, "I have done nothing wrong. I have no sin, and why do You punish me like this?"

In verse 24, Job is also asking why God hides His face from him and regards him as an enemy.

God did not hide His face from Job, but He was looking at him with blazing eyes. He was listening to every word Job said. God never hid His face nor did He consider Job as an enemy. God loves everybody.

Job's friends advised him to acknowledge his faults and repent, but he didn't listen. He only insisted that he is right, and he rather criticized his friends.

Then, through Hebrews 12:1-8, let us think of what kind of person God is.

"Therefore, since we have so great a cloud of witnesses surrounding us, let us also lay aside every encumbrance and the sin which so easily entangles us, and let us run with endurance the race that is set before us, fixing our eyes on Jesus, the author and perfecter of faith, who for the joy set before Him endured the cross, despising the shame... You have not yet resisted to the point of shedding blood in your striving against sin; and you have forgotten the exhortation which is addressed to you as sons... But if you are without discipline, of which

all have become partakers, then you are illegitimate children and not sons."

If you are carrying a very heavy burden, how much will you sweat and how difficult it will be! But an even heavier burden than any burden is the burden of sins. If we sin, we feel afflicted. We let out words from that affliction, and so, we commit more sins. We do not repent of our evil in us, but with our words we give out more evil. If we give excuses that we could not help but act that way, we will begin to tell lies, and sins will be accumulated more and more. Finally, the sins will bind us and we cannot solve that problem.

Therefore, when we have some problems that bother us, we have to endure and look up to Jesus. Jesus suffered all kinds of mocking and contempt from His creatures. Because He knew that He was going to sit on the right hand of God and there was going to be the salvation for all peoples, He despised the shame for the joy set before Him.

In this way, we have to meditate on how Jesus endured, forgave and went His way, and engrave it in our heart. For us to cast off sins, we have to struggle against them to the point of shedding blood. And because we don't do it, namely because we don't believe and obey the words of God telling us to do, not do, cast off, and keep certain things, we face God's discipline.

When children go astray, their parents will discipline them. In the same way, when His children commit sins, God also disciplines them. If there is no punishment or discipline from God, the Bible says that we are illegitimate sons.

In verse 25, Job likens himself to a driven leaf because he was cut off from life. He also likened himself to the dry chaff. A leave is a lonely and hopeless being. Dry chaff is useless thing that cannot even be used for fuel.

Job is saying all these things, with his heart twisted, to bring God down to the bottom. He cannot either die or live; he is just like a leaf that has no strength or hope. He is more useless than even dry chaff, but he is saying that God is following after him to torture him.

6. Remembering Sins in Childhood

"For You write bitter things against me and make me to inherit the iniquities of my youth. You put my feet in the stocks and watch all my paths; You set a limit for the soles of my feet, while I am decaying like a rotten thing, Like a garment that is moth-eaten" (13:26-28).

"You write bitter things against me" does not mean that God writes bitter things. In the next verse, Job says that "[God] makes him inherit the iniquities of his youth, and now he remembers his past from the time of his youth."

Namely, it means that God has recorded everything about Job since his youth. When Job thought about his past, he lived a faithful life as a father and husband, and he helped the needy and lived a righteous life. He didn't do anything wrong. During his life in his adulthood, he lived a righteous life, so he could not find anything wrong with himself.

But when he was in his youth, he must have fought with his friends or even hit some of them. Thus, he is saying that God is now punishing him for the sins that he committed long ago, when he was too young to discern between things. Namely, Job is making God out to be a very mean person.

When we accept Jesus Christ as our Savior, God forgives us of all our past sins. When we repent and turn from them with our deeds, God does not even remember our past sins and cleanses us through the blood of the Lord Jesus. But if we do not repent or turn but keep on committing sins, we will still be sinners.

Now, what does it mean that "You put my feet in the stocks"?

If your feet are put in stocks, you cannot move. You are confined, and it means you have lost your freewill. Here, the 'stocks' refers to the stocks of life. Job is saying that he can neither live nor die. God had completely confined him leaving him no freewill. Job says that God remembered his sins that he committed in his youth and put him in stocks, not allowing any room for his life.

Job is protesting against God saying that God set a limit in his footsteps, and made him like something that is rotten, like a garment that is moth-eaten. This is not a correct idea. The truth is not like a shackle that binds us but it's the light in the dark that leads us to the way of blessings.

If we dwell in the word of God, the truth will fill us, and it will set us free (John 8:31-32). If we have freedom of truth, we have hope for heavenly kingdom, although we may go the narrow way on this earth. Because we believe that God will pay us back according to what we have done, we can lead a joyful and thankful Christian life.

Chapter 14

Difference between Flesh and Spirit
- Blaming God for Everything

1. Discussing the Meaninglessness of Life
2. Job Says God Predestines Everything
   according to His Desires
3. Job Tries to Teach God a Lesson with Parables
4. Remembering His Past, Receiving God's Love

"But his body pains him, And he mourns only for himself." (Job 14:22)

1. Discussing the Meaninglessness of Life

"Man, who is born of woman, Is short-lived and full of turmoil. Like a flower he comes forth and withers. He also flees like a shadow and does not remain" (14:1-2).

In the previous chapter, Job spoke negative words in complaints, lamentation, and irritation. But because he was afraid of God, he didn't say everything he wanted to say.

But now, his arrow of resentment is directed toward woman. In this verse, Job looks down upon women. In Old Testament times, women were generally considered like maid-servants of men and they only had to obey.

Of course, God does not discriminate between women and men. But, in the Book of Genesis, we understand that sin came into mankind and they went the way of destruction through a woman. God likes what is strong and bold, but on the contrary, He does not like indecisiveness that causes one to easily change their mind due to craftiness and cunningness. Generally, more often a woman's heart is weaker and more changeable than that of a man. It's different from individual to individual, but generally, men's inner hearts are firmer than those of women.

Even in the Old Testament, God sometimes appointed women who had unchanging heart to entrust them with important duties. We find that God called some women and let them fulfill His work like Deborah in the Old Testament, who had a firm and bold heart, and in the New Testament we find the virgin Mary.

Job thought of women as trivial beings, so he says man, who is born of woman, is short-lived. Namely, he is saying that because man is born of a woman who is like a maid-servant of man and has to obey man, man's life is worthless.

Our life is usually about 70 or 80 years, and some people live more than 100 years. A man born of woman has a short life and is full of turmoil. He is like a flower that blooms and withers soon or like a shadow that disappears soon. Job is talking about the meaninglessness of shortness of life.

Ecclesiastes 12:13-14 says, "The conclusion, when all has been heard, is: fear God and keep His commandments, because this applies to every person. For God will bring every act to judgment, everything which is hidden, whether it is good or evil."

The Bible tells us that if we do not fear God and not live in His word, we are no different from animals (Ecclesiastes 3:18). God will certainly bring every act to judgment, everything which is hidden, whether it is good or evil. If we do not fear God and not live in the word, even though we may have wealth, fame, authority, and wisdom, everything is useless (Ecclesiastes chapter 1). The result will only be hell, which is eternal death.

The writer of the Ecclesiastes understood the spiritual meaning of this and said everything we do under the sun is meaningless. But Job did not understand this. He is simply saying that life is meaningless.

Literally, Job's words may seem to be right, but in spirit, it's not really right. As Job said, life is only for 70 or 80 years, so it is short. But in spirit, those who believe in God and live by His word will gain eternal life, so they will live forever in heavenly kingdom. Of course, those who do not believe in God will fall into hell and suffer there forever.

Also, Job says that life is full of turmoil, and he is bringing down not only his present life but also his past life as well. In Job's past, he had many happy moments, but because of his present suffering, he is denying even his past.

Also, 'being full of turmoil' is just the opposite of what it should be for believers. Those children of God who have received the Holy Spirit are full of joy and gladness. As days go by, the day to meet the Lord is coming nearer, and as they work hard, the kingdom and righteousness of God are accomplished, so they are joyful.

We, children of God, shouldn't bloom for a moment and wither soon like flowers. We should be full of the Spirit all the time and keep on being renewed every moment so that our soul will prosper. Men of flesh should keep on casting off flesh to change into men of spirit.

2. Job Says God Predestines Everything according to His Desires

"You also open Your eyes on him and bring him into judgment with Yourself. Who can make the clean out of the unclean? No one! Since his days are determined, The number of his months is with You; And his limits You have set so that he cannot pass. Turn Your gaze from him that he may rest, Until he fulfills his day like a hired man" (14:3-6).

How pitiable Job's circumstance is now! Job is also protesting that God opens His eyes on this kind of meaningless man and brings him into judgment Himself.

As Job said, it's right that God has His eyes on Job. But it's not that God brings him into judgment. Here, it is not that God is bringing him into judgment, but Job was causing it himself.

God has His eyes on us mankind because He loves us. He searches us to save us, to let us turn from sins and become sanctified children who are loved by God.

Job just heard about God through the stories of his forefathers. He didn't really know about the God of love.

In verse 4, Job says, "Who can make the clean out of the unclean?" He concludes there is no one! We can see that he is arrogant to make the conclusion of this kind. Moreover, what he said is not correct.

God can do everything. Before we accepted Jesus Christ, we were children of darkness and we were in the filth of sin. But when we believe in Jesus Christ, God sends us the Holy Spirit as the gift, and we can cast off unclean things and become true children who are sanctified. Job is denying this fact, and he is blocking the works of faith.

Verse 5 says, "Since his days are determined, the number of his months is with You." Job also protests that God has predestined everything. Job means that God has predestined for him to suffer as he has suffered.

Job is thinking about the God whom he heard about from his ancestors. God brought the Israelites out of Egypt, made the Pharaoh come just before the Red Sea, and parted the Red Sea to let only the people of Israel cross. When they reached Marah, God made the water bitter and then let Moses change it into sweet water. Namely, in Job's opinion, God did everything as He wished and preplanned everything to let somebody live and another die, or to forgive another. Therefore, he is saying that God has also preplanned his fate and is carrying out his plan for him.

Job may have expressed his feelings saying, "God, I am a weak man born of a poor woman. Please forgive me and let me rest now. Let me end my life in which I have to do what is spoken without any freedom."

But God does not treat men as paid-workers. God gave us freewill, so we can choose what we want. Paid-labors do not have freedom because they have to do their work to receive their payment.

Job thought that if God wanted to punish him, then God punished him. He thought that God took his children away because He wanted to do it and God also took away all his possessions and struck him with boils.

If we misunderstand the word of God, we may blame God like Job did, even though it is we who did something wrong. Then, we cannot find our faults. There are certain reasons for us to face tests and difficulties. By the mirror of the truth, we can find what we are doing wrong in the sight of God.

Job misunderstood God as a God who preplans everything, and he had problems. But he still had the uprightness to live by His word. So, when God allowed him these trials, Job finally turned from evil and came to know the way of eternal life, and he lived in great joy and hope.

3. Job Tries to Teach God a Lesson with Parables

"For there is hope for a tree, When it is cut down, that it will sprout again, and its shoots will not fail. Though its roots grow old in the ground and its stump dies in the dry soil, At the scent of water it will flourish And put forth sprigs like a plant. But man dies and lies prostrate. Man expires, and where is he?" (14:7-10)

Job had complained and said many things against God, but there was no answer; he then calmed down a little bit. Now, he is giving the parable of a woman and a tree to teach God a lesson.

Why does Job say there is hope for a tree? We can see that if we cut the tree, new sprouts bud from that place.

It says, "Though its roots grow old." If the root stays under the ground for a long time, it will grow old. Even if the stump may die in the dry soil, it will come back to life with water.

Verse 10 says, "But man dies and lies prostrate," and we can see again that Job misunderstands. Physically, when a man dies, he will go back to a handful of dust. A man expiring means that he has no strength. Namely, everything he has had, such as fame and authority, and everything he has done will go back to nothing once he dies. If he expires, we cannot find him on this earth.

And these words of Job are not really correct. Those who believed in God and died with salvation will resurrect into a resurrected body at the coming of our Lord Jesus and they will be caught up into the air. That is why the Bible says that when a believer dies he is asleep (John 11:11; 1 Corinthians 15:18). The body will go back to a handful of dust, but the spirit will never expire. It will combine again with the resurrected body and live forever.

The Pharisees at the time of Jesus believed that they had spirit. They believed that believers would go into heavenly kingdom. However, the Sadducees believed there was no spirit, and when a man died, he would just expire on the earth. Job also had a thought that was similar to that of Sadducees.

"As water evaporates from the sea, and a river becomes parched and dried up, so man lies down and does not rise. Until the heavens are no longer, he will not awake nor be aroused out of his sleep. Oh that You would hide me in Sheol, that You would conceal me until Your wrath returns to You, that You would set a limit for me and remember me!" (14:11-13)

The water of the sea seems to evaporate and go up, but eventually it comes back down as rain. The water of the sea does not decrease. If sea water were to decrease, all streams and rivers would dry up. Because he had much knowledge, Job knew that sea water would never decrease. If it did, it would obviously dry the streams and rivers. He is explaining this basic principle.

He also says, "So man lies down and does not rise." And this is not correct, either. The beggar Lazarus, who feared God, went to the bosom of Abraham. When a man dies, it is not true that he will not rise again; he can rise, resurrect, and live eternally.

Then, what does it mean that "Until the heavens are no longer, He will not awake nor be aroused out of his sleep"? It does not mean that Job knows that the heavens and earth will disappear as recorded in the Book of Revelation.

Often, when something goes wrong, we say, "This is

impossible, even if heavens and earth should change." Job is also saying this to mean that it is just not possible even if heavens and earth disappear. If heaven disappears, one may survive, but actually heaven exists forever, so it is also something impossible. Namely, Job is saying that because man will not awake until heavens are no longer, he will just stay that way forever.

Job is concluding that heavens existed before and it will exist forever, so something like heaven disappearing will not happen. In the same way, he is explaining that a man dying and rising will not just happen.

Verse 13 says, "Oh that You would hide me in Sheol, That You would conceal me until Your wrath returns to You, That You would set a limit for me and remember me!"

Job understood that Sheol was only a place where the dead would sleep forever. So, he is asking God to hide him in Sheol, which is at the state of nothingness. How painful he is feeling that he says this!

Job thinks that God is angry with his sins that he committed at his youth and giving him such hardships because of it. He thinks God punished him as He had preplanned, but someday His anger will calm down. Even between men, they may have enmity for a certain period of time but soon their hearts will give way toward one another.

So, even though it is death, he wanted God to hide him in Sheol, but he also wants God to set a limit. And he is asking God to hide him in Sheol and remember him when the time limitation set for him ends up and His anger is no more. If God does not remember him, he will die forever, and it is something he doesn't want.

So, what does Job want God to do? Job is saying that a tree

will keep on living even if it dies, but Job is a wretched person, born of a woman of no value. Furthermore, he is suffering from boils so he is even more wretched. Because he is in such a pitiful and hopeless situation, he wants God to remember him and revive him again later.

4. Remembering His Past, Receiving God's Love

"If a man dies, will he live again? All the days of my struggle I will wait until my change comes. You will call, and I will answer You; You will long for the work of Your hands. For now You number my steps, You do not observe my sin. My transgression is sealed up in a bag, And You wrap up my iniquity" (14:14-17).

Now, Job changes his argument. He asked God to remember him and revive him, even if he dies and sleeps in Sheol. But now he says that if a man dies he cannot live again.

What does it mean that "All the days of my struggle I will wait until my change comes"?

This means that Job is suffering, but if he had had hope like a tree that can live even after it dies, he wouldn't have complained against God. If he has hope that he can live again, he will endure and wait. But because the result will be different, namely because death means a complete end, he now is speaking out in words of complaint as much as he wants.

If we have a heart like Job, we have to cast off these untruthful things of the heart. Job did not receive the Holy Spirit in his heart for he lived in Old Testament times, but we can receive help from the Holy Spirit as we are God's children who have received the Holy Spirit, and should not act like Job.

Before, Job relied on God, and so, he offered sacrifices on behalf of his children, worrying that his children might have committed sin. But although Job offered sacrifices, he had never met God or heard His voice. Furthermore, even in his pains, God has not met him, nor answered him.

Job thought about his past. He thought that if God called him while he was offering sacrifices before God, he would answer Him. In order to persuade God, Job is mentioning his good times in the past.

Before, he had wealth, education, health, and everything and could influence others with his virtue. God made him wealthy at that time, and how precious God considered him!

Verse 16 says, "For now You number my steps, You do not observe my sin." He means that God changed his mind now; God is numbering his steps to observe the sin that he committed in his youth. God took away his possessions and made him suffer so much.

Job was saying, "At that time, You loved me and gave me abundance. How preciously did you consider me? If you called me, "Job!" then I would have answered. But now You have forsaken me this way, and what is the reason? And why do You treat me as a heinous criminal?"

What does verse 17 mean, as it says, "My transgression is sealed up in a bag, And You wrap up my iniquity"?

If sin is sealed up in a bag, it cannot come out. Likewise, if the iniquity is wrapped up, it cannot come out either. Job means that God is going way over the limit just numbering his steps and He is now considering him as a criminal. How much Job must be suffering to say something like this!

\\"*But the falling mountain crumbles away, And the rock moves from its place; Water wears away stones, Its torrents wash away the dust of the earth; So You destroy man's hope" (14:18-19).*

If the mountain falls, its shape will disappear. The rocks move to another position. If a volcano erupts, the top of the mountain will fly away and the whole area will be covered with lava.

Why is Job using this kind of parable before God? Here, Job likens himself to high mountains and hard rocks. He used to have renown like a mountain, be rich and have authority. But because God destroyed this mountain, he became a useless mountain and rock.

Verse 19 says, "Water wears away stones, Its torrents wash away the dust of the earth; So You destroy man's hope."

If the water flows for a long time, even rocks will wear down. Just one drop of water has no strength, but if it falls for hundreds or thousands of years, even strong rocks will have a hole worn in it.

Job says "Its torrents wash away the dust of the earth." Dust of the earth is such a small thing that can be hardly seen. Just little bit of water can wear away stones, and why does he say torrents wash away such small dust of the earth? Why does Job, who has much knowledge, say something that seems to be illogical?

Here, 'water' refers to the highness of God. Job is being sarcastic about God saying He has such great power but steps on and destroys him who is just like dust of the earth.

Job is saying, "Before You struck me, I was hard as rock and strong as steel. I was rich, and I had peace in the family. But as water wears out stones, the highness of God sunk my healthy body like rock, took my possessions and my beautiful family. Just as torrents wash away the dust of the earth, with such high authority of Yours, You washed me away, who is just like dust of the earth! You made me useless. You destroyed all my hopes."

Here, Job is misunderstanding that it is God who destroys the hope of men. But actually God gives hope to people. He wants men to be happy, and He wants to bless us in everything and give us health as our souls are prosperous.

"You forever overpower him and he departs; You change his appearance and send him away. His sons achieve honor, but he does not know it; Or they become insignificant, but he does not perceive it. But his body pains him, And he mourns only for himself" (14:20-22).

Suppose there is a fight between a 5-year-old child and a 25-year-old man. Who would have to yield? Just because a 5-year-old child is cursing and trying to fight, the 25-year-old man should not fight against this child. It would be just like spitting on his own face. He should yield or just avoid the situation.

Job is saying that God has such great authority but is trying to chase him and vanquish him who is not better than dust of the earth. "You forever overpower him and he departs" means that God tried to win against him forever, so He took away his possessions, health, and peace of his family. Finally, God will make Job leave this world and go down to Sheol.

"You change his appearance and send him away" means

Job's appearances have been changing so much, with his face turning red and blue, pale and yellow.

What does it mean by "His sons achieve honor, but he does not know it," in verse 21?

Job used to be rich and honored before. He believed in God's blessings, so he offered sacrifices of thanks before God. However, even though he did such things in the past, now he is no better than the dust of the earth. So, what is the meaning of yesterday's blessings? This is what Job is saying.

No matter how happy he used to be before, God has taken everything away from him, so he doesn't even need to remember it. So, he cannot be thankful.

Also, he says he is insignificant but he does not perceive it. He said he was not insignificant, but he had much wisdom and knowledge, and his friends should not even start talking before him. He looked down upon his friends and he also argued with God. He did not realize he was insignificant.

Because Job had gone down to a lowly place now, he should have realized his insignificance so that he could repent and turn about. But he does not realize he is insignificant. He is rather arguing that he used to be an honored man, but it's only that God made him so miserable, so he is not insignificant.

In what kind of situation do you find yourself? Being insignificant doesn't mean we have to get discouraged. We have to reflect upon ourselves with the truth to clearly realize exactly where we are. Only then can we find the way to solve our problems. If there are problems of family, financial difficulty, or problems in business, there certainly is a reason. It is a blessing to find that reason and turn away.

Those who do not find themselves but only blame others cannot have any improvement.

In verse 22, Job returns to his reality and is looking at himself. He does not perceive that he is insignificant, but in reality, his flesh is decaying, and his heart is so broken.

Because Job was blaming only God and not trying to find his fault, he couldn't either realize himself or repent.

Chapter 15

Second Argument of Eliphaz the Temanite

1. Let's Not Argue

2. Sarcasm and a Defiant Mind

3. Eliphaz' Ill-Feelings Get Fiercer

4. Eliphaz Tries to Teach Job with Words of the Ancestors

5. Eliphaz Curses with His Bursting Envy and Jealousy

"He will not escape from darkness; The flame will wither his shoots,
And by the breath of His mouth he will go away." (Job 15:30)

1. Let's Not Argue

"Then Eliphaz the Temanite responded, 'Should a wise man answer with windy knowledge and fill himself with the east wind? Should he argue with useless talk, or with words which are not profitable?'" (15:1-3)

Job's friends thought Job was a wise person, but as they were listening to him, they considered him as a foolish man. It's because a wise man does not answer with windy knowledge.

Nobody can embrace or contain the east wind. Job has kept on arguing with useless talk, and this is unprofitable argument, and unprofitable argument is like trying to catch the wind.

These words of Eliphaz are certainly true. But even though Eliphaz rebukes Job with the truth, it will be of no use at all because Job's attitude and feelings towards his friends are getting worse and worse.

When somebody's feelings are hurt, even the good and proper words will not be accepted by the person. But rather, because of those words, he will have even more ill-feelings. Therefore, if we are wise, we should keep our mouths closed in this kind of situation.

"Indeed, you do away with reverence and hinder meditation before God. For your guilt teaches your mouth, and you choose the language of the crafty. Your

Before, when Job was rich, he offered God burnt offerings with his reverent fear of God. But now, he is complaining against God and he is saying that God is a bad God. One of the reasons why Job came to argue with God is because of the argument with his friends, so his friends are also responsible for his actions.

Eliphaz says that Job is saying he is upright and righteous, but the words coming from his mouth condemn him and prove that he is a sinner.

Why does Eliphaz say that Job is crafty?

Before, Job used to fear and serve God, but now it's the opposite. That is why Eliphaz says that Job is crafty.

But Job's inner heart is not crafty. As written in Job chapter 1, he is upright and blameless. If we consider Job's words, the opinion of Eliphaz sounds right. But many times one's words and heart do not match. Right now, Job has momentarily become a crafty man because he didn't know the truth; it doesn't mean that he is crafty from his inner heart.

Eliphaz says to Job, "I do not condemn you. It is your lips that condemn you." It's the same with those who quarrel with each other. First, they just talk, but if the argument gets fiercer, they even curse. They say they are right, but in the sight of a third-party, both of them are evil.

Therefore, argument will offend others, make them feel hard in heart, get angry, and commit sins. Argument is useful for nothing. It is only nonsense. It will only cause ill-feelings in other people and make them give out more evil. The other person has become evil because of me, so it means I made that person sin.

2. Sarcasm and a Defiant Mind

"Were you the first man to be born, Or were you brought forth before the hills? Do you hear the secret counsel of God, and limit wisdom to yourself? What do you know that we do not know? What do you understand that we do not?" (15:7-9)

The very first man to exist on earth is Adam. Eliphaz knew very well that Job was not even the first one to be born. For six days God created the heavens and the earth and everything in them and then He created man. So, even before man was created, there were hills. Eliphaz is asking this question knowing hills were first to exist.

There is no way for a man to hear the secret counsel of God. Furthermore, it is absolutely impossible for Job to have all the wisdom by himself. Eliphaz is now using sarcasm against Job.

Then, why did Job's friends become so sarcastic?

It's because Job said they could not match him in any way, and that he wanted to argue only with God. But as they heard Job's argument with God, it was also nonsense. Their minds were already entangled, and they became even more cynical. Because they felt Job was so stubborn, they came to rebuke him for it.

They may have said, "Job, what you know, we all know it, too, and we understand everything you understand."

Here, we should understand that such an argument brings about disturbances, trials, and tests through the accusations of Satan. Arguments rise because both parties have knowledge. At first, they begin with trivial things, but as they keep on arguing, their tempers start to flare, and sometimes they even curse.

God's word tells us that he who serves is greater than he who is served, and urges us to overcome evil with goodness. So, what is good in insisting on our pride, and then, having enmity with others?

Jesus had much power, but He didn't argue with others. When other people did not accept His word but rather tried to stone Him, He just went away (John 8:59), and He didn't quarrel or cry out (Matthew 12:19-20). We should resemble this character of Jesus.

"Both the gray-haired and the aged are among us, Older than your father. Are the consolations of God too small for you, even the word spoken gently with you?" (15:10-11)

Here, Eliphaz is describing the appearances and circumstances of the friends. Though one is much older, if the knowledge level is similar and if the both can respect each other, they can be friends. Eliphaz is asking how Job can show such disrespect to some of his friends who were older than his father.

Until now, his friends mentioned the word of God with the heart of God.

"We console you with the word of God, and why is it that you resist us? Isn't it that you look down on us with your arrogance?"

But actually, when his friends tried to console him with the word of God, it just made him angrier, instead of consoling Job. It caused Job to express more evil and reveal sin. Job and his friends are committing the same kind of sin now.

But we should also understand that the fault of Job's friends is greater than that of Job. At the final part of the Book of Job, God rebukes Job's friends more than He does Job, and He had Job pray for the forgiveness of his friends' sins.

We should keep this in mind. If one of your brothers got angry because of you, your fault in having made him angry is greater than his fault of getting angry.

"Why does your heart carry you away? And why do your eyes flash, that you should turn your spirit against God and allow such words to go out of your mouth?" (15:12-13)

Eliphaz is arguing with Job with his feelings having reached the worst stage. He is rebuking Job for standing against God and looking down upon his friends.

"Heart carry you away, and eyes flashing" means that when people keep on arguing, each side insists that he is right, so naturally, anger and ill-feelings will grow. If they have anger, blood circulates faster, and so, their faces turn red, and sometimes even their eyes turn red. When others look at these people, it seems that their eyes are glowing. It's not glowing of goodness, but of evil.

If they keep on arguing from this point, they may even shake or have convulsions of body. If they reach this stage, they cannot control their mind at all, and their mouths will not speak truth. Job and his friends have reached this stage of anger.

Eliphaz says "That you should turn your spirit against God

and allow such words to go out of your mouth?" But he does not understand what spirit is when he said this. It's just that they have been trying to teach Job a lesson with the word of God, the Truth, but Job just ignored their words. So, Eliphaz is now saying that Job is opposing the word of God. Eliphaz knows that Job's words are not just words from the mouth, but the expression of his heart.

Sometimes, we speak words from the depth of our heart, and at other times, we just speak what is not really in our hearts. If we say something that is not in our heart, it means we are telling a lie. Also, though not intended, we sometimes speak words that we have not clearly thought through. This is also a kind of a lie. It is because what is in our heart comes out through our lips.

Sometimes, people get drunk and say many meaningless things. They sometimes accuse or blame other people when they get drunk. This is not just words they speak, but it's their real feelings in heart. They control it at ordinary times, but when they get drunk, those words that are in their heart come out through their lips.

It's natural that what is in heart will come out through the lips. If we live honestly in truth, all our words on our lips will be the same as the words that we have in our heart.

3. Eliphaz' Ill-Feelings Get Fiercer

"What is man, that he should be pure, or he who is born of a woman, that he should be righteous?" (15:14)

In the Bible, there are many people who are pure. Moses was more humble and meek than anybody else on the face of the earth, and was faithful in all God's house (Numbers 12:3-7).

When Stephen preached the word of God to the people, those evil people stoned him to death.

> "They went on stoning Stephen as he called on the Lord and said, 'Lord Jesus, receive my spirit!' Then falling on his knees, he cried out with a loud voice, 'Lord, do not hold this sin against them!' Having said this, he fell asleep" (Acts 7:59-60).

Stephen was dying without having any sin, but he prayed for the forgiveness of those who were killing him. How clean this heart is!

But why is Eliphaz saying something like this?

Eliphaz knew his unclean heart. It was evil and filthy heart. And when he considered others around him, they didn't have pure heart, either. So, he is concluding that nobody has pure heart.

Also, Eliphaz considered women worthless, so he says there is no one righteous among those who are born of a woman. This is not right either in physical or spiritual sense.

For example, there is Admiral Soonshin Lee in Korea who was loyal to the nation, faithful to his parents, and loved all his brothers and sisters. He had been wrongfully accused and exiled, and because of the country's crisis, he was ordered to come back and fight in the war. Despite all this, he didn't complain against the king who punished him. He finally sacrificed his life for the nation, his people, his parents, and for brothers and sisters.

How can we say such a person is not righteous? We can

definitely find that the righteous are even among those who are born of a woman.

It's the same in spirit. When we open the door of our heart and accept Jesus Christ as our Savior, we receive the Holy Spirit. Once we receive the Holy Spirit, our spirit that has died because of sin will revive.

Romans 10:10 says we are justified by believing in heart and saved by confessing with our lips. Those who truly believe in God will try to cast off all forms of evil and struggle against sins to the point of shedding blood. Because they cast off untruths and live in the word of God, their confession will become true, and they will be justified by God.

At this point Eliphaz becomes so furious that he can no longer control himself, and he is also speaking absurdities.

Some may ask, "How can men keep all the commandments of God and become sanctified?" But in God, nothing is impossible. He can change our heart at any time.

If we love God, keep His commands, and live in the word, then our hearts will change into good and holy hearts. If we receive the Holy Spirit and the strength from God above, we can definitely keep the commandments of God and become sanctified.

When he was a prince in Egypt, Moses had so much anger in him that he killed an Egyptian who seriously bothered one of his people. But after he went through the trials in the wilderness for 40 years, he became the meekest person on the face of the earth.

The apostle Paul also had a hot temper, but since he met the Lord, he was refined very well. He changed into an apostle of love and could receive the crown of righteousness. John and James also had short tempers but they also changed into apostles of love.

"Behold, He puts no trust in His holy ones, And the heavens are not pure in His sight; How much less one who is detestable and corrupt, Man, who drinks iniquity like water!" (15:15-16)

Being 'holy' means having no form of evil and being only good and righteous. God surely puts His trust in His holy ones. He says, "Be holy, for I am holy," and why would He not trust His holy ones? If one's feelings become furious, he begins to speak absurd things, things that don't really make sense.

Eliphaz says, "And the heavens are not pure in His sight," but why would God consider heavens impure, while He created heavens and earth and was happy about them?

Also Eliphaz says, "How much less one who is detestable and corrupt, Man, who drinks iniquity like water!" To be corrupt is to do all things leaving man's righteousness. Eliphaz is condemning Job with his fury.

Job thinks he didn't commit sins but lived a righteous life. But his friends did not comfort him in talks but only blamed and condemned him, who has been put into such a wretched situation.

Job's inner heart itself was not evil, nor detestable, nor corrupt. But his friends are saying so.

Because Job did not agree with them, his friends got angry and condemned Job. In this way, Job also released his feelings and became furious.

What caused such a result to happen? It's because of the argument. If people have more and more ill-feelings, they speak things that don't make sense, and in worst case, they even curse one another.

4. Eliphaz Tries to Teach Job with Words of the Ancestors

"I will tell you, listen to me; And what I have seen I will also declare; What wise men have told, and have not concealed from their fathers" (15:17-18).

Then, Eliphaz said, "Job, you don't listen to us, so let me tell you the words that passed down from our fathers, so that you can understand."

So far, Eliphaz has been trying to persuade Job with all his knowledge, but Job didn't listen to him. Now, he is mentioning the words of their fathers. The words that were given to Moses and other prophets had not disappeared, but had been passed down to that generation.

"To whom alone the land was given, and no alien passed among them. The wicked man writhes in pain all his days, and numbered are the years stored up for the ruthless. Sounds of terror are in his ears; while at peace the destroyer comes upon him. He does not believe that he will return from darkness, and he is destined for the sword" (15:19-22).

The land of Israel was given to God's chosen people. Joel 3:17 says, "Then you will know that I am the LORD your God, Dwelling in Zion, My holy mountain. So Jerusalem will be holy, and strangers will pass through it no more." This verse spiritually means that children of God should obey the word of God and live in it. If we befriend the world and do evil things and untruths, Satan will get into our lives, and we will face difficulties.

"The wicked man writhes in pain all his days, and numbered are the years stored up for the ruthless." What does this mean? Now, Eliphaz is rebuking Job saying that Job is a wicked and ruthless man.

Some say that evil men are prosperous. But in fact, all evil men will fall.

Psalm 1:6 says, "For the LORD knows the way of the righteous, but the way of the wicked will perish." Proverbs 24:19-20 says, "Do not fret because of evildoers Or be envious of the wicked; for there will be no future for the evil man; the lamp of the wicked will be put out."

There is judgment between what is good and evil (Ecclesiastes 12:14), so we don't have to envy when evil men seem to be prosperous.

In verse 20, the 'ruthless' refer to those who are cruel and violent. In the Bible, we can see how God reacts to evil and ruthless men. Namely, Eliphaz is saying that what God will do toward Job is already decided because Job is a wicked and ruthless man.

In verse 21, it says, "Sounds of terror are in his ears." What kind of sound did Job hear? He heard the sound of all his possessions being destroyed, his children dying, and all his cattle dying. Not only that! His wife discarded him. His relatives discarded him. Furthermore, he was hit by boils all over his body. Job kept on hearing sounds of terror.

How prosperous had Job been before? He seemed to be leading a prosperous life, but when he faced tests and trials, he heard only sound of terror, and everything just collapsed at one moment. Job had no way out of his agonizing trials.

Verse 22 says, "While at peace the destroyer comes upon him. He does not believe that he will return from darkness, and he is destined for the sword." What does it mean?

A sword is needed to cut something. Being destined for the sword refers to Job's situation in which Job is mocked and despised by many people and suffering from heart-piercing pain. Because he was destined for the sword, he could not even hope to return from darkness.

Eliphaz was saying, "Job! You are wicked and ruthless. You seemed to be prosperous, but by the work of God you were cursed. You are destined for the sword, so don't even hope to be saved from those trials. Destruction is destined for the wicked and the ruthless. What remains is only that people will despise you and laugh at you."

Can you imagine how angry Job must have become when he heard such a comment! He was being condemned as a wicked and ruthless man, while he thought that he had lived an upright life!

"He wanders about for food, saying, 'Where is it?' He knows that a day of darkness is at hand. Distress and anguish terrify him, they overpower him like a king ready for the attack, because he has stretched out his hand against God and conducts himself arrogantly against the Almighty" (15:23-25).

This is what Eliphaz means: Because Job completely collapsed, he now had to wander about for food and borrow from others. He could not get out of the darkness, and finally, he would realize that there is no way for him to recover, but he cannot do anything about it but fall into more suffering.

Job was afraid of God in his sufferings and pains. If he had not feared God, he would have spoken more recklessly, but he controlled himself because of fear. Also, if the king had prepared for so many years to attack the enemy, how easily would he have won the battle?

Eliphaz is explaining that the reason why Job is in such great agony is that he stretched out his hand against God. In the friends' viewpoint, Job has been standing against God and raising his hand against heaven.

For example, when two people have a quarrel, they sometimes raise their hands and speak with spattering. Eliphaz is explaining that this is because Job conducted himself arrogantly against the Almighty.

We should not judge others. Job's friends judged Job as a wicked, ruthless, and arrogant person merely with Job's words, but Job could not agree with them. Job's inner heart was not really wicked.

Because his friends didn't know him at all, and because they had a completely different idea from that of his, he could not help but say he wanted to argue with God, not with his friends.

"He rushes headlong at Him with his massive shield. For he has covered his face with his fat and made his thighs heavy with flesh. He has lived in desolate cities, in houses no one would inhabit, which are destined to become ruins" (15:26-28).

"He rushes headlong at Him with his massive shield" means that he is arrogant and thus disobeys God continuously. This is about Job. "For he has covered his face with his fat" means material richness. Eliphaz is saying Job had become arrogant because of his wealth.

When King Solomon became rich, he began to worship idols
and left God. When the people of Israel devotedly worshipped
God, they were very prosperous. But when they were in
material abundance and had no difficulties, they betrayed God
and worshipped idols. When God turned His face away from
them, His curses fell upon them so that they were invaded by
neighboring countries and taken as captives to become slaves.

When a country collapses, the cities become desolate, and
because nobody lives there, animals prowl around the ruins.
People wander around to find food or live between rocks in the
mountains to hide, or do farming on the hillside.

Eliphaz is saying Job is such a person. Job lost all his
children and possessions, and he fell into a wretched destination
having nothing to eat with the pains of boils. Eliphaz is trying to
teach Job the words that have been passed down from their wise
fathers.

5. Eliphaz Curses with His Bursting Envy and Jealousy

*"He will not become rich, nor will his wealth endure;
and his grain will not bend down to the ground. He
will not escape from darkness; the flame will wither his
shoots, and by the breath of His mouth he will go away"
(15:29-30).*

Now, Job's friends are cursing Job, and why are they doing
it? When Job was rich, helped others and was respected by
others, they pretended to love Job and have fellowship with him.

But in their hearts were envy and jealousy.

As Job seemed to be going the way of destruction and spoke out words against God, they rebuked him, and along with that, their envy and jealousy came bursting out. That is why they are cursing Job and saying that Job will not be rich again like before, and his possessions will not increase.

They mean that Job will not be able to come out of his situation when they say, "He will not escape from darkness."

"The flame will wither his shoots" means that even the seeds will dry, and this means there is no hope whatsoever. It means that Job will not be able to escape from curses.

What does it mean that "And by the breath of His mouth he will go away"? God created the heavens and the earth with His word. So, if God blows His breath against Job, everything will end. It means God will blow His breath against those who are arrogant.

Literally, this is right, but it doesn't really apply to Job.

"Let him not trust in emptiness, deceiving himself; for emptiness will be his reward. It will be accomplished before his time, and his palm branch will not be green. He will drop off his unripe grape like the vine, and will cast off his flower like the olive tree" (15:31-33).

At the time of Jesus, the Pharisees, the scribes, and high priests kept the law and they considered themselves righteous. But Jesus rebuked them saying they were like whitewashed tombs. They crucified their Savior without recognizing Him as their Savior even though He was in front of their eyes. But they thought they were keeping the law of Moses and were good believers in God. They were actually cheating themselves, and finally fell into destruction.

"Job, you consider yourself righteous, but you have cheated yourself. Only destruction came upon you. You have lost everything and you don't have anything left with you. Before the day comes, before you see the light, all these curses will fall on you. Destruction will come upon you before the branch will be green. Don't even dream of recovering!"

Eliphaz is telling Job not to have any kind of hope of recovery whatsoever.

As said in Verse 33, if unripe grape is eaten by worms or falls by wind, how meaningless it is! If the flower of olive tree falls by wind, it cannot bear a fruit, so even blooming is useless. Eliphaz is saying Job's life is the same.

Here, let us consider the spiritual meaning of grape. Jesus said He is the vine and we are the branches (John 15:5). Only when the branches are connected to the vine can they bloom the flower and bear fruits. If the branch falls away, it will become dry, be trampled on, and finally be burned.

If we depart from Jesus Christ, namely if we do not live in the truth, we will become like the chaff, and cannot escape being tormented in fire at the time of judgment. It's just like the unripe grapes falling from the vine.

"For the company of the godless is barren, and fire consumes the tents of the corrupt. They conceive mischief and bring forth iniquity, and their mind prepares deception" (15:34-35).

Eliphaz likens Job to a godless and corrupt man, and judges

him as an evil person who accepts bribes.

Why does he say this?

When Job was rich, he helped many people and showed generosity. From those who received his help, he also received many gifts. Job's friends saw this with their envy and jealousy, and when their arguments became more intense, they had more ill-feelings and said that Job had received bribes.

Of course, Job did not receive any bribes. Here, we can find how jealous and envious his friends were!

Chapter *16*

Job Blames Everything on God

"I was at ease, but He shattered me, And He has grasped me by the neck
and shaken me to pieces; He has also set me up as His target.
His arrows surround me. Without mercy He splits my kidneys open;
He pours out my gall on the ground." (Job 16:12-13)

1. Windy Words without Meaning

"Then Job answered, 'I have heard many such things; sorry comforters are you all. Is there no limit to windy words? Or what plagues you that you answer?'" (16:1-3)

Shaking his head Job says that his friends are sorry comforters. Why does Job say so?

'Comfort' is to make one's heart peaceful and put a person at ease. Job's friends could not become his comforters. They only made him angrier and caused him more agony in heart.

His friends kept on scolding him with their words, and as Job listened to them, Job's thinking became even more complicated. Through his friends' words, he had more agony and complexity in his heart. This is what Job meant.

Then, why does Job conclude that his friends' words are 'windy words'?

It's because no matter how good their words were, there was no following deed. For example, suppose deacon A has a sudden problem, and deacon B comes to him and says, "If you pray, the problem will be solved and you will receive blessings."

But deacon A knows that deacon B is also living in difficulties like himself. So, he cannot really pay attention to the advice of deacon B. Though he may not show it outside, in his mind he would probably think, "Why do you not pray and receive the answer first?" The advice only brings about mockery.

Not only in the church, but also in the world, we can find many windy words. There are so many words that are not beneficial but only cause more misunderstandings and ill-feelings.

In the same way, his friends' words, which were not followed by their deeds, were not helpful to Job at all. That is why Job concludes that their words are windy words.

There is no limit to windy words. They will only cause more arguments. They cannot bear any fruit. Therefore, those words cannot stand or encourage those who are disheartened. The people only insist that they are right in an attempt to win the argument, so that only Satan will have an opportunity to work.

"Friends! What is it that plagues you that you would talk this way?"

There were reasons that Job's friends were plagued. But Job thought he was perfectly right, so he could not understand why his friends were motivated to speak with such windy words.

Job complained and cursed against God saying that God is a bad God. Furthermore, he didn't even listen to the advice of his friends, but rather he only looked down on them. But he still insisted that he was upright and blameless. So in the view of his friends, he only looked ridiculous and spiteful. That is why they said such words. When one side is plagued with such agitation, it is the fault of both sides.

Some people think that they are persecuted by their family members or neighbors because they attend church and love God. But in most cases they are faced with trials and persecutions because of their mistakes and shortcomings or even wrongdoings. If we give out the aroma of the Christ, there won't be any persecutions. There are some cases where we are persecuted for righteousness in providence of God, but these are rare cases.

"I too could speak like you, if I were in your place. I could compose words against you and shake my head at you" (16:4).

Job thinks that his friends are speaking words and showing deeds that are so unreasonable and even to the point of being shocking. So, here, Job is suggesting that they should change their positions.

In other words Job is saying, "If I have in my heart the evilness that you have, I would also compose words against you and unreasonable words to plague you, and I would shake my head at you."

Composing words means they are just making up their words without having any deeds to show or back their words. It means his friends judged and condemned Job in their thoughts as they wanted. In Job's opinion, his friends had no deeds, and they just composed their words with their opinions, so he didn't trust them.

Then, why was there shaking of the head? In a fierce argument, they may get so angry that they even shake their heads. We can see how agitated the friends are now.

Even though somebody's words absolutely do not agree with our opinions, we should not shake our heads. We have to stop this habit. It will embarrass the other person, and make us judge and conclude that his word is wrong, even before he finished his speech. Therefore, it is something very rude.

Job's heart was broken because of his friends' words and deeds. He now is trying to make his friends realize their wrong deeds.

2. Job Comes to Self Realization

"I could strengthen you with my mouth, and the solace of my lips could lessen your pain. If I speak, my pain is not lessened, and if I hold back, what has left me?" (16:5-6)

Before he fell into trials, Job taught many people, strengthened the weak, and helped those in need. He had at least the fleshly deeds of goodness (Job chapter 4). Job's friends didn't have any deeds whereas Job had showed the fleshly deeds before he faced the trials.

"You tell me what to do and what is wrong with me while you yourselves do not show any deeds, but I can tell you this because I acted. If it were before I faced this trial, I could strengthen you and lessen your pain. But even though I am speaking this way, I cannot solve any of my problems. Even if I stay quiet, how can my heart be at peace?"

Job thought he was speaking only good words, but his friends just got angrier. They were so angry that they also shook their heads, for they thought Job didn't deserve to be speaking such words.

In their viewpoint, Job is under the curse of God right now.

But rather than repenting, he is arguing with God and looking down upon his friends. It was an evil thing. So, even though Job said good words, they wouldn't listen to him, either.

Job said that he could strengthen his friends and lessen their pains if it were like before, but these words only agitated his friends even more.

For example, suppose there is somebody whose current situation is not very good. He says he was a great man before and he is trying to teach others. What then would happen? Other people would not listen to him, and would probably laugh at him.

On the contrary, if he were to explain the reason why he had to face trials, this is an attitude of repentance, so it can give others a lesson and a benefit. In this way, Job is gradually finding out about himself.

He says, 'If I speak, my pain is not lessened.' This means that he is realizing the fact that at one time though he could strengthen others and lessen their pains, right now he is not able to do anything to lessen his own pain.

Then, let us think about whether Job could really give life to others before.

Before, Job's words could strengthen and encourage others because he had knowledge and wealth and people looked up to him. That is why they listened to him. But in Job himself, there was no eternal life, so his words couldn't give them eternal life.

Job spoke out evil words as a result of being sick, and his friends condemned him as a vulgar person. Flesh just perishes and profits nothing (John 6:63). That is why God had to allow Job trials to give him true life. How can a person who cannot solve his own problem solve someone else's problems?

Job says, "And if I hold back, what has left me?" Fleshly people cannot endure it when they are faced with such difficulties. They have to explode with everything they have piled up in their minds in order to feel relief.

Job was not a spiritual man, so if he held back, he had pain, and he had to let out his evil. But that way, he made his friends angry and committed great sins with his lips.

Fleshly men like spreading bad things about other people. If they keep quiet, it's difficult to hold it back. If they heard any kind of slanderous talk about somebody, they cannot keep quiet but they have to spread it very quickly. Only then will they feel relief and be at ease.

Then, why is it that they are at ease after they spread the bad things, namely after they act out evil? Fleshly men hear the voice of Satan, and when they do act in evil by spreading slanderous remarks, they make Satan feel at ease. That is why their mind is also at ease.

If we become men of spirit and have more of a positive attitude, we can change the situations to be favorable for us. But fleshly men speak negative words again and again. This way their heart becomes more and more evil, and they put themselves in traps. They make their situations more difficult with their negative words and finally, they fall into the pit of destruction.

3. Job Says that God Shrivels Job Up and Lays Waste His Friends

"But now He has exhausted me; you have laid waste all

my company. You have shriveled me up, it has become a
witness; and my leanness rises up against me, it testifies
to my face" (16:7-8).

Job is saying that it is all God who has exhausted him and
laid waste all his company. If you are spiritually exhausted, you
have no strength in heart, so you cannot do anything.

'Being laid waste' means that they are destroyed and fallen,
but spiritually, it means that the heart is corrupt and they are not
able to fulfill the duty of men. Job says that God has struck him,
so he became exhausted and has fallen into a pit, suffering all the
time. That is why he says God exhausted him.

Furthermore, he says that his friends are laid waste because
they speak absurd words and act with absurd actions to attack
him. Job doesn't realize that his friends were agitated because of
him, and is protesting that God has laid his friends as waste.

In verse 8, Job is so exhausted that he is withering. If a flower
is plucked out, it has already left the source of life, so it will soon
wither.

In the same way, Job is saying that God struck his source
of life, which is his wealth, family, health, and children, so he
is withering, not being able to bear the pains. He is saying all
the cause of his withering away is God. He is blaming God for
everything.

Also, he says, "And my leanness rises up against me, it
testifies to my face." If something withers, it becomes lean.
'Being lean' spiritually means that one has fully collapsed and
fallen to pieces.

Job's wealth, family, and health were all gone, and even his
friends stood against him. And he is blaming God saying He has

weakened and dried him up like that, and the evidence is that he became lean.

4. Job Says that God has Torn Him

"His anger has torn me and hunted me down, He has gnashed at me with His teeth; my adversary glares at me. They have gaped at me with their mouth, they have slapped me on the cheek with contempt; they have massed themselves against me" (16:9-10).

Job is arguing that God became angry with him and has torn him and hunted him down. Saying 'God has torn him' refers to the situation where Job's boils hardened and ran. From the head to toe, boils kept on hardening, splitting and running, so in Job's mind, it was no different than God tearing him.

'Hunting down' means that he is attacked by the enemy to be in agony. Spiritual meaning is that God is pointing out Job's sins again and again. Job means that God is persecuting him.

Furthermore, Job says, God gnashes His teeth and glares at him with sharp eyes to cause him more agony. Job is saying God gave him great pain by tearing him and is giving him more pain glaring at him with sharp eyes.

Verse 10 says, "They have gaped at me with their mouth." It means something negative. It's because Job's friends' words were not comforting but rather hurting him.

Job says his friends have slapped him on the cheek with contempt. Even in this world, if somebody says something unimaginably evil to us, we may feel like we are being slapped. For example, if we hear words of great contempt, then we may feel like we are being spit on, with extreme sense of being mocked.

So far, Job's friends haven't really slapped him. But now, Job is thinking about his past when he had splendor. Before, his friends used to look up to him and love him, but now, they seem to be standing against him. Because Job is thinking of his past, he is saying his friends are slapping him and are ganging up to antagonize him.

Job is actually judging and condemning just like his friends are doing. But he is in a wretched situation right now, and he feels like God is glaring at him and hunting him down.

Suppose you went bankrupt in your business or lost your job all of a sudden. Then, you may feel like people around you are treating you coldly and looking at you with sharp eyes. Even though others are not actually doing so, you may be judging and condemning that others are not the same as before to put yourself in pain.

5. The Blessings in Passing Tests

"God hands me over to ruffians and tosses me into the hands of the wicked" (16:11).

Job is saying that his friends are the ruffians and the wicked. Job and his friends are telling each other that the other is wicked.

Today, many believers blame God for their problems saying, "God tested me. He gave me this difficulty in life. He gave me this disease." But if we blame God, we cannot hear the voice of the Holy Spirit who is in our heart and we cannot find the way to solve the problem.

God never handed Job over to ruffians or tossed him into the hands of the wicked. He never told Job to argue. Right now, God is just watching him.

What God allowed Satan to do is to take Job's possessions and inflict the boils. It's not true that God gave Job a hard time. Through that trial, Job's hidden evil was revealed and it could also be removed. Job came to meet God, so we can understand that the trial results in blessing.

Job had only heard about God from his fathers but he had never met Him. But if we meet the living God through trial, we will have not just faith as knowledge but the spiritual faith with which we can truly believe from the heart.

Had Job not suffered from this trial, he would have received material blessings like before, but he wouldn't have received the spiritual blessings of clearly knowing God. He would not have discovered his sins and would not have cast them off to finally become sanctified.

After Job went through the trials, he would receive blessings. Because God fore-knew it, He allowed it to happen. Only when our soul is prosperous, not only on this earth will we receive blessings but also in heavenly kingdom can we go into a greater position shining like the sun.

Once God allows the trial to take place, whether it ends quickly or not is wholly up to the person who is going through the trial. It depends on how good or evil his heart is. If you have much evil, you will reveal more of evilness during the trial, so the test will last longer.

No matter what kind of situation you are in, if you show your faith, rejoice, pray, give thanks, and please God with unchanging faith, God will quickly remove the camps of the enemy devil and give you blessings.

When his friends first advised him, had Job said, "You are right! I must have something wrong for I have this kind of problem. I will try to find out my fault as you advised me," would his friends have argued with him? They wouldn't have refuted him. It's Job who made his friends angry.

If he had tried to find himself and turn around, God would have given him grace to realize himself. God would have helped him and given him strength. Even though Job was struck by boils all over, God would have healed him in a moment and blessed him.

Job and his friends fell into each other's pits of wickedness. Therefore, we have to discern between what is right and wrong with good hearts, and repent of our sin and turn from it.

"I was at ease, but He shattered me, and He has grasped me by the neck and shaken me to pieces; He has also set me up as His target. His arrows surround me. Without mercy He splits my kidneys open; He pours out my gall on the ground" (16:12-13).

This is what Job is saying: Before he encountered the tests, he lived in peace and comfort, but God shattered him. Just as people hold the neck of a chicken when they kill it, God grasped him by the neck and shook him to pieces. When Job thought of what had happened to him, he thought God was a cruel God.

The meaning of Job's neck being shaken suggests that Job believed that God shattered the firm will and determination of Job. It means the pillar that is supporting Job's head, namely his honor, dignity, and all the high things that he enjoyed were destroyed. That is why Job cannot help but be weak.

Job also says God set him up as a target, that God had stood him up as an exercise and the mark to be shot at with a bow and arrows.

In verse 13, Job says God shoots him from all four sides. He splits his kidneys open and pours out his gall on the ground.

Job is giving a parable for each thing. Here, the arrow is not real arrow but the arrow of God's heart. God's heart becomes arrows and He is shooting him from all four sides. Job says God is shooting His arrows at him without mercy opening his sides.

If one's side is open, it means that he lost the control over his body. If one's back is broken, he cannot use the whole body. Because his neck is broken, his will is broken, and his side is open by arrow, he has lost the balance of his body.

Also, 'gall coming out to the ground' means that the pain in his heart is so great. Because he had never had experience of meeting God, he was crying with so much pain like his gall coming out to the ground.

Even if our business went bankrupt, our children go astray, and we are inflicted by diseases, we have to keep in mind that God is always keeping us with His blazing eyes and He is our Deliverer. Because He always guides us to work for the good of everything, we can only give thanks to Him in all things.

6. Let Us Each Remove Our Horn

"He breaks through me with breach after breach; He runs at me like a warrior. I have sewed sackcloth over my skin and thrust my horn in the dust" (16:14-15).

Job is saying that God breaks through whatever defenses he has and runs at him like a warrior. Why would the almighty God break through and run at Job who is merely a creature?

Today, many of those who are suffering from difficulties and trials because of their shortcomings say that God is striking them. The cause is with them that they are suffering from difficulties, but they think of God as being fearful and say that God has stricken them.

Job is also revealing his evil while he is receiving the trial caused by his evil. To the extent that we commit acts of untruth, we receive accusations of Satan and suffer from tests and hardships.

Job is facing trials because there was a reason for it, but he is blaming God for everything, and feeling that He is a bad God and fearful God.

Verse 15 says, "I have sewed sackcloth over my skin." It means that his whole body is covered with wounds. Sackcloth is not soft but rough.

'Sewed' means that his skin keeps on running and drying. Namely, 'sewing sackcloth' means Job's skin keeps on running and drying again and again.

When Job was rich, he had the characters of a righteous man, so he must have had soft skin. But because of the boils, his skin is damaged greatly, and that is why he is likening the situation to the sackcloth, complaining against God.

He also says, "And thrust my horn in the dust." What does a horn mean?

A horn symbolizes one's pride. We form our mind as we accumulate more knowledge and education. As our mind is formed, our pride and opinion is also formed. This mind itself becomes our strength and power.

But when we accept Jesus Christ and receive the Holy Spirit, our names are written in the Book of Life in heaven from that moment, and we are recognized as children of God. Those who become children of God should remove this horn. We should get rid of the horn of pride and our own opinion, so that we will gain the power of the truth and we will only have the horn of the truth.

Accepting Jesus Christ and experiencing the Holy Spirit does not mean we have become perfect. Just as a baby is born and grows up to become a youth and adult, as we take in the word of God and practice it, we come out as men of spirit and sanctified children of God. In this way, if we have perfect measure of faith, we will gain the qualification for entering into the city of New Jerusalem which houses God's throne.

Galatians 5:16-17 also urges us to get rid of the desires of the flesh and follow the desires of the Holy Spirit.

"But I say, walk by the Spirit, and you will not carry out the desire of the flesh. For the flesh sets its desire against the Spirit, and the Spirit against the flesh; for these are in opposition to one another, so that you may not do the things that you please."

It says that the desires of the flesh are against the Spirit. Pride and insisting one's own way in an argument belong to the desires of the flesh. After we receive the Holy Spirit, these two desires fight against each other. One side wants to follow the law of the Holy Spirit, but the other wants to follow untruths going against the will of God. Thus, they are fighting against each other.

That is why Romans 7:22-24 also says, "For I joyfully concur with the law of God in the inner man, but I see a different law in the members of my body, waging war against the law of my mind and making me a prisoner of the law of sin which is in my members. Wretched man that I am! Who will set me free from the body of this death?"

When the inner being that tries to follow the desires of the Spirit and the outer being that tries to follow the law of sin fight against each other, we may lament saying, "Wretched man that I am!" Here, if we pray fervently, cast off evil, and follow what is good, the heart to follow the desire of the Spirit increases and we can lead a victorious life. From that time on we can grow up to have firm faith like a rock which cannot be shaken.

The apostle Paul said, "I affirm, brethren, by the boasting in you which I have in Christ Jesus our Lord, I die daily" (1 Corinthians 15:31). Because the apostle Paul died everyday, he could preach the gospel with manifestations of limitless power of God.

But some people think it somewhat unfair to cast off their pride. Job is lamenting that his horn has been dirtied in the dust.

Jesus and the fathers of faith did not insist on their pride, arrogance, selfishness, or their own opinions. When Moses was a prince, how strong his horn was! But after he was refined in the wilderness, his horn was gone.

It was the same with Abraham, Jacob, Elijah, Elisha, Daniel, and Jesus' disciples and the apostle Paul. After receiving the Holy Spirit and finishing all the process of refinement, they too all removed their horns, so they could be used greatly by God.

Those who live in their own opinions cannot obey the word of God. King Saul had strong opinions of his own. He did not obey the word of God and finally was forsaken by God. When Jonah did not cast off his horn of pride, he disobeyed and encountered a great storm at sea.

Job was fighting against his friends with his horn. That is why he is talking about his pride and his ego being sullied, which are his 'horn.' It tells us how strong his pride is.

Because he thinks that his horn is being trampled by God and his friends, that pain was greater than losing all his possessions and children and the pain of boils. In order for us to become perfect children of God, we have to break our horns.

7. Job Insists He is Right

"My face is flushed from weeping, and deep darkness is on my eyelids, although there is no violence in my hands, and my prayer is pure. O earth, do not cover my blood, and let there be no resting place for my cry" (16:16-18).

Job wept because he lost all his family members and because of the pain of his boils. He wept because he was forsaken by his wife and his friends. Yet even more painful was that his horn was sullied and he cried because of his sorrow. When a person cries so much, his face and his eyes turn red.

Because Job also cried a lot, his face turned red, and his eyes were also red. Because he didn't have any strength in his eyes, he seemed to be a shadow of death.

But the kind of tears that we have to shed are the tears of mourning for poor souls, tears of repentance that we shed after we commit sins, the tears to change us anew, and the tears of thanks and joy for God's grace.

Because Job didn't have life in him and he was a man of flesh, he could not help but cry. But those children of God who have life and hope will rejoice, give thanks, and pray and win the victory in any kind of trial or test. There is a major difference between those who have life and those who don't.

Job says, "There is no violence in my hands, and my prayer is pure." It is true that there was no violence in Job's hands. What is in one's heart comes out in action. Job was not so evil to show evil deeds on the outside, but he could not help but speak out evil words with his mouth. It was because he was not changed by the truth completely.

Job says his prayer is pure, so we can understand from this that he does not realize the fact that what he has been saying is wrong, but he is still insisting he is right.

Job says, "O earth, do not cover my blood, And let there be no resting place for my cry." This means that because he is righteous and pure, he is telling the earth not to cover his uprightness. When they are wrongfully accused or victimized, some people say 'Heaven and earth know I am innocent!" Job is making such a comparative statement that is explaining his situation.

But God's children don't have to use such expressions like 'Heaven knows I am right.' It's because God knows everything. If we discern with the word of God, we can also discern whether we are right or wrong.

"Even now, behold, my witness is in heaven, and my advocate is on high. My friends are my scoffers; my eye weeps to God. O that a man might plead with God as a man with his neighbor! For when a few years are past, I shall go the way of no return" (16:19-22).

A 'witness' is a person who gives a testimony, and advocate is somebody who pleads for you. Job is saying that the person who will testify to his innocence is in heaven.

He means there is nobody on this earth who can save him or solve his problems, and the only person who can do it, it is God.

Job thought his friends were mocking him, but in his friends' view, Job was not right. God's word tells us to rejoice, pray, give thanks, and ask God with faith.

But before God, Job instead was shedding tears of mourning, complaints, and resentment with judging and condemnation. So, Satan could work even more to make his disease more serious and make his pain greater.

Because Job has been insisting that he is right, he says he wants to plead with God. Here, 'to plead' is in the context of making something clear by specifically discerning between things. 'A man' that Job mentions here is somebody who has extraordinary uprightness and righteousness, discerning between righteousness and goodness, and keeping the duty of man.

Job says he wants to plead with all those who know him, namely, a man, his neighbors, and all those who heard the news and knew him. It's because he misunderstands they would think that he is a sinner who is punished by God.

Job thinks his life will end after a short while, or after a couple of years at most, but he couldn't figure out when his pains would end. That is why he concludes that he is going the way of no return.

Chapter *17*

Job Feels More Afflicted As Time Passes

1. Job Asks God for a Pledge

2. Job Curses His Friends

3. Job Mocks His Friends with Pedantic Words

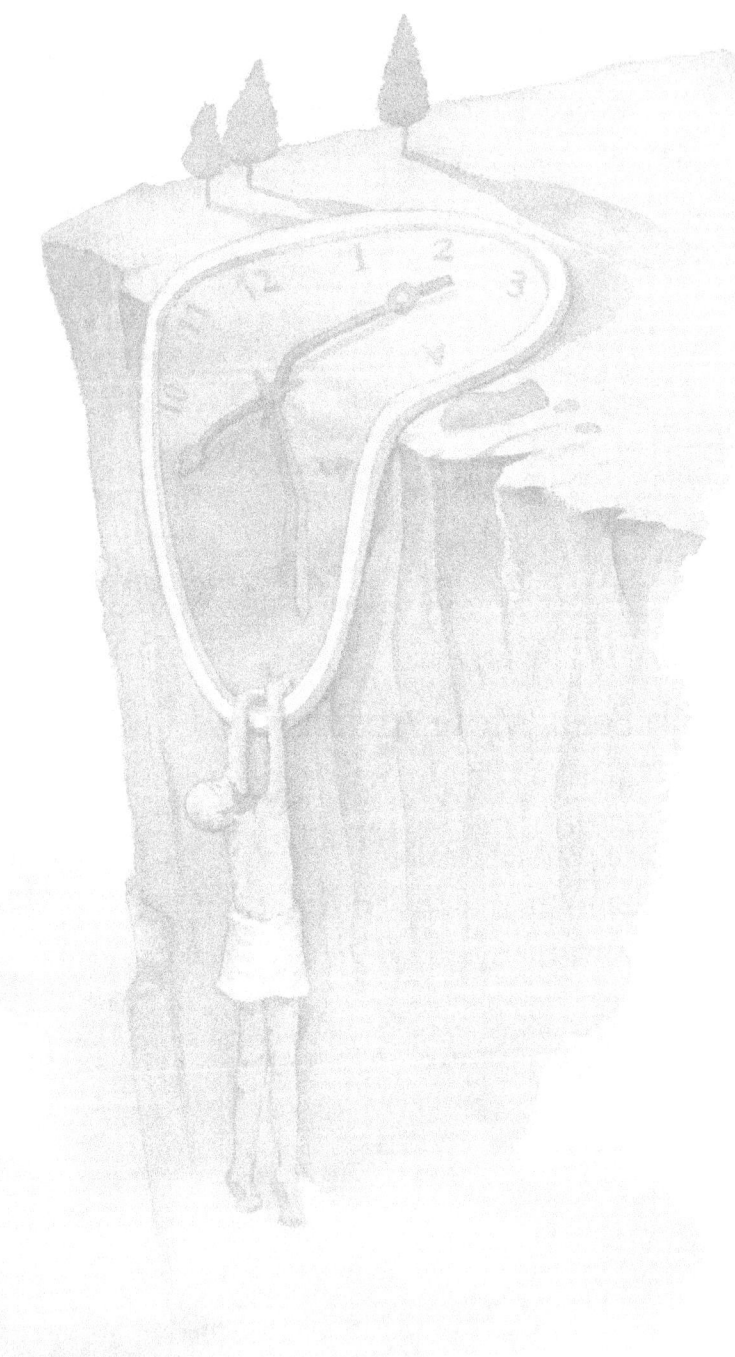

"My days are past, my plans are torn apart, Even the wishes of my heart."
(Job 17:11)

1. Job Asks God for a Pledge

"My spirit is broken, my days are extinguished, the grave is ready for me. Surely mockers are with me, and my eye gazes on their provocation. Lay down, now, a pledge for me with Yourself; who is there that will be my guarantor?" (17:1-3)

Job has been struggling with despair and pain, and he is very tired. He says that his spirit is broken, and the grave is ready for him. However it doesn't mean that he is actually prepared and ready for the grave in real life. He is just saying his life is all but ended in his opinion. He is saying if one keeps on failing in life and falls down to the bottom-most part of existence, he cannot recover and he can only wait for death.

In verse 2 Job is saying his friends are not comforting him but rather mocking him. Job actually made his friends angry but he didn't acknowledge that it was his fault. When he perceived his friends getting angry, he suffered the pain.

Suppose you borrowed some money, and because of your situation, you couldn't keep your promise to pay it back. The lender of the money got angry with you; he cursed at you and provoked you. Still, you should ask for his forgiveness. No matter what that person is doing and saying, if you say, "That's it, you have said and done enough!" or "Why are you so upset?"

it means that you have evil in your heart.

Even if somebody does something to us that is not proper, before antagonizing them, we should let them know the truth, so that they can keep their heart in truth.

A pledge is a guarantee for something, which means somebody will take the full responsibility for something. Job is asking God to make a pledge to him and be his guarantor. This means that he wants God to solve his problem as a guarantor. He is asking God to become his Master by saving him from the danger. We can see Job's desperate pleading and pains.

Unbelievers obviously try to solve their problems by means of men, so they try to find a guarantor. Just as a person who has a great amount of debt looks for a guarantor to solve the problems, Job is also asking God with this kind of desperate heart.

But even if somebody finds a guarantor, if the fundamental problem is not resolved, he will be held accountable by the guarantor. Therefore, one should solve his own problem by himself. If you have gone in the wrong direction, you should come back from it. You should correct what you have done wrong.

But Job thinks he is right, and is looking for a guarantor. He is crying loudly with the things that don't really make sense.

But when they face a problem, those who have faith don't have to seek a man as a guarantor and be held accountable to him. God is almighty, so we should first repent of our wrongdoings and follow the will of God, trying to find out the reason why we were put into difficult situations.

Job says in verse 3, "Who is there that will be my guarantor?" When he searches the front, the back, both sides, and the ground, there is nobody but God who can put him into calamity like a big storm. That is why he is saying this.

2. Job Curses His Friends

"For You have kept their heart from understanding, therefore You will not exalt them. He who informs against friends for a share of the spoil, the eyes of his children also will languish. But He has made me a byword of the people, and I am one at whom men spit: (17:4-6).

Job is saying that he taught his friends with words of wisdom, but they didn't really learn anything, but rather showed their evil, and that it was all God's work. Therefore, God will not acknowledge them, and he will not acknowledge his friends either.

If Job had taught his friends with the wisdom of God, he wouldn't have provoked his friends. Because he used man's wisdom, finally there were the works of Satan, and they were dealing with these matters with heated emotions.

Job is asking God not to raise his friends who rebuked and scolded him. He is asking God to acknowledge the fact that the words of his friends are not right.

Because Job had received severe contempt and bore such pain, he is cursing his friends' children to go blind.

Even some believers in Jesus Christ, when they are bothered by someone, curse at him. It's because they don't have faith or understand true love.

Rather than thinking about the reason why he cannot receive anything but mockery from his friends, Job condemns his friends and hurls words of curses toward them. Through this, we can understand why Job had to face trials.

Jesus said, "But I say to you who hear, love your enemies, do good to those who hate you, bless those who curse you, pray for those who mistreat you" (Luke 6:27-28).

God's word tells us to love even our enemies, and we should never hate our brothers in faith, who are not even our enemies. It's not easy to bless those who curse at us, but if we have spiritual love, we can do it. If we change into spirit, we will have compassion on even those who curse at us. So we can pray for them and leave everything with God.

Job was commended for being upright and blameless, but he still retaliated when somebody offended and attacked him. God let things happen this way to change Job's goodness formed according to the law into goodness of the heart by the Spirit.

Because God knew the uprightness and integrity of Job, He began the refining process to change Job into a man of spirit. Then, we could see Job's evils pouring out. When his friends hit him with words, he hit them back with twice as many. That's why God had to let his evil heart be revealed. When Job found his evil and cast it away, he could become a true son of God the Father who was recognized, loved, and blessed by God.

In the Olympic Games, if everybody could win the gold medal without hard training, nobody would go through such a difficult training period. The coaches don't have to train the players, and the players wouldn't want to receive the training. But only after going through the process of intense training, can the players win the medals. That is why they are willing to go through such hard trainings that feel like torment and torture.

Suppose in your church or in your workplace, a boss commended a certain person. Then, you became jealous or envious of the person who was receiving the praise.

Maybe you thought to yourself, "That person is not doing anything better than me, and why is he receiving all the praise?"

If you have this kind of heart in you, you should understand how evil a heart you have. In this case, you are not even scolded by your boss, but you are suffering because of your own evil.

Now, what does it mean by cursing the friends' children by saying, "The eyes of his children also will languish"?

Eyes spiritually symbolize the future. If you cannot see, your way is blocked and it is same as being confined. It is one of the most severe of curses. Children will continue the family line, and cursing them to go blind is such a terrible curse.

In verse 6, Job says God has made him a byword of the people, and he is one at whom men spit. Because he thinks there is no reason for him to suffer that way, he is blaming God for everything. The news about Job was widespread.

'Spitting on him' does not mean that people actually did spit on him. It is just a strong expression that people were talking ill about him since he began to show his evil.

"My eye has also grown dim because of grief, and all my members are as a shadow. The upright will be appalled at this, and the innocent will stir up himself against the godless. Nevertheless the righteous will hold to his way, and he who has clean hands will grow stronger and stronger" (17:7-9).

Job was a good writer and a man with much knowledge. He had much wisdom, too, so in his parables, there were many meanings. The spiritual meaning of 'eye' here is the foreseeable future. It's because what we see with eyes will be stored in memory and we can remember and recall it from the memory.

Then, what is the grief of Job? Job had many griefs. He lost all his possessions, and he was receiving contempt and pains. He fell to the bottom-most part of the life, and only death was waiting for him. All this was his grief.

His eye has grown dim because of grief, and it means that his future is not clear. He also says that all his members are as shadows. A shadow has the shape, but it's useless. He is referring to his life that is without meaning or purpose. He is likening the meaninglessness of his body to that of a shadow.

His body was decaying and full of worms and it had foul odor. He could not beautify it or decorate it. He couldn't do anything to his body, and he could not help but compare it with a shadow.

It's the same with our faith. We heard the word of God, and we know it. Then, we have to obey His commands that tell us to do something, not to do something, to keep something, and to cast off something. But many of us just store them as knowledge and do not practice them. When we hear and know the word of God but do not practice it, we hear the lamenting of the Holy Spirit, and our heart feels afflicted. That's why so many people seek the almighty God, but are not able to receive the answer and start wandering.

If we just look around us, many believers are in such a meaningless life. As a result, they make Jesus they believe but a shadow.

The children of God have to get into the deeper level of spirit by practicing the word of God but many of them fail to do it. They know the word, but do not practice it, and this becomes their grief.

They seem to believe the word of God, but their faith is like a shadow that is without purpose or substance. They wander around here and there without understanding what God's will really is. They sway to and fro, topple and fall down, and they may get up again. If they were only to meet God, all their problems could be solved. But because they have never seen any real works of God through the faith, they are still wandering around spiritually.

Since Job had never met God, he was grief-stricken. How pitiful this is! But God knew that Job could become sanctified and become a great vessel. And so God allowed this great trial to come upon him.

In verse 8, because his friends are accusing him of dishonesty, he is using the word 'upright' as a third-party reference to include himself among those who are upright. He is saying because he is going through all these things, the upright will be appalled at this, and the innocent will stir up himself against the godless.

When a sinless man sees another person doing such an evil thing, that sinless man may have righteous indignation. Here, Job's comparison itself is right, but he is not in a position to say it. We can use this kind of parable only when we are really full of the truth and without any falsehood. While we are not really upright, if we compare ourselves with another group of people to justify ourselves, it may cause others to fall, and it is also sin.

Actually, we often commit this kind of sin in our daily lives. So, many times, Satan accuses this to cause many disputes and conflicts.

Verse 9 says, "The righteous will hold to his way." 'Holding on to his way' means that he is faithful in what he is doing.

By saying "the righteous will hold to his way," Job is saying that he is doing what he is supposed to do without any wavering, no matter what kind of opposition he faces around him.

He means that he is right, and it is his friends who are provoking him to make him evil. So, he cannot help but argue with them, and he has to continue doing it.

Then what does it mean that "And he who has clean hands will grow stronger and stronger"?

Before, Job said "You have shriveled me up" (Job 16:8), "My spirit is broken" (Job 17:1). But here, he says he will grow stronger and stronger. So he is contradicting himself. However, from Job's point of view it is true and makes complete sense.

Job has great pride and is very stubborn, so he will plead for himself until his strength no longer exists, and he believes that he can say this because he is right. Those who have great pride will not submit even until the end.

Job's body is withering and dying, but what he says is right, so he will protest until the end with all his strength. His body is losing strength, but because he is right, he is getting stronger and stronger.

In our faith, this kind of stubbornness is useless. But rather it will only cause others to hate us. It will cause only conflicts and thus is useless. When others don't understand us, we need to check ourselves.

If we do not have peace with each other, both sides have a problem. Therefore, we should not insist that we are right. We should learn to accept one another and realize ourselves.

3. Job Mocks His Friends with Pedantic Words

"But come again all of you now, for I do not find a wise man among you. My days are past, my plans are torn apart, even the wishes of my heart. They make night into day, saying, 'The light is near,' in the presence of darkness" (17:10-12).

'Come again all of you now,' does not mean that they should go away and then come back. Job is actually telling them to check what they have been saying so far. Job also concludes that there is no wise man among his friends. He is saying no one among his friends can teach him anything, and that is why he cannot find the answer to the problem.

Job wants to say that, because he cannot gain anything from his friends, his plans and even the wishes of his heart are torn apart. He cannot solve the problem by himself, God has forsaken him, and even his friends do not have the wisdom to solve his problem. Thus, he cannot help but go the way of death.

He is pouring out his ill emotions and sufferings of heart. But this only caused Satan to work more on him. If we make our own traps with our words, keep on insisting that we are right looking down upon others, and make God a bad God, how can God help us?

The listeners dislike what we say and consider it painful, and thus, they cannot be with us but be more and more apart. It is something useless. Because Job thought his friends despised him, he was also mocking them with words.

Verse 12 says, "They make night into day." Here, night refers to darkness. Because they make night into day, darkness is their work. Job is saying this referring to his friends' heart.

Job is mocking them with these parables to mean, "What you are doing is so bad and conflicting within itself. You are pouring it on me."

"They make night into day, saying, 'The light is near,' in the presence of darkness" means that they are speaking complete nonsense just as the sun cannot rise from the west. Job is using pedantic expressions.

Although they themselves could not use these words of pedantry, Job's friends knew that Job was mocking them. So, how angry they must have been!

Today, even among believers, some people condemn others with the word of God or speak sarcastic words to them if they don't like something about others. There are even some pastors who misuse the word of God and misquote the word of God to threaten the church members. But the truth gives us peace, joy, freedom, and life; not fear or nervousness.

> *"If I look for Sheol as my home, I make my bed in the darkness; if I call to the pit, 'You are my father'; to the worm, 'my mother and my sister'; where now is my hope? And who regards my hope? Will it go down with me to Sheol? Shall we together go down into the dust?"*
> *(17:13-16)*

Job says that his hope is going down to Sheol for he is disappointed within meaninglessness. But the hope of those who believe in Jesus Christ is in heaven.

Job had no life. Everything that was his has been destroyed. That is why he says he cannot help but go down to the world of darkness, into Sheol. He also says his bed will be made in darkness.

Job also says, "If I call to the pit, 'You are my father,'" because a pit can be a shelter for his body. To those who have no hope of heavenly kingdom, when they die, the pit, the tomb will cover their bodies. Why then 'father'? The role of the father is to protect his children. If he goes down to the pit, the pit will be his father to cover him and protect him.

Then, what does it mean by "To the worm, 'my mother and my sister'"?

The mother or big brothers and sisters hug or kiss each other, giving physical contact when raising a little baby. Job is expressing his skin is full of worms and decaying. Because worms are in contact with his skin, he is saying they are his mother and sister. He is actually expressing his pain and sorrow.

He is exclaiming where his hope is. But for us, who have truth and life, our hope is not in Sheol but in heavenly kingdom, so how thankful it is!

When a man dies and is buried in the tomb, he is confined in the dust. That is why Job is saying when he rests in the dust the hope is also going with him. But the believers in God have their hope in heavenly kingdom, so they receive blessings on this earth as well.

As their souls are prosperous, all things go well with them, and they are healthy. Because they have received the eternal life, they are free from the fear of death, and they can live in joy and thanks.

To the extent that they cast off evil from heart and become sanctified, they have true peace in heart, and they are so thankful that they can get to heavenly kingdom. Other than these, there are so many blessings that believers will receive on this earth, not to mention the honor and blessings they will receive in heavenly kingdom in the future.

Chapter 18

Paying Back Evil with Goodness
- Bidad's Epitome of Evilness

"A snare seizes him by the heel, And a trap snaps shut on him.
A noose for him is hidden in the ground, And a trap for him on the path."
(Job 18:9-10)

1. Let's Not Tear Ourselves

"Then Bildad the Shuhite responded, 'How long will you hunt for words? How understanding and then we can talk. Why are we regarded as beasts, as stupid in your eyes? O you who tear yourself in your anger for your sake is the earth to be abandoned, or is the rock to be moved from its place?'" (18:1-4)

If you see your friends or relatives quarreling with each other, you probably would eventually say, "How long will you quarrel? Please stop!" When they are arguing, most people try to find words until the end to win the argument. If they are driven into a corner, they even get angry and huff.

Let us check whether or not we have kept up this kind of useless argument in an attempt to win it.

Sometimes, a third-person intervenes to stop the argument, but he himself gets involved. Bildad the Shuhite is saying, "How long will you hunt for words?" but he himself is also hunting for words.

How ridiculous this is in the sight of God! Job and his friends who are quarreling with each other are not right, but this friend who is telling them to keep quiet is not right either.

Bildad is asking Job, "Why do you regard us as beasts?" Because Job has been saying that his friends are not like men, not perfect, and they are no match for him, Bildad is saying Job regards them as beasts and being stupid.

Beasts act in any way they want without any reason or discernment. Bildad is asking Job whether Job is regarding them stupid, for Job has been saying they are 'laid waste.'

Job insulted them and disgraced them with his anger. His friends are also arguing back at him. So, they are even. Job is tearing himself in a hopeless and extremely sorrowful situation because his friends have kept on telling him that he is wrong.

Let us find out how Job is tearing himself.

Job 16:9-11 says, *"His anger has torn me and hunted me down, He has gnashed at me with His teeth; My adversary glares at me. They have gaped at me with their mouth, They have slapped me on the cheek with contempt; They have massed themselves against me. God hands me over to ruffians And tosses me into the hands of the wicked."*

He complained against God and regarded his friends as wicked saying that God has 'handed over to his friends who are the wicked and are like ruffians.' As a result Job is rending and tearing at himself with his words.

Until the time that they come into the truth and change, many believers rend and tear at themselves. They think they are victimized, and if they don't like something, they get angry and cause a commotion for themselves. In doing this they are tearing themselves by not being able to control their minds.

If we have heated emotions in our heart, we cannot help but tear at ourselves. Rending and tearing others is the same as tearing ourselves. We should look back on ourselves to see whether or not we are that kind of a person.

For example, there are some people, when they get drunk, who shout and kick at doors demanding that somebody open it quickly. When they quarrel as between husband and wife, they throw and break things in their households.

Some believers do not attend Sunday service because they have a problem with a brother in faith. To violate the Lord's Day is to commit sin before God, so if they don't attend the service, it is only damaging to them, not to others. If they stop praying just because they have gotten angry or because they have fallen into tests and trials, then it means they are also tearing themselves.

Also, only because the husband has an affair with somebody else, if the wife also goes out to have an affair as well and breaks up the family, what is the benefit in it? In the end all these actions are tearing themselves.

Verse 4 says "For your sake is the earth to be abandoned, Or the rock to be moved from its place?" It is unchanging fact that the earth and rocks stay in their places. Bildad is making fun of Job saying that no matter how angry he gets, the earth and rocks will not be moved.

Suppose a husband is angry with his wife and threw a clock down near her. If the wife says, "No matter how mad you get and break the clock, will the earth or the rocks move?" and then laugh at him, his anger would boil over.

He might have stopped at throwing the clock, but as he becomes even angrier, he may throw a TV or other furniture. The husband's action is evil, but the evil of his wife is more. If the wife makes her own husband more evil, what is the benefit of it?

But it's not only the wife who made her husband more evil, but also the husband has made his wife more evil. So, they are even, tearing one another.

Tearing each other actually makes God angry, and He has to turn His face away from these things. As a result, Satan begins to work. Families are broken up, children go astray, and they will get sick. Great trials and tests will follow. Since they are tearing each other, God turns His face away, and Satan gives them hard times as much as he wants.

In verse 4, the earth is something on which we stand, and rocks that are the size of boulders cannot be moved for they are very solid and heavy. We can feel that there is a difference between these two things.

"Will the earth be surprised by your anger? No matter how angry you are, what can you do about the hardness of rock?"

We can see that Bildad is mocking Job with his parables. Like these people in the passage, there are some people who make those who are angry angrier. They cause more heated feelings.

The truth tells us that we ought not to mock or laugh at somebody even if he did something wrong and he is the one who is getting angry. Only when we can let him understand his evil with our goodness can we stop that evil. If we react with evil toward evil, it will bring about only more evil. Therefore, to be victorious, we have to overcome evil with goodness.

In the history of Chosun Dynasty of ancient Korea, there was a concubine called Jang Hee Bin who tore herself so much. Her elder brother also tore himself so much in the strife between parties. Words and deeds that are against the truth will most certainly bring about incredibly absurd results.

That concubine tore herself with extreme jealousy. The king sentenced her to death thinking that he was carrying out justice. But because of what the king did, the tragedy continued through the son of the concubine.

If the king and his ministers knew the truth and acted according to the truth, he could have implemented another method of punishment, like confining her, because her son was going to be the king, so the history of blood would have stopped. Those who follow the truth will finally be victorious.

As we get to the later chapters of the Book of Job, the evil deep inside men's hearts is revealed, so I believe we can have realizations and understandings, gain life through it, and find out our weaknesses as well.

2. Let Us Cast off Jealousy

"Indeed, the light of the wicked goes out, And the flame of his fire gives no light. The light in his tent is darkened, And his lamp goes out above him. His vigorous stride is shortened, And his own scheme brings him down. For he is thrown into the net by his own feet, and he steps on the webbing. A snare seizes him by the heel, And a trap snaps shut on him" (18:5-9).

It is obvious that if the light goes out, there is no brightness. "The light of the wicked goes out" means that Job's hope, namely a wicked man's hope is diminishing. By saying the flame of his fire gives no light, Bildad is cursing Job by saying all the works that Job has done will collapse, because in the friends' view, they were all works of a wicked man.

Job considered himself upright and blameless because his actions were righteous. From this passage, we can find that Job's friends have been jealous of Job for his righteous acts. That is why they are mocking him as a wicked man.

In verse 5 Bildad conclusively says that the flame of his fire gives no light, and in verse 6 it says the light in his tent is darkened and his lamp goes out above him. This is an elaboration to what he said in verse 5. How evil this is, then!

Men of truth who believe in God should encourage a person like Job and give him more hope to lead him in the way of the righteousness. This is the proper duty of man.

Jesus did not break a bruised reed or snuff out a smoldering wick (Matthew 12:20). We should have this heart of Jesus. If we want to trample on a wicked man and wish him to fall, it means that our heart is also evil. Therefore, if a wicked man goes to the way of destruction, since we also have evil heart, we will also go the way of destruction.

Verse 7 says, "His vigorous stride is shortened, and his own scheme brings him down."

We understand that because Job thought he was perfect in all things he had a vigorous stride. It was a stride that was dignified.

That is why Job was a subject of his friends' envy and jealousy. But at ordinary times, this was hidden in their heart, and in the event where Job is falling down, their jealousy is clearly revealed.

This is not only about Bildad but most people. The hearts of most of men of flesh are like this.

Bildad says what Job has done before is only his own scheme, and he is falling into his own scheme. Bildad is disgracing and downgrading the works that Job has accomplished. Bildad's evil heart that used to be hidden is now revealed and spoken with words.

If we slightly feel jealous of those who are well off, if we want things not to go well with them, and if we laugh at them and express our evil when things actually go wrong with them, it means that we are very foolish. We should not rejoice when those who acted evil towards us have things go wrong, but we should pray for them with mourning.

Verse 8 says, "For he is thrown into the net by his own feet, and he steps on the webbing." What does it mean?

If there is a trap, obviously it is best to go around it. Bildad is saying that Job steps on the webbing, referring to falling into a trap.

"Job! You continuously complain and displease God in whom you believe, so it is like throwing yourself into the net and stepping on the webbing by yourself!"

Bildad didn't understand the spiritual meaning when he said this. Then, now let's look into the spiritual meaning of this verse.

Because Job has been complaining against God and spoken words that only pleased the enemy devil and Satan, he fell into a deadlock more and more. It's like throwing himself into the net of a trap and stepping on the webbing.

So, being a friend, shouldn't Bildad have helped Job so that he would not step on the webbing of the trap by himself? If his friends make him go into the net and step on the webbing even more, it means they are committing a great sin.

Job's friends, using the word of God, the word of truth, are making Job increasingly express more evil. To misuse the word of God is to violate the third commandment of the Ten Commandments, which tells us not to take the name of God in vain.

We should not be like Job who is going into the net by himself. Complaining and having evil mind is to go into the net and to step on the webbing by ourselves.

Especially, in the church, we should not be ones who cause

our brothers to become caught up in the web even more. We should help the brother and pray for him so that he will not step on the webbing.

Then, what does it mean that "A snare seizes him by the heel, and a trap snaps shut on him"? A snare is like a trap used for capturing small animals.

If an animal is seized by a snare, it will probably lose its life. In the same way, one's heel being seized by a snare means that he will collapse to the ground and be unable to get up again. It is such a fierce curse.

"Job! Just as you are falling into the net and are executed by yourself, your heel will be seized by a snare and finally, you will collapse and lose your life!"

3. If We Curse and Desire Others to Fall Down

"A noose for him is hidden in the ground, and a trap for him on the path. All around terrors frighten him, and harry him at every step" (18:10-11).

You hide a noose because your purpose is to catch something. Namely, you dig a pit in an attempt to capture something and then cover it slightly with some straw and thin layer of dirt so it can not be seen. When animals or men walk on it, they will fall into the pit.

'Noose' here symbolizes the increased suffering for Job that still lies ahead. "The noose is now hidden in the ground" means that the suffering that lies ahead of Job is now hidden and cannot be seen.

'And a trap for him on the path' means there is a trap in Job's path, so he will suffer and be destroyed. Saying 'a noose for him is hidden and a trap for him on the path' is no different from making any other threatening remark.

Bildad doesn't think that he is threatening Job now, but his hatred is coming out in this kind of a situation.

If you ever hated somebody, didn't you want that person to make a mess of things and encounter hardship? If your business was not good or you were wrongfully accused because of somebody, didn't you want the situation for that person not to go well?

God gave us His one and only Son Jesus Christ as an atoning sacrifice to solve the problem of our sin. But if we do not solve this problem of sin but still have evil hearts, what will God do?

God has to refine us to make us perfect children and to cleanse us with the blood of the Lord. Through the trials, we can pray, realize ourselves, turn back, and repent. If we have any of this kind of mind like that of Job or his friends, we should cast it off as soon as possible.

Verse 11 says, "All around terrors frighten him, and harry him at every step." Bildad is continuing to curse Job with his heated emotions.

Bildad is cursing Job that not only terrors will frighten him but also they will continue. How evil a heart this is!

4. When Original Evil Is Revealed from the Heart

"His strength is famished, and calamity is ready at his side. His skin is devoured by disease, The firstborn of

'Strength' here refers to the honor, wealth, fame, and wisdom that Job used to have. 'Famished' here does not mean a famine with no rain.

It means that Job's children were gone and everything he accumulated was gone; his pride, arrogance, and his horn were gone.

"Job, look at you. You are famished, and you are losing all your strength. Only disasters await you!"

Job is suffering from pains, and Bildad is making him feel more pain.

The 'skin' in verse 13 symbolizes everything that was formed by Job's energy. Namely, it refers to his body, children of his body, his circumstances, and all the work and achievements he has done.

'The firstborn of death' is not just death, but extremely painful death. "The firstborn of death devours his limbs" means complete death, leaving no seed of life behind. It's not just ordinary death but such a wretched death by killing each part of the body and each joint of the bones.

We can see the extremity of evil here. If you thought, "How evil Job's friends are! How can they pour out such great evil?" then, you should look back whether or not you are one of that kind of person, too.

We can see this kind of evil even today. When they have an argument and get angry at each other, they curse the other one saying, "Drop dead!" Sometimes they pour out so many curses and foul language. Even though it's not physical murder, people murder each other with their words.

Job's friends had knowledge, education, and good

personalities, too, but as the argument continued, the evil deep inside their hearts was revealed.

"He is torn from the security of his tent, and they march him before the king of terrors. There dwells in his tent nothing of his; brimstone is scattered on his habitation" *(18:14-15).*

"He is torn from the security of his tent" means that all of a person's possessions are gone and he has no place to stay. If one goes bankrupt, he has to sell his house or it will be taken away.

Then, it says, "And they march him before the king of terrors." Here, the king of terrors does not refer to some kind of demons or Lucifer. Bildad used the word king to express the accumulation of terror, which is getting bigger and bigger.

The king of terrors refers to the extremity of fear, and one's heart is taken away by fear. Bildad is making fun of Job knowing that Job is in this kind of terror.

Then, let us find out what happens because of fear.

First, people give excuses like Job.

They are afraid that they may be looked down upon by others or their inabilities will be discovered. They think that they are not properly recognized by others, so they try to explain many things about themselves and to give excuses. It's because they have fear, and finally, they may even oppose or fight with others.

Secondly, people bind themselves.

When they are not really diligent and faithful but are incapable and are not doing their duties, they will have fear. In this situation, if they do not turn, little by little they will be captured by the king of terror.

We have fear because we are hiding something that is not

right and have it in us. If we are living in the truth and we are honest, there is no reason for us to be afraid of anything. Those who have no fear will even enjoy receiving rebukes, and because they want to gain more understanding, they don't give excuses.

Verse 15 says, "There dwells in his tent nothing of his." It means that because Job's house is gone, other people will come to dwell in his place. How great a curse this is in saying that even Job's original root will not remain! It also says, "Brimstone is scattered on his habitation."

"His roots are dried below, and his branch is cut off above. Memory of him perishes from the earth, and he has no name abroad. He is driven from light into darkness, and chased from the inhabited world" (18:16-18).

After cursing Job, Bildad is finishing up with a parable of a tree. If the root of the tree is dried, it cannot help but die. But to make it worse, if the branch is also cut off, what will happen to that tree? It means complete extinction.

When we are at peace, we cannot find the evil in us. But through the tests and trials, we can find the filthiness and dirtiness of evil.

If we leave muddy water undisturbed for many days, the mud will sink to the bottom. Just seeing the surface of it, we may think that it is clean. But if it is shaken, it immediately becomes muddy water again. Therefore, to make it really clean, we have to filter out the mud in the water. God is doing the same for Job.

When Bildad is saying Job's tree will dry and his branches will be cut off, he means that every trace of Job's existence will go away. Whatever is remaining will also be gone, so there won't be so much as a trace of him left.

Verse 18 says, "He is driven from light into darkness." This means death and the loss of all hope. "And chased from the inhabited world" means that Job will disappear from this world. It's not referring to simple death, but that he should be chased from the inhabited world. Bildad means Job is trapped because he is evil, and the world and his situation didn't accept him but forsook him.

For example, when somebody seems to have no way to survive, he says, "The world and everything has forsaken me." One sometimes says the same when he has absolutely no strength to continue his life, and Bildad is recklessly saying so in reference to Job.

"He has no offspring or posterity among his people, or any survivor where he sojourned. Those in the west are appalled at his fate, and those in the east are seized with horror. Surely such are the dwellings of the wicked, and this is the place of him who does not know God" (18:19-21).

The passage says Job's children and grand children will also disappear. It is a curse saying that everything about Job will be completely rooted out.

While reading the Bible, I put myself in the shoes of Job. I couldn't but shed my tears thinking about Job. His friends did not even comfort him when he was in such a desperate situation. They only acted with so much evil towards him. How heartbroken he must have been!

If your friends do something so evil like this, how would you feel? It is explaining how Job becomes an example of the standard for a person who has received such great disasters, so people who go through the same thing will be shocked. In a cursing manner, Bildad is warning how great the sufferings will be that Job will encounter.

Bildad is further explaining that Job will encounter such dreadful things because he is unrighteous and because Job doesn't know God. Bildad is talking like this even though he himself doesn't know about God very well either.

Chapter 19

Job's Anguish and Torment
- Deeper Evil Is Revealed

1. Let Us Not Crush One Another with Words

2. Job Blames God and Gives Excuses

3. Difference between Fleshly and Spiritual Love

4. Crafty and Cowardly Hearts

"He has removed my brothers far from me,
And my acquaintances are completely estranged from me." (Job 19:13)

1. Let Us Not Crush One Another with Words

"Then Job responded, 'How long will you torment me and crush me with words? These ten times you have insulted me; you are not ashamed to wrong me'" (19:1-3).

If you are tormented your heart suffers. As Job tried to win the argument with his friends, his heart became complex and tormented. When Job said something, his friends made more parables to crush him with words, rebuking and cursing him and ignoring what he had to say.

Whether a believer or not, when he hears some words that the other speaks against him, he will try to find other words to crush the other. But it's not right to squelch others with words. You try to crush others' words because you cannot make that person understand or you don't have desire to make that person understand.

We should neither ignore nor stifle others. If we crush other's words, they will only react in evil ways. A man with love and virtue will try to make the other person understand.

Verse 3 says, "These ten times you have insulted me; you are not ashamed to wrong me." 'Ten times' here means that they did it many times.

Job was saying, "In my innocence I have been enduring the

insults until now, but you are not even ashamed to insult me and wrong me. I am inflicted by diseases because of God though I am innocent, but you are severely rebuking me. If you have consciences, you should be ashamed of yourselves!"

Job thought that a righteous man, who is himself, was suffering from so much pain, and the way his friends treated him was just unacceptable. So, he is trying to make his friends realize that their deeds are shameful.

Job had an upright heart, and if somebody could not do what he was doing in his righteousness, he advised him to go and do it. But when the other person did not accept it, he felt embarrassed.

But his friends were crushing him with words without even feeling embarrassed or ashamed.

"Even if I have truly erred, my error lodges with me. If indeed you vaunt yourselves against me and prove my disgrace to me, know then that God has wronged me and has closed His net around me." (19:4-6)

What does it mean that "Even if I have truly erred"? In Job's opinion, he had no faults. But because his friends were insisting so much, he says, 'Even if.' And then, he aimed his attack back at them asking how well they are doing and telling them to prove their righteousness.

What does it mean by, "If indeed you vaunt yourselves against me and prove my disgrace to me"?

Job says his friends are vaunting themselves against him. Job thought he had nothing to be ashamed of, so he is telling them, "If I am to be accursed, and if you are righteous as you say, prove your righteousness and prove my disgrace to me!" Disgrace is something shameful, and some kind of fault that one doesn't want to reveal to others.

When both the parties argue against each other, the other person may be right, or both sides may be wrong. Therefore, we should not argue. If they have heated emotions in an argument, people usually reveal the fault of others.

Because their words are not accepted, they get angry, and for a moment, they tend to be submitting but then soon they disclose the others' faults and wrongdoings to bring them down to the bottom. Job has this kind of intention now. We have to cast off this kind of evil mind.

Even in the church are some people who have this kind of heart. Even pastors and leaders of the church become sulky if their opinions are not accepted. Or, they just become spectators and do not cooperate, saying, "Let's see how they do it."

This kind of heart is evil of evils. If your zeal cools down and you do not cooperate with others because your opinion is not accepted even though you are working for God's kingdom, how evil this is!

In this kind of case, some people even reveal the faults of others at the back. This is abhorrence in the sight of God. This is the heart of the devil, and Satan will rejoice over it. Therefore, we have to cast it off with fasting and prayers.

2. Job Blames God and Gives Excuses

Let us look into verse 6, "Know then that God has wronged me and has closed His net around me."

Here Job is saying that God has wronged him. When Job

expressed that he was wronged, it meant he has given up on himself. It means unwilling submission done by force.

Because Job believes that he is right, he is submitting unwillingly thinking that he should not submit. Yet he is saying, "Then, does it mean you are right? It's because God has wronged me that I don't have authority and I am victimized." He is blaming and severely complaining against God.

To catch a bird or fish, we put up a net, and to catch an animal, we set a trap. Job is saying God has closed His net around him and wronged him. Job is giving excuses to his friends.

Job was caught by the net in his own evil. It's same case with some people today. They are confined within the law and yet they complain about their neighbors, the church, or even God.

For example, their business went bankrupt or they were swindled out of their money because of their mistakes, but they don't put the blame on themselves. They just blame others saying there are such evil people out there and such people took their money.

When their illegally constructed houses are demolished for redevelopment of that area, they don't complain against the government but God and blame Him. They are not even believers and they do this. How foolish this is!

"Behold, I cry, 'Violence!' but I get no answer; I shout for help, but there is no justice. He has walled up my way so that I cannot pass, and He has put darkness on my paths." (19:7-8)

In violence, there is cruelty and oppression. To suffer violence means going through a very big accident that would not usually happen.

Because Job was in such great suffering, he says that he cannot understand what he is going through, and there is no answer when he cries, and there is no justice when he shouts for help.

If we were in the same situation as Job's, how many of us will not complain against God at all? Many will complain against God and leave Him.

'Justice' here has the meaning of resolving or redressing of disappointment, frustration, anger and anxiety. Job says there is no justice because there is nobody to resolve his vexation and exasperation. He is pleading with a desperate heart.

Let us check whether or not we were like Job here. The reason why Job is not receiving the answer is because he does not realize himself.

"So when you spread out your hands in prayer, I will hide My eyes from you; yes, even though you multiply prayers, I will not listen. Your hands are covered with blood. Wash yourselves, make yourselves clean; Remove the evil of your deeds from My sight. Cease to do evil, learn to do good; seek justice, reprove the ruthless, defend the orphan, plead for the widow. Come now, and let us reason together," says the LORD, "though your sins are as scarlet, they will be as white as snow; though they are red like crimson, they will be like wool. If you consent and obey, you will eat the best of the land; but if you refuse and rebel, you will be devoured by the sword. Truly, the mouth of the LORD has spoken" (Isaiah 1:15-20).

"Behold, the LORD's hand is not so short that it cannot save; nor is His ear so dull that it cannot hear. But your iniquities have made a separation between you and your God, and your sins have hidden His face from you so that He does not hear. For your hands are defiled with blood and your fingers with iniquity; your lips have spoken falsehood, your tongue mutters wickedness" (Isaiah 59:1-3).

The reason why we don't receive answer to our prayers is because we have a wall of sin against God. If we repent thoroughly and turn back, God says He will forgive us of our sins.

Then, how can Job receive the answer?

If he had realized his inner heart, believed in God who would answer him, and prayed with rejoicing and thanks, he could have received great blessings. But contrary to the truth, he only complained and spoke of his sorrow and pains, so there was no way for him to receive the answer from God.

The truth tells us to rejoice, pray, and give thanks even in sufferings and to believe in God, but Job complained, put himself into despair, argued and gave excuses, and thus he could not receive the answer.

Verse 8 says, "He has walled up my way so that I cannot pass, And He has put darkness on my paths."

The 'path' here means a shortcut, and darkness is covering it. Job says God walled up his way so that he cannot pass, and what kind of way was Job's way?

He harvested grains, ate them, and enjoyed elegant life. He also had a good conscience and helped those who were in need. Job says God stopped him from doing these things. Yes, God did, and it was to make Job a truly spiritual man.

Job was taking the shortcut towards a good environment and future, but because God allowed darkness to be put on his path, his possessions and children were to be lost, and he was also forsaken by his wife and friends. Job is saying that all his joy is gone, and because God has put death like darkness, he is suffering such a great pain.

"He has stripped my honor from me and removed the crown from my head. He breaks me down on every side, and I am gone; and He has uprooted my hope like a tree. He has also kindled His anger against me and considered me as His enemy" (19:9-11).

A crown is something kings used to wear. Honor is the praise and fame. What does it mean that God has stripped Job of his honor and his crown?

Job was rich, and he was a comfort to many people; they were proud of him. He was also praised and loved by many people and all this became honor for him. Job is saying that all these things were gone because of God.

A crown refers to 'authority.' Just as a king wears a crown, Job had authority coming from his wealth. But because God has taken away all his wealth, his authority also disappeared.

So, we can understand that Job earned his honor and authority not through his deeds alone, but through his possessions. Through Job's confession, we can understand how meaningless it becomes when one's wealth is lost.

"He breaks me down on every side" means that God is attacking him from all four directions. Today, many people think it's same as dead if one's authority and wealth disappear. But the value of our lives is not in either authority or fame.

In Luke chapter 16, we see a rich man and the beggar Lazarus. The rich man enjoyed his life eating good foods, but did not know God. The beggar Lazarus had to beg at the gate of the rich man's house but he feared God. Which one of these lives would you choose?

When God called their spirits, the rich man had to suffer in the lower part of the Grave, in Hades, but the beggar Lazarus went to the bosom of Abraham in the Upper Grave (Luke 16:19-31). If we can see with the eyes of spirit, we will definitely say we will fear God and go to heavenly kingdom like the beggar Lazarus.

In verse 10 it says, "He has uprooted my hope like a tree." Job's hope was everything that he had accumulated. But since everything disappeared in a moment, Job is explaining that God has easily uprooted him like a tree with shallow roots.

Job's hope was in material things including his children and his possessions. Therefore, let us realize how meaningless and foolish it is to dwell in flesh, and become spiritual persons who properly know and believe in God.

Verse 11 says, "He has also kindled His anger against me and considered me as His enemy." Job is saying God became angry with him because of the pains and despair that he has. Also, because he thinks he came to suffer so much because of God, he is pouring out his ill emotions before God.

When you have an enemy, just if you see his face or hear him breathe or just by seeing his eyes, you shudder. You don't even want to see him and you may even want to kill that person. One of the most evil hearts of man is having enmity. How stunning a remark it is to say God is considering Job as an enemy, while He tells us to love even our enemies!

"His troops come together, and build up their way against me and camp around my tent" (19:12).

When did troops come and build up their way against Job?

Here, 'troops' are not really soldiers but it refers to his friends. How much was Job suffering from his friends that he would have referred to them as troops?

It may be compared with calling somebody a lion or a tiger. This is a strong expression to say that his friends are talking with very loud voices roaring against him.

'Building up their way' here does not mean building a house or embankment. It means his friends have been changing the words and intentions of Job, telling him, "This is wrong, and that is wrong."

Namely, Job believed that because God considered him as an enemy, He is changing his ways, namely his intentions and words, through his friends.

"And camp around my tent" means his friends are standing around him and attacking him. Job is blaming God even for the wrongdoings of his friends.

3. Difference between Fleshly and Spiritual Love

"He has removed my brothers far from me, And my acquaintances are completely estranged from me. My relatives have failed, And my intimate friends have forgotten me. Those who live in my house and my maids

consider me a stranger. I am a foreigner in their sight.
I call to my servant, but he does not answer; I have to
implore him with my mouth" (19:13-16).

We can surely understand the difficult situations of Job. His loneliness and hardships are becoming more and more serious.

When Job was wealthy and enjoyed honor and fame through his wealth, he could be praised by others as a righteous man, because he could give hope to others.

Job had much love for his children and offered God sacrifices for them all the time. He also had shown love to his neighbors.

But Job loved a fleshly kind of love. Fleshly love after all seeks one's own benefit, and thus, the result is miserable. Fleshly things change. When it's not beneficial for him, he turns his back.

Job is saying that his brothers left him and it is also by God's work. He says his relatives and even his close friends forgot about him.

While Job was a rich man, there were many people in his house including his servants and guests. But now, those who live in his house and his maids consider him a stranger. He is a foreigner in their sight.

The servants should obviously serve their master Job, but now they don't even answer him. Only if Job asks them a favor humbling himself before them, they may do something for him.

It must have been very difficult for Job to express all his pain and sorrow. Job must have cared well for those who were in need when he was rich. His friends must also have received much help from Job. That's why they came to visit him while he was on his sickbed.

Because Job was nice to them while he was rich, he can say

these things now. But nothing returned to him. He is receiving only mockery and contempt.

Why, then, did everybody leave Job?

Even when we spend our money, we have to spend it spiritually. It can only be perfected when it is done with spiritual love. When Job was rich, he gave hope to many people and helped them with his wealth, but it was fleshly love. So, even his brothers and acquaintances all left him.

As in 1 Corinthians chapter 13, if his love had been spiritual love to endure long, be meek, and seek others' benefits, and if his deeds had been spiritual, his brothers must not have left. He wouldn't have been forsaken by the people but rather he would have received help back from them.

If you give money to others, they may be thankful for that moment, but after some time, they forget about it. Considering the complaints and resentment coming out of Job's mouth, we can clearly understand that his love was not spiritual.

An example of spiritual love in the Bible is the love between David and Jonathan. The father of Jonathan is the first king of Israel, Saul, and David was one of his retainers. Whenever David went to a war, he won the battle, and his popularity grew among the people. King Saul became jealous of him and hated him, and finally he tried to kill him.

"Jonathan made David vow again because of his love for him, because he loved him as he loved his own life" (1 Samuel 20:17).

Jonathan knew that David was going to be the king by the plan of God and his father was forsaken by God and would fall. But he still protected his friend David. He loved David spiritually, and so did David. That's why after he became the king, David protected Jonathan's son Mephibosheth until the end, and he gave him such great love to even let him eat with him at his table.

"My breath is offensive to my wife, and I am loathsome to my own brothers. Even young children despise me; I rise up and they speak against me. All my associates abhor me, and those I love have turned against me" *(19:17-19).*

"My breath is offensive to my wife" means that his wife does not like Job being near her. Even his wife dislikes him, and then who of his brothers like him?

'Brothers' here does not mean his people, his race. The spiritual meaning is those who breathed with Job and shared their heart with him. When Job was in such a difficult situation, not only his wife but also those who had shared their hearts with him forsook him.

Before I met God, I had been sick for 7 years, but my wife did not desert me. My wife took care of me while I was on my sickbed, and she earned the living. She had to endure so much suffering.

Still, there was no improvement in my illness. It only got worse, so there was no hope for the future. But my wife did not divorce me when I had been sick. I was forsaken after I was healed of my diseases by God.

Actually, I didn't know the reason why, but when God was explaining about the Book of Job to me by the inspiration of the

Holy Spirit, He explained to me about it.

It was normal for me to love my wife in all truthfulness, without hiding anything from her. Because my wife had spent my college fee before we got married, I could not go back to college but had to get a job first. But I did not have any complaint against my wife. In any kind of situation, I did not dislike it and I did not suffer because of the situation itself.

My true love coming from my heart was always passed on to my wife, and because the truth talked, she could sacrifice for me. If I had not been faithful, my wife would have disliked me so much, feeling even my breath was offensive, and divorced me.

But whenever she felt the difficulties of reality, she said, "If I divorce you now, people will say I am a bad woman who deserted her sick husband. So I will not divorce now. But if you recover from your sickness, then, I will divorce you." Actually, she said it so many times.

These words from my wife became a trap for her, and the enemy devil surely accused her by them. After I met God and was healed of all my diseases completely, we were in great happiness planning a bright future. But the incident happened on my father's birthday.

When my mother gave advice to my wife with a good intention, my wife misunderstood that my mother was saying I fell sick all because of her, and she ran out. I was forsaken by my wife.

Later, she repented and came back and we came together again. In that process, I could see the hot-temper of my wife was gone. God worked for the good of everything.

In verse 18, Job is despised even by children. In verse 19, all his associates abhor him, and those whom he loves have turned against him.

Those he loves may be his friends, his wife, or his relatives, neighbors, or brothers. Namely, it means all people around Job became angry with him and hated him because Job kept on complaining without trying to listen to anybody.

We can also find a case like Job's around us. Suppose a person used to help many people but he became bankrupt.

Then, those who once had received help from him are now trying to give him advice telling him to do this or do that. In this situation, if the person receiving the advice thinks of only the past and does not accept any of their advice thinking, "Who do you think you are trying to tell me what to do? I am better than you in everything, and that is why I could help you before!"

Then, those who gave advice will be disappointed, and think of him like, "He has nothing and he is still boasting."

They received help from him before, but now he has gone into bankruptcy, so they give their best advice to him, but he does not accept it. Nevertheless, they should not be disappointed or hate him. They should not forget the grace they received from him before. But today, men's hearts are very likely to forget the grace they have received.

"My bone clings to my skin and my flesh, and I have escaped only by the skin of my teeth. Pity me, pity me, O you my friends, for the hand of God has struck me. Why do you persecute me as God does, and are not satisfied with my flesh?" (19:20-22)

Job's skin and flesh are dried. And as he has burning anger

from the on-going arguments, he cannot digest anything even if he eats. His whole body is covered with boils, and his skin keeps on oozing and then drying.

That is why Job's bone clings to his skin and his flesh. He was just barely managing to survive, but he was still able to speak. Almost everything in his body is dry, so how terrible it must have been for him!

Job is telling his friends to have pity on him because God has struck him.

If you fall into tests and trials and tell me, "Pastor, God has struck me. Please have pity on me," then, can I have pity on you? I cannot have pity on you because you are blaming God for the trials that are caused by your own mistakes. Of course, I may say, "How pitiful!" but it cannot solve any problem.

Here, we can understand how much Job stayed in flesh. Because he stayed in flesh, he is telling his friends to have pity on him in a fleshly way.

In verse 22, Job says something more startling.

"Why do you persecute me as God does, and are not satisfied with my flesh?"

Job is saying that his friends are persecuting him with words, and because of that persecution his flesh is drying.

Job could not digest the words that his friends told him, but he only got angry with them. That is why he felt his friends' words were like persecution. It is obvious that Job lost weight because he was suffering so greatly. But, in order to strongly express his pain, he is saying that it is as if his friends were consuming his flesh.

But if our heart is as soft as cotton, we would not lose weight. Do you have as stubborn and hardened heart as stone? If somebody slanders you or wrongfully accuses you and spreads rumors, then, wouldn't you have burning anger against him? Not being able to endure it, wouldn't you immediately go to him to argue about it? You might lose sleep because of your anger, and obviously you will lose weight. If you are the kind of person who would lose a lot of weight this way, you should understand that you have a heart that is as hardened as stone.

When we throw a stone at a piece of cotton, the cotton will just embrace and cover the stone, so there is no noise. If we have such a gentle heart as cotton, we will not have any kind of noise toward the actions of others. Even if somebody who has a hardened heart like a rock bumps into you, you only embrace him with love and gentleness, so there is no noise, and there is no reason for you to lose weight.

We should not speak words that cause pain to others. We should not be the one to cause somebody to lose weight. Job says he is losing weight because he cannot accept the word of his friends, but his friends are still talking to him! What is the point in doing that? If Job had accepted his friends' words, he wouldn't have lost his weight but his problem must have been solved.

Also, the other person who keeps on talking that way is also committing a sin. If we make our hearts as gentle as cotton and become one grain of wheat that dies in the ground, wherever we are, it will be heaven there, and our families and workplaces will be evangelized.

"Oh that my words were written! Oh that they were inscribed in a book! That with an iron stylus and lead they were engraved in the rock forever! As for me, I know that my Redeemer lives, and at the last He will take His stand on the earth. Even after my skin is destroyed, yet

from my flesh I shall see God" (19:23-26).

An 'iron stylus' is like a pen.

Job is saying if he writes what he is going through in a book, it may be erased or the book may be torn apart, but if it is inscribed on a rock, it will last a long time. He means that he has the sole desire to permanently record about how great his pain and sorrows are.

Before you did not believe in God and suffered wrongfully or were victimized, haven't you said something like, "Who knows my situation? Will the heaven or earth know? Where can I record this unfair suffering?"

You might say these things because you have evil in your heart. If we endure and leave everything and rely on God, God works for the good of everything (Psalm 37:5). So, there is no need to record anything.

In verse 25 it says, "I know that my Redeemer lives." It is not something that he knows for sure, but just what he had heard before.

There is a great difference between at the level of sure faith and at the level of shaking faith. If your faith is not sure, you may have doubts, befriend the world, and commit sins.

Verse 26 says, "Even after my skin is destroyed, yet from my flesh I shall see God." It is also just what he has heard.

Even unbelievers say things like, "Heaven has done too much harm on me!"; "God is being so mean to me!" and "I think I will go to heaven because I lived a good life." But all these words will end up in vain. They are spoken only to comfort oneself.

4. Crafty and Cowardly Hearts

"Whom I myself shall behold, and whom my eyes will see and not another. My heart faints within me! If you say, 'How shall we persecute him?' And 'What pretext for a case against him can we find?' Then be afraid of the sword for yourselves, For wrath brings the punishment of the sword, So that you may know there is judgment" (19:27-29).

Job has heard about God and served Him, so he cannot walk before God as a stranger. Before, Job had faithfully served God. But now, he is complaining against Him and saying that God is a bad God. So, how will he see Him later? When Job thought about the situation where he would meet God, he felt nervous and his heart grew faint.

Verse 28 is one of the more difficult passages to understand. It is supposition. The 'he' here refers to Job. His friends are speaking continuously to crush Job with words and make him surrender.

Job's friends have been saying that all the cause of the problem is with Job. But Job did not acknowledge it. He just felt victimized and wrongfully accused saying the cause is with God who struck him. He wants God to surrender and blames God for everything.

Job's friends are blaming Job for everything, and Job is blaming God!

But even though Job explained to his friends, they didn't listen. So, Job's heart fainted. And now, Job went a level higher to make supposition with his friends. He is escaping the arrow of their attack with tricky words and blaming both sides.

We should not blame others for anything nor make random guesses in judging somebody. But Job is blaming others for something that he had caused. He was making a conjecture. He blamed both God and his friends.

Job could do this because he had much knowledge, but we should not let anybody suffer because of something that was caused by our own fault. If we can, we must take the responsibility for what we have done. If we blame somebody else, it is done with a cowardly and crafty heart.

In verse 29, Job concludes that wrath brings the punishment of the sword. This is truth. Because people get angry, there are fights, violence, and even murders. Job is making a rather threatening and forceful conclusion by saying the end of wrath is the punishment of the sword.

It means, "You with your anger tortured me, so as a result, there will be punishment for you!" Anger does not bring any benefit. God will certainly judge between what is good and evil. Right now, Job is using these words to threaten his friends.

Even if the other person may get angry with us and spit on us, we should not threaten him. How did Jesus act? He was flogged, wore the crown of thorns and suffered on the cross but still, He prayed to God saying, "Forgive them, for they do not know what they are doing."

Stephen was being stoned by people while preaching the gospel, and he also prayed to God, "Lord, do not hold this sin against them!"

A man of truth will not threaten another person, even if he acts with evil. A man of truth will only forgive and pray with love. We should never become an evil man who threatens others.

Chapter 20

The Outcome of Being Wicked
- The Second Argument of Zophar

1. Let's Not Be Agitated
2. What Kind of Heart Do We Have?
3. The Outcome of Being Wicked
4. Let Us Cast Off Ill-Feelings

"The heavens will reveal his iniquity, And the earth will rise up against him.
The increase of his house will depart; His possessions will flow away
in the day of His anger." (Job 20:27-28)

1. Let's Not Be Agitated

"Then Zophar the Naamathite answered, 'Therefore my disquieting thoughts make me respond, even because of my inward agitation. I listened to the reproof which insults me, and the spirit of my understanding makes me answer.'" (20:1-3).

The 'fainting heart' of Job (19:27) and the 'agitation' of Zophar here are a little different in meaning. Job's 'fainting heart' refers to the future when he meets God and Job is saying that having complained about God, he will have pain and suffering before God. Zophar's 'agitation' is his self-realization. Zophar together with his friends, rebuked Job, but Zophar realized the contents of the rebukes also actually applied to Zophar himself as well. Because Zophar had some conscience, he felt agitated by it.

Today, many people do not take responsibility for what they say. Some people with good consciences may have a sense of shame, but some others don't feel anything at all.

If a man will not take responsibility for what he has said, he loses confidence. This kind of person will have agitation of heart and feel shame.

In this case, if he just closes his mouth and stops the argument, he will not be ashamed any more, but Zophar and his friends are trying to comfort themselves by speaking more evil words.

Verse 3 explains why Zophar was agitated.

Zophar listened to a reproof that made him feel shameful, and the spirit of understanding caused him to respond. The reason why Zophar became agitated with a sense of self-rebuke is because his conscience told him that the words he had spoken toward Job with his friends were coming back equally applicable to himself. He felt that he was not doing what he had said, just like Job.

As Zophar was rebuking Job together with his friends, he had qualms of conscience. We are able to realize that he had some conscience left.

Here, we can understand "the spirit of understanding makes me answer," only when we discern it with the truth. Namely, how can an agitated man speak with wisdom?

If you give advice to somebody and tell him to do what you cannot do, you will have some pricks of conscience, that is, if you have some conscience. It means that you are rebuking yourself, and so, in another way, you try to make excuses to defend yourself.

In this case, let us see what Zophar is doing.

Because his words were piercing him, and Job was also piercing him, he tries to give excuses now. He tries to attack in many words in an attempt to change the situation.

I can see this kind of case very often in the ministry, too. When I give some advice on what went wrong, they don't try to repent but only try to give excuses. If they accept my advice and repent and turn away, they will be able to have the heart of truth in several months. So, I feel very sorry about such a thing when they don't try.

People don't want their shortcomings to be pointed out, and because of this, they try to hide them. They have crafty hearts and give excuses, not revealing their inner opinion. This is seeking their own benefit. If we do not cast off these kinds of heart then we will not be able to change our hearts for a long time.

When a person is agitated because he feels the pricks of conscience, he feels that he has to make excuses. When somebody pointed out some of your mistakes, didn't your heart become agitated and didn't you think quickly to make excuses? "How can I get away from this situation? What kind of excuses are there? How can I find his weak points and counterattack that person?" Didn't your heart become hurried with this kind of thinking?

Those who try to reverse the situation are the same as Job's friends. They cannot be deemed clean because God looks at our inner heart.

2. What Kind of Heart Do We Have?

Those who live in the truth should never feel agitated in any kind of situation. The righteous will think deeply to find an answer to give the other. If somebody is colliding with you, it's better to stop talking with him. It is better for you not to quarrel but to have peace.

We have to keep this in mind. If we get agitated in a conversation, we will have heated emotions. Once we have heated emotions, our faces and eyes turn red and the skin around the eyes also moves and wrinkles. If this goes further, we cannot hold it any more and we may even strike out at the other person with foul language. God dislikes this, but the enemy devil will enjoy it.

Those who are agitated and emotional this way cannot hear the voice of the Holy Spirit. The Holy Spirit's voice is heard in a heart that is as calm as lake. When they have agitation and heated emotions, they cannot hear the Holy Spirit's voice. We can hear His voice only when we break off our fleshly thoughts in us and remove evil within us. No matter how much we pray and how much knowledge of the word of God we have, if we just insist on our own way of thinking, we cannot hear the voice of the Holy Spirit.

In order to hear the Holy Spirit's voice, we have to break our personal way of thinking. And we have to cast off the untruths in our hearts, and it will help us break the frameworks of our thoughts.

Those who have good consciences will turn back or keep quiet when their mistakes are pointed out. But those who are evil will only give poor excuses and try to speak more. They not only give excuses but also try to blame somebody else, showing many kinds of evil works.

And they think themselves wise with the excuses they created.

For example, when somebody hits them once, they hit him back two times. If somebody attacks them, they also counterattack. Then, they think, "This is the way it should be. I am wise." It's an evil heart.

When somebody pointed out one of your mistakes, and you pay him back by pointing out two mistakes of his, do you feel good about it? When you see the other person not being able to answer, you feel you won the game.

This kind of thing comes from evil heart seeking one's own benefit. Reflecting this upon the truth, how foolish and cruel this is! We can see the characters of that person, that how evil and cruel, and foolish this person is.

3. The Outcome of Being Wicked

"Do you know this from of old, from the establishment of man on earth, that the triumphing of the wicked is short, and the joy of the godless momentary? Though his loftiness reaches the heavens, and his head touches the clouds, He perishes forever like his refuse; those who have seen him will say, 'Where is he?'"(20:4-7)

Here, we can find the reason why Zophar thought of himself as being wise. It was because he considered Job an evil man.

Zophar was saying to Job, "Don't you know the triumphing of the wicked is short, and the joy of godless momentary? Thus, aren't you both the wicked and the godless?"

After piercing Job with this word, he thought he spoke words of wisdom.

A godless man does not revere God, and thus his actions are not proper. Because Job had much knowledge, Zophar continues saying, "Don't you understand?"

We find in the history of Israel or in modern history that the victory of the wicked ends very quickly. Here, what Zophar said is correct, but it doesn't apply to Job.

Zophar's pointing does not apply to Job, but Zophar himself

thinks he is right and wise, so how foolish he is actually!

Those children of God who live in goodness and in truth will receive blessings from God above, so that they will be rich on this earth, and they will enjoy eternal life in heavenly kingdom. Worldly people say the wicked are more prosperous, but when we look at the result, we can see it's not so.

Verse 6 says, "Though his loftiness reaches the heavens," and it means that the authority and honor of the wicked and the godless are revealed to the world and their names are known. It is the explanation of the authority and honor of the wicked one. In verse 7, the word 'refuse' appears. Refuse is useless garbage that is dirty and has smells. This is being used in comparison with Job, but Job himself is not really a wicked or godless man, so it cannot be applied to him.

In history we can find many people who seemed to be able to enjoy great fame and prosperity forever, but in one moment they were put into situations comparable to refuse. They were both forsaken by people and received insults. That was worse than just being refuse.

Because they followed only their own benefits with the greed of man, they only followed the controlling of the enemy devil and Satan. Many people became victims and had to shed innocent blood. It was the history of pain and sorrow.

Let us check whether or not we have this kind of wicked heart. And if we find such a heart, let us repent and turn away.

"He flies away like a dream, and they cannot find him; even like a vision of the night he is chased away. The eye which saw him sees him no longer, and his place no longer beholds him. His sons favor the poor, and his

hands give back his wealth. His bones are full of his
youthful vigor, but it lies down with him in the dust"
(20:8-11).

If we speak with heated emotions and evil, we speak as if
the other person were a sinner although he is not really a sinner,
or we may speak as though he is not really innocent even if he
is innocent. But, those who only act with the truth, not being
controlled by their heated emotions, will not make these kinds of
mistakes.

In verse 7 it says, "Those who have seen him will say, 'Where
is he?'" It means that his works were all evil and they collapsed.
People don't even try to remember them, and they cannot
remember anything good about that person. Rather, they will
remember only bad things about him and spit on him.

In verse 8 it says, "He flies away like a dream." A dream is
just meaningless after waking up, no matter how good it was.
Zophar says the wicked and godless will fade away like dream
even though they may enjoy momentary fame, honor, and
prosperity.
Job was showing his resentment about his past, thinking of
his past. When his friends saw it, they were making fun of Job
this way. They were judging Job with their evil. Job did not think
of himself as wicked, but his friends were criticizing him, so he
felt victimized.

Then, the passage says, "Even like a vision of the night he is
chased away." Even the king of a nation can be chased away and
sent into exile. He will give up his palace, and he will go inside
a mountain to find a shelter. Everything about him will come to

collapse.

Zophar continues, "Job, because you were wicked and godless, your fame, honor, and prosperity were taken away, and everything disappeared like a meaningless dream." We can see how evil Zophar was in the sight of God. We can understand what kind of strong and fearful words Job's friends spoke to Job, and how great Job's pain was.

Verse 10 says, "His sons favor the poor, and his hands give back his wealth."

Job's friends were full of fury and insulted Job with things that were not really related to Job. 'His sons favor the poor' means the children of the wicked are asking for grace of the poor. In the Bible, we can find how wretched the ending of the wicked persons were such as Saul and King Ahab's children.

The poor here do not only mean those who are financially poor, but those who have relatively less fame and authority. And now, the wicked will ask for the mercy of those poor people.

For example, a king or a president at one time came to ask for the mercy of his previous subordinates after the situations changed. It is to favor the poor, as said in the passage. When some corruption is found out and the president steps down, he has to ask for the favor of the poor, and he has to give out the wealth he has previously accumulated.

Job acted with goodness toward others, but now, his position changed and was being condemned by his friends. He must have felt so much pain as if his flesh was eaten.

Job had said that it was like his friends were consuming his flesh. But it was actually Job eating at himself as well. Those who have as gentle and soft heart as cotton will embrace everything, even severe words that are like a rock, so no noise of collision will happen to them. But those who have hardened hearts like slate or concrete will make a loud noise when they collide with the other. Therefore, isn't it the same as Job eating his own flesh?

When we speak, we should be careful about our words. We should not offend or hurt the feelings of our brothers in trying to make them understand and turn away from wrongdoings.

Verse 11 says, "His bones are full of his youthful vigor, But it lies down with him in the dust."

We can understand this very well from history. There have been many kings and queens who had great authority, but still their lives were so miserable in the end.

"Your youthful vigor that you had is gone because of your evil. Now, your strength is gone and you have to lie down in the dust like a dead person."

Likewise, Job's friends are assaulting him so painfully.

Some people think the wicked are more prosperous and envy them, but this is not right. Finally, wickedness surely falls.

Even if some people gained great wealth or success with wicked ways, we don't have to envy them at all. Even if somebody has earned millions of dollars by swindling others, what benefit will it bring to him?

They will live in nervousness worrying whether or not their money will be stolen or whether or not their crime will be revealed. Those who earn money that way will not be able to spend it properly. They end their lives after enjoying meaningless pleasures.

Also, their children get into wretched situations, and the final destination for them is hell. Therefore, we would rather be poor and live a righteous life to enter into heavenly kingdom. This is much more blessed life.

4. Let Us Cast Off Ill-Feelings

"Though evil is sweet in his mouth And he hides it under his tongue, though he desires it and will not let it go, but holds it in his mouth, yet his food in his stomach is changed to the venom of cobras within him. He swallows riches, but will vomit them up; God will expel them from his belly. He sucks the poison of cobras; the viper's tongue slays him" (20:12-16).

"Though evil is sweet in his mouth and he hides it under his tongue" means evil is hidden, so it can be used any time. In Zophar's opinion, Job had to cast away his evil, but he considered it sweet and hid it under his tongue, so that he could use it any time he wanted.

Here, Zophar says the complaint of Job against God is evil. He is saying the friends have been admonishing Job until now, but he is not casting off his evil but has hidden it under his tongue to use it any time.

But in fact, his friends considered even greater evil sweet, hid it under their tongues, and acted in evilness, so how ridiculous it is!

Actually, Job's friends are more evil than Job, but they are saying only Job is evil. They are not discovering their own evils at all.

Though he was deemed upright and honest among men of flesh, Job was not a man of spirit. He did wrong according to the truth. But he failed to realize his faults but only thought he was right.

Many of us think we know the truth, but we reveal our evil when we pierce the other with our words or point out his mistakes and faults.

However, we may actually consider it sweet. We hide it under our tongues and keep on assaulting others, but we don't think it is evil. We may intend to point out others' mistakes to make things better and benefit them, but it rather may have the opposite effect.

If the others don't accept our advice, they will rather lose their strength and get discouraged. So, we should not let this kind of thing happen.

In verse 14, because Zophar does not understand about heart or soul, he is giving an illustration of food.

He says the evil hidden under the tongue becomes evil and goes down to the stomach. It refers to 'heart.' If the evil becomes food, goes into the stomach, and becomes venom of cobras, how fearful a thing this would be!

Cobras are very scary. They bring death. Spiritually, the venom of the cobras refers to death, and the cobra, which is a poisonous snake, is the same as the enemy devil. Venom is also something bitter and dirty, and is stronger than the cobra itself. The venom of the cobra brings death, and the venom of the cobras refers to stronger evil.

"It becomes venom of cobras in the stomach" means Job has strong and a great amount of evil. Zophar is saying Job is a man of such evil.

Right now, Zophar is increasing the intensity of his assault with his ill-feelings. Saying one is like a poisonous snake is actually a very strong way to say one is an evil person, and since he is saying the word venom of a cobra, it is even more evil thing. So, how angered Job must have been hearing this!

Verse 15 says, "He swallows riches, But will vomit them up;

God will expel them from his belly." Zophar did not say this because he understood the will of God, but he only said what he had heard from his fathers, with his heated emotion.

God lets us reap what we sow and pays back to us according to what we have done. If we do evil, it is obvious that we will finally reap evil. When we look at the world history, we can see that those who did evil finally died very wretched deaths.

This is the principle in the spiritual realm and the law of God. Suppose you took the evil way following your benefit right now. The other person is cheated by you, and it seems that things are going in a very favorable way for you. But it will last only for a moment. Because God is living, those things will be turned upside down, and finally you will have to shed tears.

And this will not end only on this earth, but in eternal world, you will have to suffer forever in the fire.

Verse 16 says, "He sucks the poison of cobras; the viper's tongue slays him." What does this mean? The poison of cobra means something evil and brings death. 'To suck the poison' means that because Job did evil, he would face the consequences.

"He does not look at the streams, the rivers flowing with honey and curds. He returns what he has attained and cannot swallow it; as to the riches of his trading, he cannot even enjoy them. For he has oppressed and forsaken the poor; He has seized a house which he has not built" (20:17-19).

It says, "He does not look at the streams, the rivers flowing with honey and curds." This means Job has lost all his land and everything from which he could enjoy prosperity, and he will not be able to see them any more.

It's because, in his friends' opinions, Job has collapsed completely. They believe that Job will not be able to stand back up ever again.

Do any of you think that you have fallen down completely without having any strength to stand back up again just the way Job did? Then, it is not of faith, but only of human thought. If God begins to work, things can happen in a moment. Even though you have collapsed, if you repent and turn back, and please God with your faith, then, you can stand back up in a moment. You can be better-off than before.

Verse 18 says, "He returns what he has attained and cannot swallow it." This means that even though Job has gained something in a just way he will not be able to take it but it will only disappear.

So, the verse 19 tells us why this happened. It was because Job oppressed and forsook the poor; he has seized a house which he has not built. Job has never done such a thing, but Zophar is wrongfully denouncing Job with his own feelings.

In the history, many of the authorities such as the presidents or ministers did not care for the poor. It's same as oppressing and forsaking them. Because those authorities only sought their own benefit, it's the same as taking the houses from the poor people.

But Job was not such a person. With his ill-feelings, Zophar was fabricating what is not truth. We have to understand how foolish and useless our heated emotions and ill-feelings are. It is to commit great sins and to give hard times to others.

When our words are getting twisted by our emotions, we have to avoid words that contain and transfer ill-feelings.

Because of ill-feelings, quarrels and fight arise, so we have to cast off any kind of ill-feeling. The outward expression of these ill-feelings makes the other become upset and get angry or causes complaint against somebody. This is surely not right according to the truth, so we have to get rid of this kind of ill-feelings.

When we pray continually and fervently on a regular basis, we can dwell in the grace and receive the strength of God the Father and the help of the Holy Spirit. Thus, we will be able to cast away our ill-feelings. If we offend others with our ill-feelings and express our heated emotions in our relationships in dealing with others, we will commit many kinds of sins.

"Because he knew no quiet within him, he does not retain anything he desires. Nothing remains for him to devour, therefore his prosperity does not endure. In the fullness of his plenty he will be cramped; the hand of everyone who suffers will come against him. When he fills his belly, God will send His fierce anger on him and will rain it on him while he is eating" (20:20-23).

Here, 'he' refers to an evil man, but actually Zophar is referring to Job. When greed comes into one's heart, he is not satisfied with anything. The greed gets bigger and bigger. If the seed of our faith grows up, we can even move a mountain, but when lust is conceived, it gives birth to sin.

"Then when lust has conceived, it gives birth to sin; and when sin is accomplished, it brings forth death" (James 1:15). If one has lust about money, fame, or authority, he cannot control himself from using unrighteous methods and he will commit sins.

If we have greed for money, we may even try to harm the other by making schemes and swindling that person.

Some people do not care about what kind of ways they are implementing to get fame or authority. They sacrifice so many people and even cause the problem of bleeding, until they actually get the power.

Zophar is looking at Job in flesh, and that is why he keeps on criticizing him. But God was refining Job to make him a better vessel and to give him greater blessings. It is not true that because Job was evil he did not give thanks for his possessions and or children and lost everything.

Verse 21 says, "Nothing remains for him to devour, therefore his prosperity does not endure." This word itself is true. Zophar is saying what he has heard from his ancestors.

Namely, when greed is conceived, it may seem that everything is going well in the beginning, but all things will be taken away by people, and they will disappear in various ways.

In the world history as well, when the head of the country thought and acted in greed, everything including their fame, authority, and prosperity collapsed and disappeared in a moment.

Also, there was a Korean president who would have been greatly respected if he had just followed the law properly. But, because greed was conceived in him, he changed the constitution and thus he performed the presidency twice. His promises were not kept, and he issued another plan. Finally, he had to face a miserable death.

Verse 22 says, "In the fullness of his plenty he will be cramped." What does it mean?

Being cramped means there will be unfortunate and difficult things. Because the fullness is of evil, it cannot be kept, and the prosperity cannot last long, so he cannot help but be cramped. It means Job's prosperity did not last long, and he collapsed, so he will be 'cramped' because he is evil.

Verse 23 says, "When he fills his belly, God will send His fierce anger on him and will rain it on him while he is eating." To fill his belly means he is enjoying his prosperity and is securing his abundance.

For example, one president did many works and handed over his power after his term, but because he did it with evil, God's wrath fell on him. So, he cannot but stay in darkness, and all his possessions are to be taken back.

Then, what does it mean that 'His fierce anger will rain on him while he is eating'? Right now to Job, how many things have turned into arrows that are falling on him? Because Job was evil, he was surrounded by his friends, and he is being assaulted.

"He may flee from the iron weapon, but the bronze bow will pierce him. It is drawn forth and comes out of his back, even the glittering point from his gall. Terrors come upon him, complete darkness is held in reserve for his treasures, and unfanned fire will devour him; It will consume the survivor in his tent"(20:24-26).

It says, "He may flee from the iron weapon, but the bronze bow will pierce him." This can be explained in two aspects.

The first meaning is the following: "Job! You are trying to avoid the advice of your friends, so we cannot help but give you advice with words that are so piercing. Even if you can avoid our advice, the bronze bow that you cannot avoid is waiting for you."

Another meaning is that when iron weapon is attacking, you may block it or avoid it, but because a bow's arrow follows in a moment, it's not easy to avoid it. It means a bronze bow is more fearful and more painful than iron weapon.

Verse 25 says, "It is drawn forth and comes out of his back, even the glittering point from his gall. Terrors come upon him."

When an arrow is stuck in a person's body, he will have unbearable pain. But when the arrow is taken out, the pain should go away, but it says terrors come upon him.

This verse is not easy to understand if we try to understand it only literally. For example, a person is swindled out of his money. He is so angry and he cannot bear it. Suppose this man killed the person who cheated him.

He killed that person following his desire, but when he sees that person dead, he will have the terror thinking, "I have become a murderer." When everything is finished, he will have fear and terror, and regret what he has done.

"Job! After the arrow is taken out, you will have such pain and terror."

Zophar is threatening Job to make him afraid. We should not do this to cause pain and terror to another person.

So, towards the end of the Book of Job, the anger of God falls on the three friends, and through the intercession of Job, they were forgiven.

Verse 26 says, "Complete darkness is held in reserve for his treasures, and unfanned fire will devour him; It will consume the survivor in his tent."

Generally speaking, Zophar was jealous of Job's great possessions. That is why Zophar is telling Job that because Job had greed for money and accumulated his wealth like an evil man, darkness fell on him, and he cannot move now. So, he has to be confined or wander around.

It is like saying, "Job, the disasters on you have come because you are evil. God turned His face away and Satan is working on you. Thus, it is not any man who brought disaster on you, and you cannot help but perish."

In darkness, we cannot interact with others or move about freely. We will be confined or only be able to grope around. The fame, authority, and money will go away because people's hearts turn their backs on us.

> *"The heavens will reveal his iniquity, And the earth will rise up against him. The increase of his house will depart; his possessions will flow away in the day of His anger. This is the wicked man's portion from God, even the heritage decreed to him by God" (20:27-29).*

Zophar is saying that because God reveals Job's iniquity, all his ways are finished. If the heaven does not forgive, everything in life is meaningless. Thus, his house, his possessions, and everything in life will disappear.

The earth can give all the material blessings to men during their lives, and Zophar is saying even all these things will disappear. He says that everything Job is experiencing is the very inheritance that the wicked man will obviously receive from God.

But we should know that God did not preplan everything that would happen to Job, as Zophar says. God has set a boundary in the principles of this world, as to what will happen if we act in such a way.

The almighty God knows everything in the future, and He is a God of foreknowing and preplanning in perfect justice. He has set the boundary, but He does not decide what would happen beforehand.

He has just set the boundary of salvation through the law, and thus, whether or not we go into that boundary solely depends on our freewill.

If God had predestined the fate of each one beforehand, He cannot judge us nor does He have to judge us at all.

The Author:

Dr. Jaerock Lee

Dr. Jaerock Lee was born in Muan, Jeonnam Province, Republic of Korea, in 1943. In his twenties, Dr. Lee suffered from a variety of incurable diseases for seven years and awaited death with no hope for recovery. One day in the spring of 1974, however, he was led to a church by his sister and when he knelt down to pray, the Living God immediately healed him of all his diseases.

From the moment Dr. Lee met the Living God through that wonderful experience, he has loved God with all his heart and sincerity, and in 1978 he was called to be a servant of God. He prayed fervently so that he could clearly understand the will of God, wholly accomplish it and obey all the words of God. In 1982, he founded Manmin Central Church in Seoul, Korea, and countless works of God, including miraculous healings and wonders, have been taking place at his church.

In 1986, Dr. Lee was ordained as a pastor at the Annual Assembly of Jesus' Sungkyul Church of Korea, and four years later in 1990, his sermons began to be broadcast in Australia, Russia, the Philippines, and many more through the Far East Broadcasting Company, the Asia Broadcast Station, and the Washington Christian Radio System.

Three years later in 1993, Manmin Central Church was selected as one of the "World's Top 50 Churches" by the Christian World magazine (US) and he received an Honorary

Doctorate of Divinity from Christian Faith College, Florida, USA, and in 1996 a Ph. D. in Ministry from Kingsway Theological Seminary, Iowa, USA.

Since 1993, Dr. Lee has taken the lead in world mission through many overseas crusades in the USA, Tanzania, Argentina, Uganda, Japan, Pakistan, Kenya, the Philippines, Honduras, India, Russia, Germany and Peru. In 2002 he was called a "worldwide pastor" by major Christian newspapers in Korea for his work in the various overseas Great United Crusades.

As of August 2009, Manmin Central Church has a congregation of more than 100,000 members. There are 9,000 domestic and overseas branch churches throughout the globe, and so far more than 132 missionaries have been commissioned to 25 countries, including the United States, Russia, Germany, Canada, Japan, China, France, India, Kenya, and many more.

As of the date of this publishing, Dr. Lee has written 57 books, including bestsellers *Tasting Eternal Life before Death, My Life My Faith I & II, The Way of Salvation, The Measure of Faith, Heaven I & II, Hell, and The Power of God.* His works have been translated into more than 41 languages.

His Christian columns appear on *The Hankook Ilbo, The JoongAng Daily, The Dong-A Ilbo, The Munhwa Ilbo, The Seoul Shinmun, The Kyunghyang Shinmun, The Hankyoreh Shinmun, The Korea Economic Daily, The Korea Herald, The Shisa News, The Christian Press and The Nation Evangelization Newspaper.*

Dr. Lee is currently leader of many missionary organizations and associations: including Chairman, The United Holiness Church of Korea; President, The Nation Evangelization Newspaper; President, Manmin World Mission; Founder, Manmin TV; Founder & Board Chairman, Global Christian Network (GCN); Founder & Board Chairman, World Christian Doctors Network (WCDN); and Founder & Board Chairman, Manmin International Seminary (MIS).

Heaven I & II

A detailed sketch of the gorgeous living environment the heavenly citizens enjoy and beautiful description of different levels of heavenly kingdoms.

The Message of the Cross

A powerful awakening message for all the people who are spiritually asleep In this book you will find the reason Jesus is the only Savior and the true love of God.

Hell

An earnest message to all mankind from God, who wishes not even one soul to fall into the depths of hell! You will discover the never-before-revealed account of the cruel reality of the Lower Grave and hell.

Tasting Eternal Life Before Death

A testimonial memoirs of Dr. Jaerock Lee, who was born gain and saved from the valley of death and has been leading an exemplary Christian life.

The Measure of Faith

What kind of a dwelling place, crown and reward are prepared for you in heaven? This book provides with wisdom and guidance for you to measure your faith and cultivate the best and most mature faith.

www.urimbooks.com

www.ingramcontent.com/pod-product-compliance
Lightning Source LLC
Chambersburg PA
CBHW061554120626
46550CB00004B/1486